The
GENESIS
RACE

The
GENESIS
RACE

Our Extraterrestrial DNA
and the True Origins of the Species

WILL HART

Bear & Company
Rochester, Vermont

Bear & Company
One Park Street
Rochester, Vermont 05767
www.InnerTraditions.com

Bear & Company is a division of Inner Traditions International

LIBRARY OF CONGRESS CATALOGING-IN-PUBLICATION DATA
Hart, Will, 1946-
The Genesis race : our extraterrestrial DNA and the true origins of
the species / Will Hart.
p. cm.
Includes bibliographical references (p.) and index.
ISBN 978-1-59143-018-6 (pbk.)
1. Civilization, Ancient—Extraterrestrial influences. I. Title.

CB156.H36 2003
001.942—dc22

2003019570

Printed and bound in the United States

10   9   8   7   6

This book was typeset in Sabon with Agenda and Avenir as display typefaces

Contents

Making the Case for Extraterrestrial Intervention

*We shall postulate that on some distant planet, some four
billion or so years ago, there had evolved a form of higher
creature who, like ourselves, had discovered science and
technology, developing them far beyond anything
we have accomplished.*

Sir Francis Crick,
Life Itself: Its Origin and Nature

Future shock now seems like a permanent feature of postindustrial
civilization. The everyday world of modern society has already
trumped the tales of the most imaginative science fiction writers of
our age: We penetrated the mysteries of the atom a generation ago,
and at this time our space probe on Mars is collecting information,
the latest of which reveals evidence suggesting the presence of water
and some kind of life on the red planet in its distant past.

We are in the midst of an information explosion. Scientists estimate that the human knowledge base is doubling every five years—an
expansion rate impossible to keep up with for most of us, including
specialists in every discipline who work full time just to stay abreast
of developments within their fields. Science and technology are supposed to explain how the universe works, to help to make life a little
easier, and to solve problems. But in the past 50 years we have learned
the painful lesson that they can also generate problems.

While this book was being written, three amazing stories grabbed headlines: In December 2002 a company called Clonaid announced that the first human clone had been born—a 7-pound baby named Eve. Clonaid is an offshoot of a religious sect founded in France 30 years ago by a French journalist who now calls himself Rael. The Raelian movement reports having some 40,000 members worldwide, and one of its main goals is to clone human beings and eventually achieve immortality through this process. While the truth of Clonaid's claim has not been proved by means of DNA testing, scientists agree that such cloning will be a part of our future. The technology and methods have already been used to produce clones of a number of animal species.

Also in 2002, the Public Consortium, a nonprofit research group, announced that it had finished the first draft of the human genome— it had mapped the human genetic code. This may seem like an altogether novel breakthrough, but in fact it is a logical step in a historical progression. We have been altering the gene pools of plants and animals for thousands of years: A canine subspecies that did not exist before has been created by a method as yet unidentified. Similarly, we have caused some species to become endangered and others to go the way of extinction. In short, we have been "playing God" for a long time. The fact that we do not recognize this is due to acceptance, over time, of our practices of selective breeding and re-engineering of the natural environment. What is to stop us from experimenting with human cloning? While there is considerable resistance to the idea of human cloning today, resistance is a common reaction to scientific breakthroughs. In all probability this response will melt away in a generation and cloning will become commonplace.

A third story occurred in 2001 and was reported from London by Reuters under the headline "Scientists Build Tiny Computer From DNA": "Following Mother Nature's lead, Israeli scientists have built a DNA computer so tiny that a trillion of them could fit in a test tube and perform a billion operations per second with 99.8 percent accuracy."[1]

What exactly is this machine and how does it work? Professor Ehud Shapiro of the Weizmann Institute explained matter-of-factly to the reporter, who was probably as mystified as the average reader of the article, "We have built a nanoscale computer made of bio-molecules. . . . When a trillion computers run together they are capable of performing a billion operations."

You may say that these three stories do not seem shocking or incredible. Maybe we do not have the capacity to be shocked anymore; maybe nothing is incredible in this age of continuous scientific breakthroughs and technological revolutions. We seem to be caught in an ever-accelerating spiral of such mind-numbing announcements and advances, and new ones are perpetually leapfrogging those that were introduced yesterday or last week or last month.

Yet while we rush headlong into an uncertain future that is growing more complex every day, we seem to have forgotten our past. But how can we really come to know the universe—appreciating, for instance, that life once existed on Mars—without first knowing the truth about our own origins and history? At the core of our psyches significant facts confront us: We do not know how we got here; we do not know how human life was created. Our ancestors lived our history but we have lost the threads to complete the tapestry of their legacy.

We are puzzled and awestruck by the wonderful and mysterious achievements that the very earliest civilizations left behind in the sands of Egypt and Mesopotamia, in the high mountains of Peru and the jungles of Mexico, in the Indus River Valley and on the plains of central China. At a time when the majority of Earth's human population was still living very primitively in small tribal units with relative equality and a reasonably fair distribution of wealth, power, and resources, advanced civilizations with a very different way of life sprang up suddenly at these six distinct points on the globe. (See fig. 1, page 5).

Beginning in 8000 B.C.E., followed by a major developmental thrust between 3500 B.C.E. and 1500 B.C.E., there was a sudden explosion of innovation in these distinct areas of the planet. These first civilizations shared an amazing number of similarities that were completely unlike anything human beings had yet exhibited: All of them built monumental structures—especially pyramids—constructed urban centers, and replaced hunting and gathering with agriculture. They each invented new tools, used the strengths and efficiency of an organized workforce and specialization within that force, and created the sophisticated aesthetic and intellectual features that define civilized society. And four of them originated key agricultural crops that we still rely on today—corn, potatoes, rice, and wheat.

These similarities lead to many questions: How and why did these six human civilizations originate—and why do they share so many characteristics? Why, for instance, do we find pyramids in Sumer, Egypt, Mexico, and China? How did both the Sumerians and the Maya acquire advanced astronomical and mathematical knowledge? Why did these societies abandon the hunter-gatherer way of life, which had been successful for hundreds of thousands of years, in favor of dependence on agriculture?

A further, defining characteristic of our ancestral civilizations, often noted but never really explained, is a social organization entirely different from that of the previous millions of years of human evolution: The existing simple egalitarian system became a complex pyramidal system with a divine king at its apex. Why was the appearance of our earliest civilizations accompanied by this radical social transformation? What caused such an extreme shift?

Our scientists have unlocked the human genetic code, but we have yet to find the key to solving the riddles in the great and beautiful cities whose ruins haunt us today. We have yet to understand the legends these ancient cultures share, or why they are shared by peoples so distant from each other geographically—the stories of a great deluge, of the origins of agriculture, of giants that once roamed the earth, and of a race with superhuman powers that created and taught people how to be *human*. The creation myths from these six points in the world—all quite distant from each other—are in fact remarkably similar. In each, gods—seemingly humans, though far

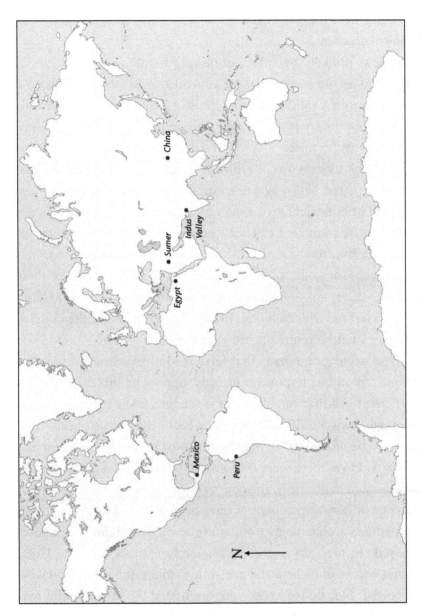

Fig. 1. Sites of the world's six primary civilizations: Mexico, Peru, Egypt, Sumer, the Indus Valley, and China

superior to humans in knowledge and power—descended from the heavens to create human beings as we now exist, to give humanity the gifts of civilization, and to leave behind a theocracy based on the idea that the king has descended from the gods or has been appointed by them.

It seems unlikely that the astonishing number of similarities in these myths is the result of mere coincidence, which leads us to a larger question: Could it be that those stories that we have long considered myths are in reality factual accounts? The evidence seems to support this premise.

This book focuses on collecting evidence to prove the theory that Earth was visited by an extraterrestrial race of human beings who intervened in biological processes, a race that bioengineered modern humans in their image. I call this the theory of *intelligent extraterrestrial intervention*. Once this creation was accomplished, this Genesis race—or gods, as they are referred to in the myths of these ancient civilizations—taught humans the arts and skills of agriculture and civilized life, including those required to build the colossal monuments whose remnants are visible today.

These stone monuments that have stood like silent sentinels for millennia are in fact important records supporting this theory. It has been determined that the blocks of stone that make up these monoliths weigh between 20 and 400 tons each; they are so heavy that they could be moved today only by the most modern equipment and machinery. How, then, were they moved thousands of years ago? As chapter 7 will make clear, the construction of the massive pyramids in Egypt, for instance, could not have been achieved using the primitive methods archaeologists and anthropologists claim the builders employed. In fact, no one can adequately explain how the Great Pyramid was built or how the megalithic stones of Tiahuanaco were transported. Nor do we know who originated the idea to build pyramids and ziggurats or how it was decided to make these structures geodesic markers by aligning them to true north.

Perhaps the greatest question is why it is that we don't know the answers to all these questions. Why have we forgotten our own past? Rather than having forgotten, maybe up to now we have not had the knowledge and understanding that would allow us to see the answers that have been with us all along.

The theory of intelligent extraterrestrial intervention explored in these pages is predicated on the following points related to the six initial civilizations on our planet, each of which is supported by existing evidence:

- These civilizations appeared suddenly, without precedent, which, the theory contends, was due to the external stimulus of an advanced race.
- These civilizations departed completely from humanity's primitive past by exhibiting, without precedent, corporate architecture, metallurgy, agriculture, and other manifestations of accelerated technical advancement. Further, over a long period of time some of these developments eventually spread from the six specific geographic locations that were first to exhibit them.
- Four of these six primary civilizations were first to develop and grow some of the agricultural crops that have since become staples of the world's people—crops including wheat, potatoes, corn, and rice.
- The rest of the world lagged far behind these six cultural centers in all the technical, corporate, legal, bureaucratic, and organizational features that comprise civilization, which explains why we have not found in other parts of the world the remains of pyramids or ziggurats or sophisticated irrigation systems dated to the same time period as those found in these first areas. Nor were cities, large-scale agriculture, process metallurgy, wheeled vehicles, advanced systems of math and astronomy, civil engineering, or writing in evidence anywhere else at the time they were flowering in the six centers.

- Among these six locations there is a convergence of literary and oral traditions relating to creation legends and to how these peoples acquired the arts and sciences.
- There are a large number of especially provocative enigmas and anomalies associated with these ancient civilizations.
- Human civilization is much older than we have estimated—beginning perhaps 10,000 to 20,000 years ago.

As this book will show, the theory of intelligent extraterrestrial intervention is strongly indicated by evidence in all these areas. While some excellent, groundbreaking books have delved into some of the topics contained in this work, here we will cover new ground from a scientific perspective, synthesizing disparate observations, data, and other findings into a coherent paradigm. Here we will ask questions, look at hard research, explore information and evidence that have not appeared in other related works, and make connections based on uncompromising logic and common sense.

When I began investigating the subject matter that led to this book, I did so with no preconceived conclusion in mind. The results of my search that I share here surprised me—and they are conclusive. Our past is littered with mysterious anomalies that do not fit our fixed ideas and accepted theories of how human history evolved. This alone suggests that perhaps it may have come about differently from how we have imagined.

Nevertheless, scientists try to explain away these enigmas. Or they silently ignore the fact that something must have intervened in our history to lift us up to the level of awareness and ability that would allow us to create civilizations. That this intervening "something" was extraterrestrial is, as we shall see, a logical conclusion, for the Book of Genesis states: "Let Us create man in Our image." While this interpretation of our ancient texts may have seemed far-fetched a generation ago, does it seem so fantastic today?

Questions about our origins and about the anomalies in and similarities among ancient cultures have piqued human curiosity for ages, but only a fraction of these questions have been satisfactorily answered. Perhaps some answers have waited until we arrived at the level of sophistication in biotechnology, computerization, and knowledge of space and the universe that we have today. The knowledge we have acquired in these areas may enable us to take a fresh look at the evidence contained in the total record. As the three recent stories at the start of this introduction indicate, we actually possess or have within reach extremely advanced computer capabilities, the ability to genetically engineer organisms, and a new understanding of our own genetic code. Perhaps we finally stand at a technical level that can enable us to decode the myths and artifacts of the past to learn the story of our origins.

In the end, our history must make sense. Unraveling the mysteries of our origins will allow us to understand the past without prejudice or fear—and this can be accomplished by starting with what exists, with the facts, regardless of how awesome or strange or unlikely they may be.

Before we go further, it is important to address the term *civilization,* a controversial and subjective one whose meaning can depend entirely upon its context—who is using it and how it is being used. Throughout this text I use the term to indicate a particular model of a society that is technologically advanced and that shows evidence of the kind of structural and engineering projects commensurate with such advancement; that is both socially stratified and differentiated according to skill and employment; and that has in place codified laws and hierarchical government.

We have before us a tremendous quest that must begin with an open mind. Do we have the collective will to find what we seek? We will begin with Darwin's theory of evolution and the biblical account of Genesis—and then rethink everything from a revolutionary new perspective.

ONE

Reconstructing Our Ancient Past

NEW DISCOVERIES

Some believe that the Age of Discovery is over. But the Earth is vast and full of unsolved mysteries. Human history itself remains an enigma, a complicated puzzle with missing pieces that have yet to be found and placed. Some of them lie at the bottom of the ocean or are buried in the jungle, and others are secreted in hidden caves waiting to be discovered.

These are exciting times for anyone who is curious about the origins of humanity and our enigmatic past on planet Earth. The number and the magnitude of new discoveries are increasing at an almost breathless pace. New technologies combined with new interdisciplinary approaches and the fresh perspective of independent researchers are rapidly changing the entire antiquities field.

There is a new breed of researcher in the field of archaeology, one who is making the science far more interdisciplinary. Today, archaeologists work in tandem with hydrologists, agronomists, geologists, and a variety of other specialists geared to reintegrating the many complex pieces that make up the puzzling ruins of a lost city or civilization. They employ advanced technology, including computer-based reconstructions, high-resolution aerial photography, remote

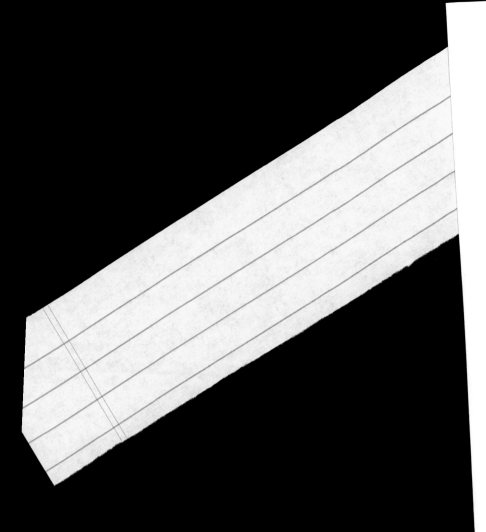

sensing, infrared photography, and geophysical surveys that lead to precise maps. For underwater investigations, advanced robotics and submersibles are employed in conjunction with sonar, 3-D photogrammetry, and digital video. Archaeologists are also successfully using the technology known as ground-penetrating radar (GPR). Invented in the 1970s, it was originally used for military purposes such as pinpointing the location of land mines and military tunnels. These new technologies have put a powerful set of tools in the hands of investigators into our human past, which can mean only that the rapid pace of fascinating new discoveries will continue.

At this writing a Canadian exploration company with solid credentials—they have discovered and retrieved several Spanish galleons and located the USS *Maine,* the warship that exploded and sank in 1898, igniting the Spanish-American War—announced a startling find in the Caribbean. They had located a "lost city" at a depth of 2,100 feet off the coast of Cuba and less than 50 miles east of the Yucatán Peninsula.

Using side-scan sonar equipment, the team noticed a large underwater plateau with "clear images of symmetrically organized stone structures that looked like an urban development partly covered by sand. From above, the shapes resembled pyramids, roads and buildings," one of the researchers reported.[1] The researchers then sent in an underwater robot probe—a Remotely Operated Vehicle (ROV)—to film parts of the 7.7-square-mile plateau. The resulting images confirmed the presence of monolithic blocks of cut stone sized from 6.5 to 16 feet in length and positioned in perpendicular and circular formations. Some of the blocks were stacked and some were exposed to the sea.

Who built this ancient city? The team declined to speculate, but they did say they thought that it must have been built when the current sea floor was above the surface—a logical assumption—which would have been at least 6,000 years ago. That would make it the oldest such site in the world, predating the cities of ancient Egypt by 2,500 years, those of the Olmec civilization by 3,500 years, and those of the Maya by almost 4,500 years. By virtue of their proximity to the Yucatán Peninsula, the ruins are in the same general region as those of the Mayan civilization. In fact, it's apparent that if the sea level were lower, Cuba, the Yucatán, and the ancient city would be part of the same landmass.

Mayan legends tell us the Mayan people came from a land to the east at the time of the Great Flood. Quetzacoatl, the bearer of their culture, also came from the east. Likewise, the Aztecs refer to their original home, Aztlan, as being to the east. The Aztec empire's capital city, Tenochtitlan, was laid out in a pattern said to resemble that of Aztlan, which must have been an island because the Aztec capital was an island in the middle of the relatively shallow Lake Texcoco.

But the Canadian explorers were not the only ones to make such an amazing discovery. For generations local inhabitants of the region around Lake Titicaca in South America told of a sunken city beneath the lake's surface. Although this legend had been recounted ever since the Conquistadors arrived, it had been summarily dismissed as pure fiction for almost 400 years.

Then, in the summer of 2000, an international research team comprising archaeologists and scientists from South America and Europe discovered an ancient structure submerged 66 feet beneath the surface of the lake. After diving for 18 days they identified a temple 160 feet wide by 660 feet long, a terrace for crops, a 2,600-foot retaining wall, and a pre-Incan road.

The chief Bolivian scientist on the team, Eduardo Pareja, told reporters, "I strongly support the hypothesis that what was found by the *Atahuallpa* 2000 expedition are the ruins of a submerged pre-Columbian temple."[2] This dating is quite significant because archaeologists have always ascribed a fairly recent date to Tiahuanaco as well as other local ruins located on the Island of the Sun. We will explore this in detail in chapter 12.

In June 2000 French marine archaeologist Franck Goddio announced his latest discoveries in the Bay of Abourkir in Egypt. Using electronic instruments, Goddio first created an underwater map of the bay region, which revealed a very large accumulation of ruins located next to the remains of Napoleon's sunken fleet about 20 feet below the surface. Then, using the latest high-tech underwater equipment, the archaeologist was able to locate and retrieve many artifacts including statues, gold coins, and precious jewelry. He also discovered a previously unknown sunken city that had been submerged so quickly that people did not even have time to grab important items and flee.

Goddio's discoveries are corroborated by the accounts of ancient Greek historians such as Herodotus, who described the temple of Hercules in Herakleion in 450 B.C.E., and Strabon, who told of the luxurious lifestyle of the cities of Canopus, Herakleion, and Menouthis in the second century. Even in ages past, however, the cities were mysterious because they had slipped beneath the waters of the bay for reasons that are still unclear.[3]

Chinese archaeologists recently announced that in Fuxian Lake, in central Yunnan province, they had found the submerged ruins of an ancient complex, which they named China's Pompeii. The expedition used the *Blue Whale* submersible to examine and photograph the site comprised of stone walls that are 50 to 75 feet long and about 10 feet wide. Flagstones and the complete walls of eight buildings and flagstones were found scattered over a 1.5-by-.5 mile area.

The scientists believed the city was part of the ancient Yunnan kingdom that local legends say simply disappeared. Central Yunnan is prone to earthquakes and Yu Xixian—a prominent Chinese archaeologist who led the underwater investigation—pointed to the fractures and subsidence tracks on the surrounding mountains as evidence of what might have happened to the ruined city: It either sank directly into the lake or was inundated after a landslide blocked an outlet.

Other such discoveries made in recent years in various parts of the world will be recounted in later chapters, and now that the technology exists for deep-sea exploration, more can be expected in the decades to come.

From lost cities submerged beneath the waters of seas and lakes we turn to the riddle of the Taklamakan Desert in eastern China. There one of the great mysteries of modern archaeology started to be unearthed in the 1970s and 1980s. Dozens of bodies that are thousands of years old were discovered, each perfectly preserved by the area's alternately hot, dry desert air of summer and frigid temperatures of winter. The mummies—known as the Tarim Basin people—had essentially been desiccated and freeze-dried, which, amazingly, left their skin, hair, features, and clothing intact.[4]

But scientists soon learned they were only at the beginning of deciphering this new, enigmatic chapter of human history. In the course of their study they discovered that the mummies of central Asia were Caucasian! Though no one is quite sure why they were there or why they disappeared thousands of years ago, we do know now that their culture thrived for at least 1,500 years. According to the folk traditions of local tribes, a non-Chinese people had settled the region in dim prehistory.

As determined from the mummies, the Tarim Basin people had dark blond, reddish, or yellow-brown hair, deep-set eyes, and long limbs. Many clues to the culture of these people are revealed in the clothing worn by the mummies. It seems that the Tarim Basin people buried their dead in brightly colored clothing and boots. They tended sheep and cattle, used horses, practiced some form of farming, and made clothing from the wool of their sheep: After dyeing wool brilliant colors, they wove intricately designed fabric and stamped motifs on this handmade woolen felt.

At least 1,000 mummified bodies have been unearthed so far and countless sites remain to be excavated. Regardless of where they came from originally, the remains of these people found near the old Silk Road reveal that humankind's history on the earth is far richer and more complex than we have imagined.

Dolkun Kamberi, a man with medium brown hair and Caucasian features, is an archaeologist born and raised in this region of the Chinese desert. He believes he is a direct descendant of the

Tarim Basin people. In the course of his work in the area, he found a portion of a human skull determined to be a half million years old, definitive evidence that people were in the region 500,000 years ago.

The discovery of the Tarim Basin people promises to turn upside down the notions of both orthodox historians and those in the Chinese government, who are not pleased to find that non-Asian people settled on Chinese soil in ancient, predynastic times. Kamberi thinks that central Asia will be an archaeologist's dream for the rest of the first century of the new millennium. We will uncover more mysteries and controversies in China in chapter 9.

In South America as well a recent discovery has forced us to rethink history's time line, pushing back the date of urban settlement of the ancient Americas. "Our findings show that a very large, complex society had arisen on the coast of Peru centuries earlier than anyone thought," says Jonathon Haas, Ph.D., MacArthur Curator of Anthropology at Chicago's Field Museum.[5]

Although the north coast of Peru is not nearly as well known for its excavations as the Andean archaeological sites, the coastal region is home to dozens of very impressive finds. Radiocarbon dates of plant fibers from one of these sites, known as Caral, indicate that not only was it established as early as 2627 B.C.E. but it also already exhibited monumental corporate architecture and irrigation agriculture at that time. Caral is one of 18 massive contemporary urban centers in the Supe Valley. (We will delve into this region in detail in chapter 10.)

Another recent find in the coastal region, this one in the Casma Valley, one of the largest monument centers in the New World, is Sechin Alto. Using laser-aided mapping and kite photography combined with classic techniques, Peruvian archaeologist Ivan Ghezzi has made a series of discoveries at this site over the past few years. In 2000 his team uncovered the Thirteen Towers section of Chankillo, which sits on a hilltop. It had long been considered a fortress, but his team has shown that the towers were in fact positioned to mark the dates of the solstices, equinoxes, and months.

These astro-archaeological findings indicate that Chankillo actually served as a celestial calendar and as a center for public rituals.

On March 23, 2001, an international press conference was held in Spain in conjunction with the Peruvian Embassy to announce a startling find by the Koricancha Project at the Incan Temple of the Sun, now the Santa Domingo Church in Cuzco, Peru. "The scientific investigation and GPR [ground-penetrating radar] data obtained recently in the Santa Domingo Church-Koricancha by the Bohic Ruz Explorer Society will open one of the greatest mysteries of our time," the press release stated.[6]

Using ground-penetrating radar, researchers had located a number of subterranean structures and tunnels beneath the church. Indeed, many independent explorers over the past 50 years have claimed that a maze of underground tunnels and galleries exists between Sacsayhuaman and the Temple of the Sun and connects to many other sites. However, these reports had never been substantiated by any scientific exploration until the work at Koricancha confirmed them. "These discoveries will capture the imagination of the world and have the potential to rival the finding of King Tut's Tomb of Egypt," said Anselm Pi Rambla, president of the explorers club.

Ground-penetrating radar studies have also been conducted in Egypt. However, the findings there have been steeped in controversy. Some researchers contend that a system of galleries and tunnels has been discovered under the Sphinx and the Pyramids. Others, however, dispute exactly what the GPR data has revealed and the Egyptian government remains tight-lipped about the alleged findings.

NEW BLOOD AND
RENEGADE "INDIE" RESEARCHERS

The field of archaeological and anthropological investigation has also been transformed by a number of independent researchers and scholars. The work of David Rohl demonstrates how small errors in interpretation combined with oversights can lead to critically inaccurate conclusions about history. While studying to be an Egyptologist, Rohl had a heretical insight. A mounting suspicion that something was wrong with accepted Egyptian chronologies prompted him to launch an all-out assault on what is probably the most conservative bastion in the entire science of anthropology.

Because Egyptologists are notoriously hidebound, he knew that publishing his criticisms and revealing his new ideas to colleagues was risky. Yet Rohl realized that his insight was far-reaching and would have profound ramifications if his thinking proved to be correct. It had the potential not only to revolutionize the accepted chronology of the ruling dynasties and the prevailing ideas about Egyptian and Israeli history, but also to settle a very old and bitter set of disputes between believers in the Bible and skeptics.

When Rohl introduced his theory in *A Test of Time: The Bible from Myth to History*, it appeared against a complicated and emotionally charged background. Archaeologists and skeptics had long questioned the authenticity of the Bible as a historical document, despite the powerful faith of believers. In the 1800s skeptics pointed to the Gospels' references to the towns of Capernaum, Chorazin, and Bethsaida, claiming that these places had never existed and that the accounts were just myths that should not be regarded as real history. Eventually, however, archaeologists discovered these forgotten cities and they are on tourist maps today.

The skeptics then turned to the Old Testament accounts of Nineveh, the capital of Assyria, claiming that no such city or country ever existed. But in 1840 Henry Layard, a British explorer, decided to prove them wrong. He set out to see if he could find ancient Assyria and dug up the city of Nineveh in the process.

By the beginning of the twentieth century, the skeptics turned their attention to the Hittites, claiming they were nothing but fictional people, even though the Bible mentions their empire at least 40 times. Sure enough, archaeologists uncovered a Hittite city in Turkey in 1905.

In spite of this string of proof—and these instances are only a small sampling—archaeology had failed to confirm the stories of the key patriarchs of the Old Testament. This posed a serious challenge to the historical accuracy of the Bible. There was no archaeological evidence to substantiate the accounts of Abraham and Moses. Nor was there any supporting evidence for the books of Saul, David, and even Solomon. It was not for lack of effort to find confirmation; many scholars and archaeologists had tried to validate the accounts of the Old Testament patriarchs, but all had failed. This large question remained: How could several million Jews reside in Egypt, migrate across the Sinai to Canaan, and then proceed to conquer the land without leaving a trace of evidence?

Because archaeologists could not find the footprints, their conclusion was that the events recounted in Exodus never really happened. That led scientists to assert that the Old Testament in its entirety—including not just Exodus, but Saul and David and Solomon and the rest as well—was not an accurate historical record and that Jews and Christians alike erred in believing that its literary stories or tribal legends were true accounts.

Without the required substantiation and corroboration of extra-biblical sources, the conclusion of the scientists was seemingly indisputable. The nail in the coffin came in the form of the famous excavation of Jericho in 1952. The lead archaeologist concluded that no city had existed there at the time the Israelites were said to have entered the land and to have fought the famous Battle of Jericho. According to the findings from the excavation, the mound of Jericho had already been in ruins for several hundred years by the time the Jews had crossed the Jordan. As far as traditional archaeologists were concerned, the door was now closed. Needless to say, believers did not agree.

David Rohl did not set out to prove the Bible right or wrong; that was not his priority. What Rohl realized and wanted to demonstrate was the fact that scholars had missed several crucial details while building the Egyptian chronology. He understood that these errors in interpretation had thrown off track everyone who had used that chronology as a basis for comparison with events described in the Bible.

Rohl's book details his thorough detective work and sound reasoning. He proved that the many educated guesses made by Egyptologists during the process of formulating Egyptian chronology had been based on incomplete data and were, in fact, wrong. One fundamental problem with the traditional chronology, for instance, had to do with the failure to take into account the phenomenon of parallel dynasties: In Egyptian history there were periods when there was no central controlling dynasty; several pharaohs ruled simultaneously over fragmented territories.

After resequencing Egyptian chronology, Rohl then made some necessary adjustments to biblical chronology. He shortened the sojourn in Egypt from 430 to 215 years, declaring that the sojourn of 430 years began at the time the Hebrews came into Canaan rather than at the time they entered Egypt. He also adjusted the length of time of the wilderness wanderings, the conquest of Canaan, and the period of the Judges, increasing it from 220 to 417 years.

It is easy to see how Rohl's book stirred up a major controversy. But when archaeologists began applying his revised chronologies to their work, they started making profound discoveries. It was as though a light suddenly illuminated a path that was there all along but had been obscured by darkness.

The new chronologies matched up characters and events in a completely different way from the old one. These new realizations spurred the scientific review of ancient documents such as the Amarna Letters, discovered in Egypt in 1887 and consisting of 380 cuneiform tablets of correspondence sent to the pharaoh by foreign kings. Scholars had assigned the letters to the house of correspondence of the pharaoh Akhenaten and as a result, Egyptologists had never bothered to search the tablets for correspondence from the United Monarchy of Israel—according to the old chronology, Akhenaten had lived and died before Israel was even established. Rohl's new chronology, however, placed Akhenaten at the beginning of the reign of Saul. In this light scholars began to make sense of letters that had defied previous analysis—letters from the rulers of Palestine that made copious references to Hebrews: The rulers of Palestine were unhappy because David and his army of mercenaries were pillaging the countryside to stay alive. The Egyptian record and the Bible now coincided.

There are other examples of this newly discovered relationship between the two chronologies: Rohl's revised time line put Dudimose at the end of the thirteenth dynasty, which seemed to correspond to biblical references to the plagues of Moses. In his history of Egypt, written in the third century B.C.E., High Priest Manetho laments: "In his [Dudimose's] reign, for what cause I know not, a blast from God smote us . . ."

This new link between the pharaoh Dudimose and specific events allowed a new perspective on a finding that had puzzled archaeologists. Excavations at Tel ed-Daba (the biblical Goshen), located in the Nile delta region, revealed "plague pits" into which hundreds of bodies had been thrown, verifying the plague referred to by both Manetho and the Bible. An inspection of tombs in the area resulted in the discovery that the people who populated the area were from Palestine and Syria: the children of Israel.

Rohl's fascinating book, with its wealth of information, has revolutionized the fields of both Egyptology and biblical archaeology.

While such groundbreaking intellectual work has been going on in the arena of scholarship, similar revolutionary work has been occurring out in the field. James O'Kon, a self-taught archaeologist, made his first trip into the mysterious land of the ancient Maya in 1969, which sparked in him a lifelong passion to understand this lost civilization. In 1989, on an expedition to the city of Yaxchilan, which archaeologists had been studying for 100 years, he visited a remote site along the Usamacinta River, the natural border that separates Mexico and Guatemala.

Yaxchilan is situated in the rain forest between two of the ancient Maya's most important sites: Palenque, approximately 100 miles to the north, and Tikal to the south, across the river in the Peten jungle of Guatemala. As the dugout canoe in which he was traveling approached the shore, O'Kon noticed a rock formation. To his eye its ancient function was immediately apparent.

"That's a bridge pier!" he declared, without any doubt in his mind.

The archaeologist who was leading the tour dismissed his observation. After all, the scientists who had studied the area could conclude only that the mound of rocks was a puzzling phenomenon. But O'Kon was already visualizing the construction of the bridge and the length of the span. As a well-known and highly respected forensic engineer and as a former chairman of the Forensic Council of the American Society of Civil Engineers, he had an arsenal of modern technology at his disposal to help prove that his premise was correct.

He gathered data at Yaxchilan, then used computers, aerial photos, and maps to develop a 3-D model of the site of the rock formation and to determine a variety of important engineering coordinates. When all of his calculations were complete, the results were astounding: They demonstrated that the Mayan engineers had designed and built the longest bridge span in the ancient world, a 600-foot suspension structure with two piers on each side of the river and two supports in the river itself.

His findings were published in the January 1995 issues of *Civil Engineering* and *National Geographic* magazines. Yaxchilan had in fact needed such a bridge because it was located on high ground at a bend in the Usamacinta River, which bordered the city on three sides. This part of the rain forest receives 150 to 200 inches of rain between June and January—so much that during the rainy season, "Yaxchilan became an island city," O'Kon states.

This important discovery is only part of O'Kon's work. He is convinced that the Maya were not a "Stone Age" people, referring to them instead as a "technolythic" race that "used jade, which is harder than steel, for their tools." His reasoning is difficult to refute: "The nearest iron was fifteen hundred miles away," he told me during a recent discussion I had with him. "The Mayans were very sophisticated mathematically and scientifically. They had the concept [of] zero seven hundred years before the Europeans."

O'Kon has now turned his attention to the enigmatic road system of the Maya that connected their sites. O'Kon has already discovered that a 60-mile-long road that stretches from Coba to Yaxuna is as perfectly straight as a road can be—truer than modern roads, with only a negligible deviation. This discovery has raised again a question that has long plagued researchers: Why did the Maya feel compelled to build wide, paved, level roads when they did not have wheeled vehicles or dray animals? Another modern explorer in the field of Peruvian antiquities has been turning myths into history for four decades. Now in his seventies, Gene Savoy is still an active researcher with a far-flung reputation in South America and a collection of real-life exploits that seem to rival those of Indiana Jones.

Savoy spent his childhood in the northwestern United States and says he can't recall a time when he did not want to be an explorer. He had an early passion for the history and folklore of North American Indian tribes (Savoy claims a one sixty-fourth Cherokee ancestry). By the time he was in his twenties he had already formulated some theories that he wanted to test by exploring the mountains and jungles of Peru.

He had noticed similarities in the pictographic symbols and design motifs of various ancient North American and South American peoples that suggested there must have been contact among them. Fueled by his theory of transcontinental contact, Savoy made some startling discoveries long before Machu Picchu became a tourist site. His first expeditions took place in the 1950s and early 1960s, with his daring treks into the eastern Andes leading to the discovery of the fabled Vilcabamba, the Incas' last city of refuge from the invading Spaniards.[7]

In 1965 he found another important site, which he named Gran Pajaten, in the northeastern jungles of Peru near the Rio Abiseo drainage. The subsequent discovery of 40 additional ancient ruins in this region could be credited to him. But evidence of the "mythical" Chachapoyas—the tall, fair-skinned warriors who preceded the Incas and whom the Incas were said to have used as guards—was what he sought most passionately.

In 1984 Savoy returned to try to find clues to their legendary civilization and this time he was successful. His expedition uncovered spectacular cloud forest ruins near the Vilaya River that he subsequently named Gran Vilaya, and after exploring the ruins, his expedition mapped out the region. This huge site in the Department of Amazonas, west of the Utcabamba River, presented many curious artifacts. It comprises well over 24,000 oval-cut stones covering an estimated 100 square miles.

In 1989, as the Gran Vilaya expedition was nearing its completion, Savoy and his team scrambled into a cliffside cave, where they found a set of inscribed tablets. On them he noticed a familiar symbol, one used by King Solomon to mark the ships he sent to the land of Orphir to recover gold and precious stones for his temple in Jerusalem. This sent the tireless explorer on a new journey, a seagoing expedition, with the goal of retracing the possible routes used by ancient Old World mariners to reach the New World.

Savoy has opened up many new and mysterious historical realms. To date science knows very little about the Chachapoyas, whose name means "cloud people," other than the fact that they built numerous walls across the misty mountaintops to guard their secret cities, which clearly dominated the cloud forest. It was on an Andean peak in their realm that ice mummies were found in 1995. To date archaeologists have also uncovered tombs and other artifacts, but they have yet to penetrate the enigma of the people of the perpetual mist.

However, despite these and other mysteries whose explanations have eluded us, the discoveries of the last 100 years suggest that we are standing on the threshold of a great leap forward in our understanding of ancient history. The onset of the third millennium holds out the promise that we will finally penetrate the heart of those mysteries that have confounded generations. Using new technologies, innovative methods, a multidisciplinary approach, and the fresh perspective of independent researchers, we may well unlock the secrets of the ages.

However, as there have always been, there are today potent forces committed to maintaining the status quo. What would serve best is a wholesale review of the orthodox interpretations of ancient history, one based on a revolutionary way of looking at the origins of human civilization. In short, we need a full commitment to uncovering the truth, a commitment that is free of preconceptions and open to possibility.

TWO

Mysterious Origins: Descended from Apes?

Any new theory of the genesis of life, humankind, and civilization must begin by addressing whether the traditional or prevailing dogmas are adequate. Those who subscribe to the alternative history school of thought have not yet fully examined how Darwinism has been applied to the development of history and culture. But before we can do this here, we must begin by first looking at what makes up Darwinism.

Darwin's theory of evolution is based on the mechanism of mutation—accidental alteration of the genetic code—and the feedback mechanism of natural selection, which follows the principle that the fittest survive while the weaker die out.

Interestingly, though the concept of evolution has been attributed to Charles Darwin, he did not actually originate the theory. It had been around for two centuries when Darwin began examining it. Nor did Darwin invent the idea of natural selection, which had been observed in great detail by other scientists studying heredity. It is Darwin, however, who began piecing together these hypotheses in a scientifically plausible way, bringing them to a cohesive whole in his voluminous work *The Origin of Species*.

But should Darwin's theory of evolution still be considered the definitive explanation for the evolution of all Earth's life-forms? In his 1986 book *Evolution: A Theory in Crisis*, author Michael Denton looks at Darwin's theory and makes a distinction between two types of evolution: *microevolution* and *macroevolution*. The first involves natural selection within genotypes, a horizontal process that is readily observable in the artificial selective breeding of domesticated plants and animals, in the variation within genotypes explained by Darwin in his theory, and in the geographical distribution of many living species. The process of microevolution mirrors natural selection in some ways, though in an accelerated form. We will see in chapter 3, however, that artificial selection is really very different from the natural process and that the results produced in a short time are the opposite of those produced by natural selection.

In his book Denton claims that it is the process of macroevolution that Darwinism cannot explain.[1] Macroevolution involves the creation of the first cell of a new organism with a new genotype or the leap from one genotype to another. This change across type—a vertical rather than a lateral process—is what is so hotly debated. The main tenets of evolution indicate that species evolve from random mutations, resulting in their gradual rise up the ladder from simple to complex forms of life, not their horizontal development into new genotypes.

Recent discoveries made by a public consortium working on the human genome project have also raised significant questions about Darwinian theories of evolution. Although some of these issues are being hotly debated by the scientific community, the media have not focused much attention on the implications of these discoveries. As a result, the public has not really assimilated or analyzed what they mean in terms of the prevailing and generally accepted ideas (at least in science) about the origins of life on Earth, especially in regard to how humankind has evolved.

Cracking the code of the human genome has produced at least two startling results. Scientists had previously reasoned that simpler life-forms might have as few as 500 to a maximum of 2,000 genes, while humans, being the most complex species, have the greatest number of genes, perhaps 60,000 to 80,000, with the average estimate being 100,000 to 140,000, far more than any other species. This prediction, based on Darwinian theory, was not, however, borne out by the results. Once our genome's code had been broken, the human gene count turned out to be a disappointing 30,000—only a little more than double the 13,601 genes in a fruit fly.

The second disturbing bit of news was the consortium's revelation that the human genome contains 223 genes that do not have predecessors on the genomic evolutionary tree. Because 223 represents a small percentage of our 30,000 genes, their existence may seem inconsequential—nothing to fuss about! When referring to genes, however, even small numbers can make all the difference. For example, though it may be difficult to accept, human beings are separated from chimpanzees by only 300 genes, a 1 percent difference! At the genetic level chimpanzees and humans are 99 percent alike. To some, that human beings and chimpanzees differ genetically by only 1 percent clearly proves the theory of evolution. Instead, it actually makes it more difficult and more critical to explain human uniqueness. What is contained in that 1 percent to make us so different from chimps?

MORE DISSENTING OPINIONS

When his now famous book was published in 1859, Darwin knew that his theory of evolution had weaknesses. What's more, he was well aware of the exact portion that was his Achilles' heel:

> The number of intermediate varieties, which have formerly existed on earth must be truly enormous. Why then is not every geological formation and every stratum full of such intermediate links? . . . [This] is the most obvious and gravest objection which can be urged against my theory.[2]

What Darwin was getting at is that though the truth of his theory *should* be supported by indisputable substantiation in the fossil record, some intermediate supports are missing. We all know this as the problem of the "missing link," which is generally assumed to refer to the lack of a precursor only for modern humans. However, the problem is much broader and deeper. As the late Louis B. Leakey, preeminent anthropologist, told his audience during a lecture at the University of the Pacific in response to a question about this topic: "There is no one missing link—there are hundreds of links missing."[3]

According to Darwinism, the two processes of mutation and natural selection worked together gradually over time to change fish into amphibians, amphibians into reptiles, reptiles into birds, and eventually birds into mammals. The theory predicted that the ultimate proof that this is the way life developed on earth would come from the fossil record. But to date excavations have not fulfilled this prediction.

"It was the absence of transitional fossils that first made me question Darwin's idea of gradual change," science writer and recovering Darwinist Richard Milton told a reporter during an interview about his book, *Shattering the Myths of Darwinism.*[4] Milton was an ardent Darwinist who had spent his weekends studying geology and paleontology in his native England. One day he realized that something was amiss. It occurred to him that much of the thinking that proved Darwinism was circular, as were the methods used to justify the theory. For instance, he points out that rocks are used to date fossils and fossils are used to date rocks.

Once Milton's natural skepticism was aroused, he left no stone unturned. He became an almost daily visitor to the prestigious Natural History Museum in London, where he subjected to intense scrutiny every piece of evidence that was used to support Darwin's theory. He looked at the theorized evolution of the horse, the Archaeopteryx, half reptile, half bird; the peppered moth; the Galápagos finches; and all the other "unquestionable" pieces of the Darwinian puzzle. He found that the supposed histories of their development could not hold up under routine journalistic investigation.

The scientific community likes to present the image of being united. It insists that the majority of its members are on board the Darwin bandwagon (or the good ship *Beagle,* as the case may be) and would like the public to believe that the only criticisms of Darwinism come from unscientific religionists (or creationists—those who believe that the world was created by God, as recounted in Genesis), who have an ax to grind, even though this representation is inaccurate. In fact, several eminent scientists, notably Dr. Francis Crick, the codiscoverer of the structure of DNA in 1950, and astronomer Fred Hoyle, have published criticisms of Darwin's theory and presented alternate theories for consideration.

That Crick—the man who made it possible to decode the human genome—does not accept Darwin's theory of evolution is especially telling. In his book *Life Itself* Crick raises 100 rigorous questions that he does not think Darwinism can answer. He goes on to offer an alternate theory called *panspermia,* which we will examine in more detail in the next chapter. No one would deny that Dr. Crick is an eminent scientist with impeccable intellectual credentials, yet the scientific establishment largely ignored his criticism of Darwin and his innovative theory was likewise dismissed.

Crick and Hoyle are by no means the only scientists to question the foundations of evolution. A number of other books expressing criticism of the theory have been published in recent years, and not long ago a declaration titled "A Scientific Dissent on Darwinism" was signed by 100 scientists and released to the press in time to coincide with the scheduled airing on PBS of a seven-part pro-Darwin series called, appropriately enough, *Evolution.*

The scientists who signed the declaration made up a diverse lot, including biblical creationists, though they did not make up the majority. One statement from the document indicates just how direct their dissent was: "I am skeptical of claims for the ability of random mutation and natural selection to account for the complexity of life."[5] The signers went on to offer reasonable and rational support for intellectual questioning of the theory: "Careful examination of the evidence for Darwinian theory should be encouraged." But the strongest criticism came from chemist and Nobel-nominee Henry "Fritz" Schaefer, who chided Darwinists for "embracing standards of evidence for evolution that as scientists they would never accept in other circumstances."[6]

BUT WHAT DOES THE EVIDENCE SHOW?

The process of macroevolution—of change from one genotype to another—has never been observed: No person ever witnessed reptiles changing into birds or nonflowering plants emerging as flowering plants. So to find the missing links between reptile and bird or between a nonflowering plant and one bearing blossoms, scientists have turned to the fossil record. Thus the most extensive scientific effort in history has gone on continuously since Darwin's day. Armies of scientists and weekend Darwinists eager to get dirty for the cause have participated in excavations around the globe in the interest of achieving one goal: to prove that the theory of evolution is valid. This long and massive effort has turned up roughly a quarter of a million fossils that are housed in museums all over the world—but has found no intermediate fossils of any significance.

This fact alone poses a serious threat to Darwin's theory. If life slowly evolved from simple to complex forms through a series of mutations in response to changing environmental conditions, as Darwinism claims, then there should be a superabundance of intermediate forms. Yet the fossil record does not bear this out. The picture of life on Earth as shown by fossils is that new, fully formed species appear out of nowhere, remain the same for long periods of time, and then disappear.

This picture is the secret that paleontologists and Darwinists have been keeping to themselves. The late paleontologist Stephen Jay Gould actually dared to admit, "All paleontologists know that the fossil record contains precious little in the way of intermediate forms; transitions between major groups are characteristically abrupt."[7] This truth is obviously what prompted Gould to publish his controversial theory of *punctuated equilibrium,* an attempt to explain why there are missing links and why species appear and disappear as if by magic instead of following Darwinism's slow progression of small incremental changes. But Gould's colleagues quietly dismissed his theory, saying that "the theory of evolution already accounted for it"[8] despite the fact that Darwin included in his hypothesis nothing about abrupt, discontinuous appearances and disappearances.

One of Darwin's most vexing conundrums was trying to account for the sudden appearance of flowering plants. All of the primitive plants had propagated and survived successfully for hundreds of millions of years via asexual reproduction. Then, about 100 million years ago, flowering plants inexplicably emerged. Darwin referred to it as the "abominable problem."

This sudden appearance is confusing for several reasons. First, there are no transitional species in the fossil record. If Darwin's theory is correct, however, there should be thousands of such examples. Cycads and ferns, which existed 300 million years ago as they do today, are nonflowering, primitive plants that are abundant in the fossil record. Flowering plants have existed for 100 million years and have become the dominant plant species in the world—there about 250,000 species today. Like nonflowering plants, they too are plentiful in the fossil record. But where are the fossils of transitional species linking nonflowering and flowering plants? If these intermediate plants in fact existed, their fossils should be just as abundant. There is no Darwinian explanation for this absence. Evolutionists are very aware of the lack of support from the fossil record and, in an attempt to find a way out of this dilemma, typically offer two spurious arguments: 1) the fossil record is incomplete; 2) a future excavation will turn up these missing links.

In addition to the conundrum of the absence of fossil evidence, there is no mechanism in Darwin's theory to explain why a successful species would mutate and invest energy in new structures such as petals, stamens, anthers, pollen, and nectar in anticipation of an insect co-evolving to eventually pollinate it. Such a mutation implies the intelligent design that Darwinists dispute—even more so because along with plants developing flowers in anticipation of insects to pollinate them, a similar anticipatory intelligence would have had to have been present in insects so that they might develop into pollinating bees and butterflies.

The theory of evolution is appealing because it is a simple way to explain how life evolved on Earth. If viewed from a broad perspective, it seems to make sense. As we see here, however, building a model of the evolution of a particular species using Darwinian principles reveals the holes in the hypothesis. The sudden change in plants from nonflowering to flowering calls into question the Darwinian insistence that evolution is a random process of accidental mutation. And the tremendous expenditure of energy required to mutate an efficient non-flowering plant into a less efficient, less competitive flowering plant defies the Darwinian law of natural selection. Darwinism simply does not allow for the complexity of the coexistence of plants with two vastly different types of reproductive systems.

Yet another concern lies in the fact that cycads and ferns are still with us and flowering plants are abundant, but the more developed alleged intermediate forms are not. Nor do we find transitional species of those insects and birds that would have had to evolve simultaneously with flowering plants. There is, in short, no evidence of the coevolution of flowering plants and the creatures required for their reproduction.

THE MEDIA AND THE PUBLIC

We are left to wonder why the media have taken such a pro-Darwinist stance. The PBS program *Evolution* came out in strong support of Darwinism, though it was presented as a fair, impartial documentary reporting the established facts. The producers left out two critical elements, however: They failed to include any dissenting voices and they failed to address the now apparent holes in Darwin's theory.

When questioned about the program's presentation, the producers responded that it presented "facts and the accumulated results of scientific inquiry, which means understanding the underlying evidence behind claims of fact and proposed theories, and reporting those areas where the science is sound. . . . In keeping with solid science journalism we examine empirically tested explanations . . . but don't speak to the ultimate cause of 'who done it'—the religious realm."[9]

This response sounds very much like the rhetoric of neo-Darwinists. In fact, the critics of Darwin's theory do not argue that the "religious theme" should be avoided. They simply wish to raise important questions based on their own research and the empirical evidence they have gathered against the theory of evolution.

But it seems that Darwinists have been more comfortable debating creationists than dealing with the serious criticisms levied by other scientists or fielding pointed questions from tough-minded journalists. Indeed, the war between evolutionists and creationists has heated up over the past decade. Creationists like to characterize evolutionists as Godless intellectuals who dogmatically embrace a secular theory of life that they cannot prove, while evolutionists have portrayed creationists as dogmatic biblical fundamentalists. These characterizations have lead to nothing but polemics and contentiousness—and to a neat diversion from the scientific criticisms of Darwinian theory.

Actually, for all their claims of avoiding the religious theme, the program *Evolution* had quite a lot to say about God and religion, though not from a believer's perspective. The viewer was reminded numerous times by a bevy of scientists that Darwin was "in" and God was "out." But none addressed the issue of whether Darwin's theory is viable or seriously flawed.

Meanwhile, the American public has insisted on steering a middle course. A recent survey showed that "83 percent of those questioned generally support the teaching of evolution." That may sound as though most Americans believe in Darwin's theory and want it taught to their children as established fact. But that is not the case: "71 percent of those respondents say biology teachers should teach both Darwinism and the scientific evidence against Darwinian theory."[10]

This seems a fair and objective approach. The public is not asking that creationism be taught; it merely wishes to have alternative theories presented in the classroom. But ever since Darwin's theory became part of standard public school science curriculum, no effort has been made to present contrary theories. Nor is there a plan for instituting such a balanced approach in the future. The unvarnished truth is that Darwin's theory—once it was accepted by the scientific establishment—has been taught in an uncritical way to generations of schoolchildren here in America, throughout Europe, and in much of the rest of the world.

Any other theory that had been allowed so many opportunities to prove itself yet had failed and still exhibited major flaws would have been tossed aside by now. Why has Darwin's theory persisted? And if this notion of evolution is not the answer, then what is?

THREE

Origins II: Evolution or Extraterrestrial Intervention?

How did life begin? One of the paradoxes that Darwinism—if we embrace it—leaves us with is the notion that order comes out of chaos, that something that begins as a random event eventually becomes organized. To the adherents of Darwin's theory, human beings are the outcome of an evolutionary process that began long ago in the chaos of primordial soup.

Many human cultures have sought to explain the mystery of the origins of life through their creation myths, which often include humans being fashioned from mud (primordial soup?). If our modern civilization were to collapse, as so many other civilizations have in human history, perhaps future anthropologists would boil down our myths and evolutionary theory and reconstruct it like this: This ancient lost civilization believed that humans were created from a swampy "mud soup," a notion that was obviously a product of their primitive imagination. According to their understanding, what had been created from mud became a worm at some point and eventually transformed into a monkey and then a human being.

Of course, this characterization of Darwinism is an exaggeration, but it is true that Darwin never did address the sticky issue of the origin of life; for him this was the province of religion, and natural evolution presented no answer to this riddle. Nor do neo-Darwinists claim to have an explanation for what caused life to begin. In fact, the theory of evolution accepts only mutation and natural selection as causal factors in the universe at large.

Nevertheless, evolutionary theory has been used as a template to explain everything from the origin of the cosmos (the Big Bang) to the development of agriculture, civilization, and the existence of social hierarchies (the richest are the fittest). The theory assumes that everything evolves out of disorder in gradual, incremental steps toward the ultimate triumph of the winner in nature's grand lottery. But in its findings the human genome project has created additional obstacles for the theory of evolution. The project proved that there is only one tree of life and that it developed only once, which does suggest that the tree was planted—that intent and design, and not chance, were at work. It also shortened the time span during which life was to have evolved from the simplest forms to the most complex via random mutations.

Fred Hoyle, however, sees no support for the belief that life on the planet evolved from random mutations: "In short there is not a shred of objective evidence to support the hypothesis that life began in an organic soup here on Earth . . . Life did not appear by chance."[1] He once declared that the emergence of a living cell from an inanimate chemical soup is about as likely as the assembly of a 747 by a whirlwind passing through a junkyard!

The mystery of the origin of life is compounded by the fact that any chance mutations and the process of natural selection had only a few hundred million years to accomplish what still ends up being a miracle, though Darwinists can call it whatever they want. Darwin himself made it clear that his theory could be disproved: "If it could be demonstrated that any complex organ existed which could not possibly have been formed by numerous, successive, slight modifications, my theory would absolutely break down."[2]

In the recently published book *Darwin's Black Box: The*

Biochemical Challenge to Evolution, Michael Behe claims that biochemistry has indeed demonstrated this. We have to keep in mind that in Darwin's day a cell was thought of as an indistinct entity and no one knew anything at all about DNA. The technology to penetrate the cell and determine its biochemistry did not yet exist. Behe makes it clear that for "the Darwinian theory of evolution to be true, it [modern biochemistry] has to account for the molecular structure of life."[3] In his book he proves that it does not.

Every researcher, regardless of his or her ultimate position relative to Darwin's theory, has to admit that the origin of life is a tricky problem that seems impossible to account for statistically. As one scientist put it: "The probability of not only getting all the right ingredients together in one place, with the right amount of energy, but also organizing those ingredients into a complex organism capable of replicating itself seems extremely small."[4] Around the issue of life's very beginnings, we can divide the two sides of the scientific community into "improbable-ists" such as Francis Crick and Fred Hoyle and "inevitable-ists." Crick once commented that the origin of life seems to be ". . . a miracle, so many are the conditions which would have to be satisfied to get it going."[5] But in his book *Climbing Mount Improbable* Richard Dawkins counters, ". . . my guess is that life probably isn't all that rare and the origin of life probably wasn't all that improbable."[6]

Behe contends that "[b]iochemistry has pushed back Darwin's theory to the limit. It has done so by opening the ultimate black box, the cell, thereby making possible our understanding of how life works."[7] What he observes in the basic cellular processes are systems and dynamics that are irreducibly complex, and this evidence, he concludes, overwhelmingly disproves Darwin's theory: Cells could not possibly have been assembled piecemeal over any length of time.

In order to share the rationale for his conclusion, Behe takes us to the microscopic level, where we can see that the theory of evolution fails to explain certain molecular and intracellular processes.

He examines five main phenomena: blood clotting; the human immune system; cilia, oarlike bundles of fibers; transport of materials within the cell; and the synthesis of nucleotides, the building blocks of DNA. In every instance he finds systems that are so complex that no gradual, incremental, Darwinian route could produce them.[8] "The result of these cumulative efforts to investigate the cell—to investigate life at the molecular level—is a loud, clear, piercing cry of 'design!'"[9]

But his sense of having achieved a scientific breakthrough has clearly been dampened by its reception: "But no bottles have been uncorked, no hands slapped. Instead a curious, embarrassed silence surrounds the stark complexity of the cell."[10] We have encountered this strange silence before when other scientists have critiqued Darwinism. The Darwinist establishment seems to regard as defectors those who question the theory. But though it knows how to fight the unscientific creationists, refuting those whose credentials are not so easily dismissed is another matter.

Richard Milton sees in this cold reception only a basic human need to conform: ". . . Then I began to discover one by one the many scientists around the world who had already realized the emperor has no clothes, but who cannot speak out without jeopardizing their careers and even their jobs."[11]

LIFE FROM EXTRATERRESTRIAL ORIGINS: PANSPERMIA

While each focuses on different phenomena, the scientific critics of Darwinian evolution all arrive at the same conclusion: The origin of the species is not to be found in random mutation and natural selection. Crick, Behe, and Hoyle go further by arguing for a theory based on intelligent design.

The first half of Nobel laureate Crick's book *Life Itself: Its Origin and Nature* is devoted not only to taking apart Darwin's theory of evolution, but also to showing why life could not have originated on Earth. He then proposes that life was seeded on Earth from spores that arrived from outer space. Although this seemed like a novel idea when the book was published, the theory of panspermia, as the process is called, first originated with a Swedish physicist named Svante Arrhenius in the nineteenth century. But what distinguished Crick's theory from the original version was his proposal that life had evolved on another planet to a technical level higher than we have reached up to now. Once this extraterrestrial civilization reached a certain level of development, it began sending rockets containing spores (primitive life-forms similar to bacteria or viruses) throughout the universe. This conscious spreading of the seeds of life is called *directed panspermia* and is a mechasnism we ourselves could theoretically employ now by loading a space module with bacteria and mold and sending it toward another planet.

When it was published in 1983, Crick's book met with strong skepticism and harsh critical reviews from within the scientific community. The objections revolved around the lack of any empirical evidence for this hypothesis and unlikelihood that such organisms would survive the extended time period required to travel great distances in space.

Following Crick, Fred Hoyle—originator of the steady state universe theory—and his coauthor N. Chandra Wickramasinghe used the first part of their book *Lifecloud: the Origin of Life in the Universe,* to prove that life did not originate on Earth. The evidence they present is as solid as that in Crick's work. After establishing an extraterrestrial origin of life on this planet, the authors propose that the seeds of life traveled on comets that crashed into Earth. This theory and the book's authors were received with ridicule. In his review in the journal *Nature,* astronomer Fred Whipple probably represented the consensus of those in the scientific community: "I am charmed but not impressed by the picture of life forms developing in warm little ponds, protected in their icy igloos from the cruel cold and near vacuum of open space; and falling to primitive Earth at speeds exceeding eleven kilometers per second."[12]

Though ridiculed and dismissed, the theory refuses to go away due to new experimental and observational data that disproves some of the main objections hurled against it. Twenty years have elapsed since Crick's and Hoyle's books were published and reviewed and some very interesting developments have occurred that have changed negative attitudes toward panspermia. In the late 1960s a common bacterium of the throat, *Streptococcus mitus*, was inadvertently taken to the Moon on one of the cameras mounted on the Surveyor 3 landing module. The Apollo 12 mission rescued the lander without contaminating the bacterium's sterile conditions and found the bacterial growth had survived and remained viable after more than a full year of exposure to the extremely inhospitable conditions of the lunar surface.

This unplanned experiment accidentally opened the door to panspermia that Darwinists believed to be securely shut. Life was not supposed to be able to survive the brutal conditions of outer space, neither the extreme cold nor the intense levels of radiation, which were thought to be the main obstacles to life arriving on Earth via any interstellar excursion. The fact that the bacterium did survive supported the idea that life could have evolved in space and that this life-form already has the proper defense mechanisms that would allow it to get to any planet. This resistance and vigor were confirmed when it was discovered that another bacterium, *Deinococcus radiodurans,* was able to resist enormous doses of radiation. It is now clear that life has evolved mechanisms to deal with radical universal conditions. In essence, and as Crick and Hoyle have suggested, life may well have originated elsewhere in the universe and been brought here by a higher civilization or far-ranging comets or even interstellar space probes designed expressly for the purpose.

The evolution of human beings is seldom addressed in the debates on evolution. But in the final analysis, we must be able to fit the human race into any grand scheme of the origin and subsequent development of life. Even if evolution could be proved to be substantially factual, one crucial anomaly remains: *Homo sapiens sapiens*. Darwinism insists that humans are part and parcel of biological evolution and thus should not exhibit any extraordinary or wildly divergent traits or propensities not found in other primate species. There is, then, no Darwinian accounting for the human being's single-minded dedication to tool making, domestication of plants and animals, agriculture, and all other aspects of civilization. In fact, as we have recently realized quite contrary to the theory of evolution's insistence on the development of a species toward greater likelihood of survival, these capabilities all seem to lead to antievolutionary outcomes such as destruction of habitat, extinction of fellow species, and harm to ourselves. If Darwin's theory cannot account for our own history, then how can we expect to use it to penetrate to the very creation of life itself?

The human record does offer us some potential answers, however. The earliest written and oral accounts converge on a hybridized form of the theory of panspermia that I have called intelligent extraterrestrial intervention. These accounts come from Sumer, Egypt, Mexico, Peru, China, and India: those exact places where civilization originated.

For instance, the Maya, the Incas, and the Aztecs all tell of a time when a white, bearded man in a cape walked among them, teaching the arts of civilization. The cultures gave him different names but the accounts of his deeds are identical. He brought agriculture, tools, and laws to the people before he and his assistants departed, saying they would return one day. This story has been dismissed as a myth and the man (Quetzacoatl or Viracocha) has become a god in the mythical pantheon.[13] As we shall see, some of these legends have proved to contain much truth and have led to many significant discoveries. In fact, the deeper we dig into nature's mysteries and the stories of our ancient predecessors, the more possible it seems that we are the progeny of some extraterrestrial beings who somehow sent their seed to Earth.

FOUR

The Genesis Account

One of the earliest and most important written historical records we have is contained in the Bible. But the meaning of the history contained within the Old Testament is not easy to decipher, though generations going back several millennia have all made their attempt. Perhaps the true meaning of the Old Testament's accounts—especially the account of Genesis—has eluded us because the technical development of our cultures has not been sufficient to make sense of seemingly conflicting descriptions of how life on earth originated, how human beings were created, and who the God referred to is. Adding to the difficulty is the fact that for centuries humans from childhood through adulthood have been given instruction on the traditionally accepted interpretations and meanings of biblical accounts. These "lessons" have entered the deepest parts of human imagination.

From the time since author Erich von Däniken opened the door by suggesting a new interpretation of scripture, legends, and lost civilizations, many writers have focused on specific verses of the Book of Genesis and the Book of Ezekiel to reassess our origins. And while it is not really possible to understand all that the Old Testament has to tell about human history by considering only a few verses of its entirety, Genesis is perhaps the best place to start because it provides a fascinating and complex picture of creation and the origin of humans.

There is a code contained in Genesis, though it involves no complicated supernatural interpretations, no allegorical or metaphorical leaps, and no magical thinking. On the contrary, unlocking the truth of the Bible requires a clinical approach, uncompromising logic, a fearless determination to stick with the literal meanings of the words on the page, and the effort necessary to compare new interpretations and established facts using common sense.

Rigorous analysis of Genesis 1 and 2 makes one point clear right away: There were in fact two creations of humankind. This is a crucial distinction, for though, to my knowledge, biblical scholars and theologians have never made it, the early chroniclers of human history did, which is why they included two different sequences of creation in two separate chapters of this book of the Bible.

It is important to note at the start that blurring Genesis 1 and Genesis 2 creates insoluble confusion. A great deal is missed in assuming that the two chapters are describing only one series of events. Nowhere is it indicated that the second chapter is a further elucidation of the first chapter, least of all in the accounts themselves, which differ so completely.

We can begin by comparing these two creation sequences. Genesis 1 tells us that God created the elements of the universe in the following order:

1. Heaven and the earth
2. Light
3. Day and night
4. Expanse and waters
5. Dry land, earth and gathering waters, seas
6. Plants and trees
7. Stars, the Sun, the Moon, and the planets
8. Living creatures
9. Humans, both male and female

This first chapter concludes with Genesis 1:31: "And God saw all that He had made, and behold, it was very good. And there was evening and there was morning, the sixth day."[1] The second chapter starts with "Thus the heavens and the earth were completed, and all their hosts." (Genesis 2:1) The work of the creation is finished. God rests on the seventh day.

But in Genesis 2:4–9 we are given a brand-new creation account in which God creates:

1. Man from dust
2. The Garden of Eden
3. Trees, two of which are the tree of the knowledge of good and evil and the tree of life

After this, God does the following:

4. Divides the river into four rivers
5. Places man in the Garden of Eden to cultivate it
6. Instructs man that he may eat from any tree, "but from the tree of the knowledge of good and evil you shall not eat"
7. Forms "every beast of the field and every bird of the sky"
8. Causes Adam to fall asleep and takes a rib from his side
9. Fashions Eve from his rib

The two versions of creation in Genesis 1 and Genesis 2 are obviously completely different, but separating the information into two distinct acts of creation—a literal reading of the biblical content and structure—can clear up the confusion. Genesis 1 is the original creation. In it the Hebrew word used for the God who creates the heavens and the earth is Yahweh, the singular designation for the Almighty Lord. This is the One Supreme Being responsible for the creation of the universe of solar systems and galaxies.

In Genesis 1:27 we read: "And God created man in His own image, in the image of God He created him; male and female He created them." The meaning of this passage has long been a subject of debate. If we interpret it in a strictly literal way, it tells us that the physical form of human beings is a copy of the form of their creator. But if the One Eternal God has no form and is a purely spiritual, omnipotent, omniscient, and omnipresent being, how can humans have been made in his image?

Although theologians, biblical scholars, and the teachings of the church have insisted that this verse be taken in a metaphorical or spiritual sense, its meaning is much more straightforward. To understand what the ancients were trying to tell us in this verse, we have to look closely at the preceding passage, Genesis 1:26. In it the Hebrew word used to refer to God suddenly changes from that used in the verses up to verse 26. It is no longer Yahweh but Elohim, a *plural* word for deity: "Then the gods said, Let *Us* make man in *Our* image, according to *Our* likeness; and let them rule over the fish of the sea and over the birds . . . and over every creeping thing. . . ." Theologians have traditionally ignored this crucial switch to the plural voice, and though it exists quite clearly in the text, and is used in later passages, we can be forgiven for any confusion: Is there one God or a number of gods, or can God somehow change into a plurality? A single God creates Heaven and the earth, light, and creatures, while gods—the genesis race or superior humanlike race—confer and decide to create humans.

Though 1:26–27 seem to fly in the face of monotheism, any biblical text is subject to interpretation. Fundamentalists, who are usually also creationists, insist that Genesis be taken literally and that we regard the contents of the Bible as historically accurate, yet they themselves do not take these two passages literally. In reality, however, these verses actually make perfect literal sense when we understand that the One Supreme Being that created the universe and life is simply not the same as Elohim, the gods who came after the universal creation. Who, then, were these superior, godlike yet humanlike beings?

I offer the possibility that they were very advanced humans from an Earth-like planet who traveled through space and arrived on

Earth with knowledge and techniques that were a million years ahead of ours developmentally. Beings so superior to early humans—with the capability of intervening in human genetics— would certainly have been referred to as gods and lords by the humans they created.

This interpretation has been ridiculed as being "far-out" science fiction. But given the three recent news stories outlined in the introduction to this book, given what modern science has already accomplished, is this interpretation so impossible to accept? In fact, at this point in our civilization we are nearly mirroring the Elohim of Genesis 1: We are exploring space and experimenting with genetic manipulation.

Bear in mind that nothing in Genesis 1:26–27 refers to humans being created by supernatural means. We are obviously physical beings, part of a living biological world, and from the biblical account it is clear that the gods were creating physical beings. Of course, we do not know exactly how they accomplished this. The process is not explained in Genesis 1 and our ancestors could not possibly have understood or expressed it even if their creators had told them exactly how it was achieved. But at this point in our history we can make a very educated guess as to their methods. We already have the answer in sperm banks, retorts, computers, and genetics labs. We ourselves genetically alter plants and animals. We can even buy genetically modified organisms in our supermarkets! If the Elohim created humans in their image, then it is likely they had a very sophisticated knowledge of genetics and bioengineering, knowledge that modern scientists are on the cusp of now.

It is important to note that Genesis 1 does not make any references to humans having an inner being or a soul—in fact, it does not refer to anything of a spiritual nature. Some theologians assert that "God made man in his image" actually means "God made man in his *spiritual image*," but the account of human origin in Genesis 1 is concerned with only physical creation—biology, not spiritualism. At this stage of creation humans are animals. God creates the earth and then the gods bioengineer humans, who are to live off the land very much as other creatures do.

Genesis 1:29 explains God's (here, the gods') plan for human survival as it is presented to the first human: "Be fruitful and multiply . . . and rule over the fish of the seas and over the birds of the sky. . . . Behold, I have given you every plant yielding seed that is on the surface of the earth, and every tree which has fruit yielding seed: it shall be food for you." Here, then, is all that an early human would need to live: animals, plants, and fruits. This establishes that these first humans were to live not as tillers of the soil but as hunter-gatherers.

Genesis 1 is actually an account of the creation of proto-*Homo sapiens sapiens*—Neanderthals and their precursors who would become the humans of today. These early humans roamed the earth, living the way the gods ordain at the end of Genesis 1. Ultimately, Neanderthals failed to survive, though science has no explanation for why they became extinct about the time modern humans emerged as a slightly superior species. But at the end of Genesis 1 these early humans are new. The text has made clear that male and female have been created at the same time in the image of the gods and, as spelled out in verses 29–31, that they are to be hunter-gatherers in the natural world created for them.

There is no explanation anywhere in the Book of Genesis for the existence of the second story of creation found in Genesis 2. A direct comparison of chapters 1 and 2, however, reveals that chapter 2 describes an entirely different sequence of creation and introduces an entirely different kind of human from that in chapter 1—a human who is more developed, who is capable of self-awareness, of acquiring new skills, embracing a whole new life. It is this human who, at the end of chapter 3, is sent from Paradise and compelled to change his hunter-gatherer existence to a farming way of life.

We can speculate that the early humans of chapter 1 were not fit for an agricultural civilization. This, however, does not explain what became of them after the creation of the more advanced humans of chapter 2. I suggest the possibility that a global cataclysm wiped out the original human prototypes, an event on the order of the gods' history-changing interventions described in later chapters of Genesis—the Flood, the destruction of Sodom and Gomorrah, and so forth.

Genesis 2:7 tells us: "Then the Lord God formed man of dust from the ground, and breathed into his nostrils the breath of life . . . ." Man has been created. But what of the world around him? What kind of world does he enter, and how does it compare with the world of plants and animals in Genesis 1? A careful reading of Genesis 2 reveals that the conditions on the earth are different: "Now no shrub of the field was yet in the earth, and no plant of the field had yet sprouted, for the Lord God had not sent rain upon the earth; and there was no man to cultivate the ground." (Genesis 2:5) The world that was lush and alive in Genesis 1 now appears barren, almost post-cataclysmic. We might think of the world at the time of the dinosaurs, teeming with megaflora, that was then decimated by some sort of planetary cataclysm.

Humans have lived most of their time on the earth as children of nature, hunting, gathering, moving according to the dictates of weather and season. We know from science that the human race has progressed very slowly, that elementary reasoning abilities came only after millions of years. The early stages of development revolved around inventing stone tools and learning how to control fire, and even this glimmer of mental capacity represented a giant leap forward. Only within the past 10,000 years have humans become gardeners or tillers of the soil.

Adam, the new prototype (the one who replaces the Neanderthal), is *Homo sapiens sapiens*. Ultimately, he will leave the garden of Eden and usher in the agricultural revolution. In Hebrew Adam means "the one who has a different purpose." That he is different is further revealed when he names the creatures around him—a detail entirely missing from Genesis 1 and one that indicates that Adam has rudimentary intellectual and language skills—and later, when he receives a commandment from the gods regarding the two special trees they have planted in the Garden of Eden.

Interestingly, Eden itself is also absent from the account of chapter 1, although the earth is mentioned numerous times. Part of the confusion in understanding the true meanings of Genesis 1 and 2 has stemmed from the mistaken interpretation that Eden is the same as the state of wild nature found on the earth in chapter 1. A garden, however, implies something altogether different from the kind of arrangement and growth that occurs freely in nature. It suggests plant selection and cultivation and special attention to their growth, which puts an altogether different spin on the purpose and mission of humanity. In Genesis 2:9, we are told that God (the gods) ". . . caused to grow every tree that is pleasing to the sight and good for food," along with "the tree of life also in the midst of the garden, and the tree of the knowledge of good and evil"—two specimens that we know were considered special. Finally, in Genesis 2:15, man himself is situated in the garden: "Then the Lord took the man and put him into the garden of Eden to cultivate it and keep it." Here, the word *cultivate* implies that Adam is meant to act as caretaker in the garden—for its plants are clearly already established.

The differences between chapter 1 and chapter 2 reach beyond the physical environment and the nature of man, however. Genesis 2 specifically describes the creation of woman, an aspect entirely missing from chapter 1: "So the Lord God caused a deep sleep to fall upon man, and he slept; then He took one of his ribs, and closed up the flesh at that place." The Lord (here, the gods) then fashions Eve out of Adam's rib. The images and words here almost suggest a surgical procedure as performed by a person, a physical being. It does not say the Lord's spirit came over Adam—remember, there are no spiritual references in this account and in fact any such interpretation would be a departure from the actual words of the scripture.

Here we have, then, a new type of human—both man and woman—who is quite different from the one created in Genesis 1, and a new place—a garden—in a world that has become barren. But is there any more information about the creator? The next chapter,

Genesis 3, gives us more corroboration for the assertion that the gods who appear throughout Genesis after the universal creation are actually physical beings. Genesis 3:8 says: "And they heard the sound of the Lord God walking in the garden in the cool of day, and the man and his wife hid themselves . . ." God (one of the gods) is clearly somewhere in the garden, for how could Adam and Eve hide from the all-seeing, all-knowing, omnipresent Lord that theologians find in these passages? And how could God himself walk in the garden if he were not a physical entity? Further, he soon asks to know where Adam is hiding: "Then the Lord God called to the man, and said to him, 'Where are you?'"(Genesis 3:9) But why would an all-seeing God have to search for two of his creatures in the garden of his own making?

Continuing in the third chapter, after this god rebukes Adam and Eve for eating from the tree of the knowledge of good and evil, he makes "garments of skin for Adam and his wife" to clothe their nakedness. Could this refer to him—a physical being—actually showing his human creations how to make rudimentary clothing from skins? We know that soon, as a result of their infraction, he will send them from the garden into wild nature with a new mission: to farm the land. Would he do so without providing his creations with the knowledge and skills required to survive—including how to clothe themselves and how to till the land? Accounts of the gods instructing primitive human beings in the arts of agriculture and civilization can be found in the ancient cultures of Sumer, Mexico, and Peru. It seems obvious that Adam is taught how to cultivate the land in Eden.

This leads us to a discussion of the central action of Genesis 3—the eating of the fruit from the tree of the knowledge of good and evil, Adam and Eve's new understanding of their nakedness, and the command that they leave Eden and live instead in the wild outside it. Over time, these events have been the recipients of a great deal of interpretation and study.

In Genesis 3:7 we are told that after Adam tastes of the forbidden fruit of the tree of knowledge he and Eve became aware of their nakedness. This is usually interpreted to mean that Adam and Eve discover their sexuality. But God's reaction and their own reaction to this new awareness would imply that there is something negative or shameful in their sexuality, that God had somehow attached shame to their sexual differences and therefore to the fact that Adam and Eve are meant to procreate. The entire scenario played out in Eden thus takes on the connotation of a trap set by God, with sex being the forbidden fruit. Along with this interpretation comes the sense that God's purpose in decreeing that Adam and Eve must not eat the fruit of the tree of the knowledge of good and evil is to give them a test that he knows they will fail, with the result being a permanent state of guilt or shame. But the Old Testament is certainly full of explicit sexual references including incest, homosexuality, and adultery. If this assumption about God's purpose for the commandment not to eat from the tree is correct, there is no reason his plan should be so veiled here.

It is certainly clear that Adam, the gardener in the Garden of Eden, is allowed to eat from every tree but the two special trees, and there is no question that this is a test of Adam's capacity to obey orders, which he fails miserably. Once Adam shows his inclination to defy the gods' commandments by eating from the tree of knowledge, he is removed from the garden. But we might wonder at the gods' extreme reaction to Adam and Eve's disobedience. Why are they told to leave Eden as a result of their action?

The answer to this can be found in Genesis 3:22, a passage that hearkens back to Genesis 1:26 in the Lord's use of the plural in referring to himself: "Then the Lord God said, 'Behold, the man has become like one of Us, knowing good and evil; and now, lest he stretch out his hand, and take also from the tree of life, and eat, and live forever . . .'" The text continues with verse 23 and the removal of the couple from the garden. The reason that the gods sent them from Eden is very clear and stands in complete contradiction to mainstream Judeo-Christian theology: The gods of Genesis 2 and 3 do not want these humans to be immortal! Eating from the tree of the knowledge of good and evil might lead to eating from the tree of life, after which these humans would live forever, becoming like gods.

Interestingly, there is no mention anywhere in Genesis of the gods creating an eternal soul for—or conferring eternal life upon—humans. It is not hard to understand why: This is the next step in human development. We must remember that Genesis comes at the very beginning of the story of human beings and is focused mainly on the physical creation of the earth and humans; up to now nothing has been said of human character or psychological makeup—though this changes in Genesis 3.

What Genesis becomes at this point is the story of humans gaining awareness of the distinction between themselves and the rest of the animal kingdom. Eating from the tree of the knowledge of good and evil gives them the sudden realization that they are different from other animals. It gives them feelings of shame and guilt for the first time—the initial budding of the human conscience, which demonstrates that humans have free will (never possessed by animals)—and gives them an awareness of their nakedness.

In Genesis 1 humans live as other animals do, though it is made clear that humans are superior and have potential dominion over the earth. In Genesis 2 the two humans are first presented as animals—"Man and his wife were both naked and were not ashamed" (Genesis 2:25)—as creatures who have not yet risen to the point of knowing they are any different from the rest of the animal kingdom (whose creatures have always been naked). Though we do not know for certain, it is likely that this shift toward human consciousness occurred 40,000 years ago, when the Neanderthals inexplicably died out and modern humans became the dominant *Homo sapiens* species. (For more on this, see chapter 19.) Genesis 2 and 3, then, mark our first small steps toward civilization.

We know now that Genesis 1 and Genesis 2 do not have the relationship so often attributed to them: The latter is not merely a detailed account of what happens in the former, for the outcomes are entirely different. Further, while Genesis 1 and 2 do not go together, Genesis 2 and 3 certainly do. In Genesis 3:19, after the gods have excoriated Adam, they tell him that he will have to toil and earn his living and "eat the plants of the field; by the sweat of your face"—a way of life altogether different from that of the protohumans described at the end of Genesis 1. In Genesis 3:23 a distinction is made between the garden and the world of nature outside the garden, which will be the home of Adam and Eve: "Therefore the Lord God sent him from out of the garden of Eden, to cultivate the ground from which he was taken." The word *cultivate* here implies that he will prepare the soil and plant from scratch. Adam and Eve are to become farmers, taking the first major leap toward civilization.

In scientific terms, what we have in the first three chapters of Genesis is a bare-bones history of human development from the hunter-gatherer protohuman who was little different from the earth's animals to the Neolithic horticulturist. In this decoding we find that the first chapters of the Book of Genesis are aligned with the findings of modern science and the known path of human history.

FIVE

Genesis Continued

We have seen in Genesis 2 and 3 that the genesis race—a race of gods—creates both man and woman and uplifts them to the level of modern *Homo sapiens sapiens*. When Adam is first placed in the garden, his task is merely to tend the world as it is—"Then the Lord took the man and put him into the garden of Eden to cultivate it and keep it"—and it will provide the food he needs, just as wild nature provides for all animals and just as it provided for early humans who lived as hunter-gatherers. But upon leaving the garden, Adam's task will involve breaking ground, plowing the soil, and raising his food from "nothing." Thus the gods, upon sending him from the garden, give him the knowledge, tools, and principles of agriculture. In later chapters of Genesis we can find further support for extraterrestrial intervention in the course of human development.

After the tragic fratricide—Cain's murder of Abel—recounted in chapter 4 of Genesis, it is Cain's DNA and inherited traits that are passed on. In Genesis 6 we find that the human population is growing. But there is an underlying problem: humans' violence against one another, which is perhaps rooted in Cain's DNA—a genetic predisposition to violence that increases as chapter 6 unfolds.

One element of great importance throughout Genesis is that of genetic inheritance. Detailed records of genealogies are related time and again, and sometimes entire chapters are devoted to genealogies, such as Genesis 4 and Genesis 7. Keeping track of the genetic line was obviously very important to the chroniclers, perhaps because it was important to the gods, who may have instituted these genealogies.

It is interesting to note that Genesis 6:2 introduces another branch of the genealogical tree: ". . . the sons of God saw that the daughters of men were beautiful; and they took wives for themselves, whoever they chose." Who are the "sons of God"? From this passage we can determine that they are definitely physical beings, for if they were not, they could not mate with women. Yet a distinction is made between them and ordinary human males. One inference is that the sons of God are the descendants of the advanced race that created humans in Genesis 1 and that has been living on the earth for some time. This corroborates the suggestion in chapter 4 that the *our* in "in our image" (Genesis 1:26) refers to the gods who were, in fact, advanced humans.

There is a startling correlation between the Old Testament version of the creation of humanity and the account of the Sumerian civilization, known as the Enuma Elish, preserved on cuneiform tablets. In both cases the gods create humans and bestow the gifts of civilization. The cultures that produced these accounts are in fairly close proximity. That this small geographic area has been proved to be an original home of civilization is an amazing correspondence.

What natural evolutionary mechanisms explain why civilization first grew here and why those in the Fertile Crescent made quantum leaps forward in agriculture and civilization when the rest of the world lagged behind? Before answering these questions we must step back and ponder the enormity of the archaeological finds among the ruins of ancient Sumer. Excavations have unearthed libraries full of intact books in the form of cuneiform tablets on such subjects as mathematics, school curriculum, agriculture, poetry, and the payment of taxes. These Sumerian writings and other artifacts attest to the fact that the ancient peoples in this area had a sophisticated understanding of a 360-degree circle, the zodiac, the actual number of planets in the solar system (they included Pluto, which was not rediscovered until 1927), and much more. All of these were thought to have first been understood thousands of years later.

Where did all this advanced knowledge come from? According to the cuneiform texts, the gods taught these people all of this. The records claim that their technological breakthroughs, rather than coming by way of their own ingenuity, were handed to them by the gods—including how to write, set up irrigation canals, grow barley, and smelt metal.

As we shall see, the advanced civilizations of the Incas, Maya, and Aztecs on the other side of the world report similar helpful intervention. The fact that these ancient cultures do not take credit themselves for their achievements only supports the conclusion that the gods were indeed the source of the amazing explosion of growth and innovation that occurred from 3500 B.C.E. to 3000 B.C.E. and has never been equaled since.

While there are obvious parallels between the Genesis of the Old Testament and the accounts of the creation inscribed on the cuneiform tablets discovered in Sumer, the Sumerian accounts are clearer about who the creators were and what they looked like. The tablets tell of a time when a superhuman race descended from the stars in "bark" and "fire" ships.[1] These beings, the progenitor race from another world, rather than looking like the spindly, large-headed aliens popularized by the media over the past 25 years, were human. This, of course, is what we would expect of beings that created humans in their image and seems to be corroborated by Genesis 6:3: "Then the Lord said, 'My Spirit shall not strive with man forever, because he also is flesh.'" This clearly suggests that the gods are human and are aware that at some point "man"—the race they have created—is going to come into conflict with them, the inevitable result of a process they had sought to slow in the Garden of Eden by keeping humans from having access to the tree of life. They are aware of the potential and character of humans because humans are their progeny.

Further evidence of the human nature of the gods can be found in the next verse, 6:4, in which we discover that the interbreeding of the "sons of God" and women produces some unexpected results: "The Nephilim were on the earth in those days, and also afterward when the sons of God came in to the daughters of men, and they bore children to them. Those were the mighty men who were of old, men of renown." *Nephilim* has been translated as "giants" or as "those who came down." The text suggest that they were either actual giants or that they had superhuman, or "giant," attributes. This verse leaves the impression that several advanced races were living on earth with human beings. With this we are reminded of the tragedy of Cain's violent genetic legacy. The traits inherited from Cain and those present in the descendants of the interbreeding of humans and the "sons of God" appear, in 6:5, to have created severe problems—as if, perhaps, a genetic experiment had gone terribly awry: "Then the Lord saw that the wickedness of man was great on the earth, and that every intent of the thoughts of his heart was only evil continually."

The situation is grim and the gods find man's behavior intolerable. Whatever the exact nature of events, circumstances are now out of control. The gods seem to have but one choice: "I will blot out man whom I have created from the face of the land, from man to animals to creeping things and to birds of the sky, for I am sorry that I have made them." (Genesis 6:7)

What could have gone so terribly wrong to cause the creator to destroy his own work? The descendants of Cain, the other inhabitants, and the Nephilim (the descendants of the interbreeding of the sons of God and daughters of men) do not seem to get along. In 6:13 the gods say that they are corrupt and "the earth is filled with violence because of them; and behold, I am about to destroy them with the earth." It may be that the gene pool has become so polluted that it must be cleansed, the slate wiped clean except for Noah, whom the gods instruct to build an ark and collect animals, "two of every kind into the ark, to keep them alive with you; they shall be male and female."(Genesis 6:19) Here is recorded, as in the traditions of

230 cultures around the world, the great cataclysmic Flood that completely changes the earth.

We find the themes of Genesis 6 in the creation myths of Sumer and in Mayan and Incan accounts. The human race is created and then found unfit for one reason or another. These first humans are destroyed in an event of cataclysmic proportions and either a new and improved race is created or a "remnant" survives. These themes are so common around the world that they must commemorate an actual catastrophe whose memory lies in our collective unconscious.

One important aspect of Genesis—and the source of much confusion—is time. An event that seems to have huge consequences for humanity—the Flood—is related in a compact synopsis, and brief chapters containing from 200 to 400 words describe long spans of time. The events described in Genesis 11, for instance, obviously occur long after the Flood. In 11:1 the earth has recovered from the global catastrophe: "Now the whole earth used the same language and the same words." It would seem that those who have repopulated the earth, having all come from the small group of Flood survivors, would naturally speak the same language. This "bottleneck" is corroborated by the latest findings in the human genome: DNA findings based on analysis of mitochondria studies indicate a point in time when the human race branched from a very small population (see chapter 19).

The survivors then spread out and become ambitious, as we discover in 11:3: " 'Come, let us make bricks and burn them, thoroughly.' And they used brick for stone, and they used tar for mortar." This development does not meet with the gods' approval. They monitor the work of the new population closely as the builders continued to speak among themselves about their plan and why they should execute it: " 'Come, let us build for ourselves a city, and a tower whose top will reach into heaven, and let us make for ourselves a name; lest we be scattered abroad over the face of the whole earth.' " (Genesis 11:4)

What gives them cause to believe that they will be dispersed to the four corners of the globe? More important, why do their efforts offend their creators? Could it be that they are duplicating the "sky vehicle" of their creators? The gods come down to earth to inspect the city and tower the "sons of men had built" (11:5): "And the Lord said, 'Behold, they are one people, and they all have the same language. And this is what they began to do, and now nothing which they purpose to do will be impossible for them.'"

This reference to "one people" would lead us to conclude that the people of the earth are now genetically more homogeneous and unified, which makes sense, given that Noah and his family were the sole survivors of the Flood, charged with the task of regenerating the earth's population. But this outcome is apparently not what the gods had expected. It appears that the new race is evolving too quickly, something that the gods want to prevent, much as they had prevented Adam from eating from the tree of life. In 11:7 they decide upon a course of action: "Come, let Us go down and there confuse their language, that they may not understand one another's speech."

The gods return to the earth and scatter the builders who "stopped building the city." Thereafter the Tower of Babel becomes a symbol of disunity and confusion. Exactly how the people were scattered is not explained. But in this chapter it becomes clear that differing interpretations of just one word—*Us*, which is viewed traditionally as the (singular) God—changes the entire meaning.

Chapters 1 through 11 of Genesis are concerned with the earliest origins and histories of humans on Earth. From the Tower of Babel episode on, after the population is scattered, Genesis focuses on the history of the Israelites, the Jewish tribes. How does all this square with the Sumerian account of genesis?

According to the Sumerian tablets—the Enuma Elish—the gods came to earth and created man: "We need servants. Let us create them."[2] When we compare this to Genesis, in which Adam is created to tend the garden of Eden, we find a close correlation. In the Enuma Elish figures are made out of clay and life is "blown into" them: Nintu, also called Mami, the mother goddess or womb goddess and midwife of the gods, is credited with creating human beings with the help of Enki. She mixes clay with the blood of the gods in order to shape and birth seven men and seven women. The early prototypes are unfit but finally acceptable prototype humans are created to be servants and bear the workload of the gods.

One thing is clear in both the Enuma Elish and the Bible: Humans are inferior beings created in the image of the gods, with some of the blood of the progenitors mixed with their earthly animal blood. The gods determine their character and ultimate destiny, but humans do have free will. It is likely that we would insist on this same order if we were to create or genetically alter a primate species, for instance, and attempt to uplift it to the point at which it could understand reason, philosophy, law, and science. The gods give humans the gifts of higher intelligence and agriculture both in Genesis and in this Sumerian tablet: "According to our belief, our gods have made ready these cities and roads and institutions in them. They created us and said 'take your cities.'"[3]

While the Sumerian gods, like their Old Testament counterparts, live forever, man remains mortal "lest he stretch out his hand, and take also from the tree of life, and eat, and live forever." (Genesis 3:22) Sumerian history, in fact, is laced with tales of the gods unleashing disasters that claim the lives of men, including disease, minor floods, drought, and the Deluge. The Sumerian deluge, which predates that of the Old Testament, is very similar to the Flood in Genesis; the Sumerian history tells us that the Ut-napishtim are the long-lived survivors of the disaster that wipes out the rest of humanity.

Just like the Ut-napishtim, Noah and his line live to very old age, which has always baffled biblical scholars, but it is not at all surprising if early humans were indeed a mixed race and the extraterrestrials who created them were as long-lived as the Sumerian gods were said to be. Further, although the first generations of humans to live after humanity had been genetically uplifted might have reached very old age, the human life span eventually shortened to about

72 years, as the gods predicted. (Psalm 90:9–10 states: "The years of our life are threescore and ten or even if by reason of strength fourscore . . . ")

Archaeologists are still puzzled by the sudden and unexplained ingenuity and sophistication of the seminal Sumerian civilization. Its origin and its language, which are unrelated to others in the region, remain mysteries, though scientists today still dismiss as nothing but polytheistic myth the Sumerian accounts of their origins and how they became civilized.

Yet there remains much that is unexplained in the Bible as well. What, for example, are the angels? Are they supernatural beings or physical beings? And are some of the events in the Bible actual historical occurrences or are they myth? The following account from Genesis 19 combines both angels and the type of calamitous event that could well be historically true: "Now two angels came to Sodom in the evening, as Lot was sitting in the gate of Sodom. When Lot saw them, he rose to meet them and bowed down with his face to the ground." (Genesis 19:1)

The passage says nothing of the angels being insubstantial, ethereal beings. Lot invites them into the house: "So they turned aside to him and entered his house; and he prepared a feast for them, and baked unleavened bread, and they ate." (Genesis 19:3) Nowhere in this story or in the rest of the Bible does the text say that angels have wings. They fly, but they do not have wings. In fact, it was Christian artists who turned the angels into winged creatures thousands of years after Genesis was created—and we still depict them that way today. But wings or no, these angels sit down and eat bread with Lot. What further evidence do we need that they are corporeal and human in appearance? Certainly that the men of Sodom see them enter Lot's house is evidence enough. They ask him: "Where are the men who came to you tonight? Bring them out to us that we may have relations with them." (Genesis 19:5)

The crowd then becomes unruly and the angels grow impatient with them: "And they struck the men who were at the doorway of the house with blindness." (Genesis 19:11) What type of weapon these "human" angels use to strike the men blind is not revealed. But perhaps it is awesome enough that the comparatively primitive people of Sodom see the two visitors as supernatural "gods" and winged "angels." The next day Sodom is destroyed for its wickedness: "Then the Lord rained on Sodom and Gomorrah brimstone and fire from the Lord out of heaven." (Genesis 19:24) We too send bombs that can destroy whole cities. It has happened many times in our recent history.

As we have seen, with a fresh perspective the biblical account of Genesis can be perceived in a light that allows us to explore anew what is real and which aspects of the history of our very beginnings can be proved. In the next chapter we move along the time line, exploring the mysterious events that created Earth's first civilization along the Tigris and Euphrates Rivers.

SIX

Sumerians: The Strange Black-Headed Tribe

During the late Neolithic era, circa 5000 B.C.E. to 4500 B.C.E., the tribes of the Nile Valley were living in semi-subterranean oval houses, roofed with mud and sticks. They made simple pottery and used stone axes and flint arrowheads. Meanwhile, tribal cultures across Scandinavia and Eastern Europe were largely still pursuing a hunter-gatherer way of life. They created yarns out of plant fibers, made wooden paddles, and, by 3500 B.C.E., began to construct megalithic monuments in strategic places around their local landscapes.

Most of the human populations in the Americas, Asia, and Africa were living much the same way as the Europeans, some even more primitively, while others were starting to experiment with producing food and living in small villages. Agriculture was in its infancy. The earliest records of settled village life based on producing a few supplemental cereal crops come from the hilly flanks of the Fertile Crescent, from 7000 B.C.E. in Jarmo (in what is now northern Iraq), and from 6000 B.C.E. in Catal Huyuk (in what is now southern Turkey).

Jarmo and Catal Huyuk are two of the most extensively studied Neolithic sites in the world. These early settlements with their experiments in agriculture were very small and very modest. One hundred and fifty people lived in Jarmo in 20 mud-walled houses. At Catal

Huyuk pottery, woven textiles, and mud-brick houses were spread around a 32-acre area. They reaped grain with stone sickles, stored their food in stone bowls, and kept domesticated goats, sheep, and dogs. This does not mean that their sustenance depended solely upon their livestock and the crops they grew. They still relied on hunting and gathering their food.

In these settlements—representing the most advanced peoples of that era—there were no doctors, merchants, engineers, architects, mathematicians, carpenters, stone masons, musicians, or metal-smiths. There were no wheeled carts or plows and no system of writing. In short, the majority of people on Earth were living in close association with nature, just as thousands of generations had done before them. There was nothing to foreshadow the explosive events that would begin to take place in six distinct points on the globe: Egypt, the Indus Valley, China, Mexico, Peru, and along the Tigris and Euphrates Rivers.

The Ice Age was a dim memory by then. Earth had warmed, the sea levels had risen, the rivers had swelled, and the land had been flooded. Around 4000 B.C.E., a strange foreign tribe speaking an unknown tongue settled near the mouths of the unpredictable Tigris and Euphrates Rivers in what is now southern Iraq. We still do not know where they came from or the origin of their language, which is unrelated to the primarily Semitic languages of the tribal cultures in the region at that time.

The newcomers soon set about the stupendous task of draining the marshes and building embankments to control the swiftly moving floodwaters of the Tigris, diverting them into a well-planned system of irrigation canals and ditches. The Tigris is a rough, fast-flowing river that historically has been known for changing course. The Sumerian word for the waterway is *idigna,* which means "fast as an arrow." To tame it for large-scale irrigation required an extensive, well-organized workforce.

We often hear scholars talk of how ancient civilizations settled in river valleys as if it were quite easy and natural for our ancestors to do this. We are led to believe that such settlement was only logical, bringing them nothing but benefits and few challenges—at least none they could not handle. But is this an accurate representation—especially with regard to settlement around the Tigris and the Euphrates?

Prior to the settlement of these rivers by the Sumerians, our human ancestors—stretching back 100,000 generations—had no experience with hydrologic control. They had not developed the specialized technical skills or corporate organization required to undertake such a challenge. There simply were no previous human cultures that were experienced and knowledgeable enough to tame rivers for irrigation, nor were any of the Sumerians' contemporaries in other parts of the world attempting such a project.

Sumer covered about 10,000 square miles of flat, river-made land with no minerals, almost no stone, and no trees. It was not exactly the benign, resource-rich land of milk and honey to new settlers. Why, then, did a people who had been wandering around the countryside from an unknown point of origin suddenly arrive in Mesopotamia with the idea that they could tame a formidable river, drain the marshes, and create a civilization? How did they come to believe that they could manage a Herculean task that no other culture anywhere in the world had even tried?

Sumer, a land of violent, erratic forces, was pummeled by blistering heat for 5 months of the year, blasted by frigid north winds in the winter, then inundated by floods in the spring. Today, the land that the Bible referred to as Shinar is a brutal desert, its ancient cities buried beneath layers of sand. It is common to see temperatures soar from 110 to 125 degrees Fahrenheit. No rain falls there for 8 months of the year and sandstorms frequently rage across the land. It seems that agriculture and civilization would begin under more favorable conditions.

The wandering tribe that surveyed this land, finding deserts, rivers, and marshlands, had only simple stone tools at its disposal—no wheels, no carts, and no dray animals. Even today, the floodwaters of the river can be used for agriculture only when the fields are shielded by a complex system of interdependent dams, dikes, and canals. But who among these newcomers had the understanding, insight, and expertise to envision and then implement such a sophisticated system?

In order for the Sumerians to settle along the Tigris with the intent to engage in large-scale irrigation for agriculture, they would have necessarily arrived with high-level knowledge of how to do this to ensure adequate food for themselves. They indeed knew that the first step required to turn Mesopotamia into productive farmland was to take charge of the rivers and marshes.

But where could they have gained such a body of knowledge? Scholars have uncovered no evidence to explain how Sumerians acquired their agricultural and irrigation techniques or the rest of their technical knowledge so far in advance of the rest of the world. Their settlement occurred at a point in history prior to the advent of cities (which they themselves would later invent) and social stratification and preceded the specialization of labor. Keeping these details in mind, it hardly seems likely that a major river valley would be the first and most logical choice for the settlement of a primitive tribe. In addition, at this time in history the world was neither overpopulated nor lacking in alternative choices for settlement. There were no nations and no sovereign armies to worry about, and people did not have a track record for success with a settled way of life and growing crops in hill country.

We may ask if it's possible that the climate and environment were different in this geographic region 6,000 years ago. If so, then it might account for the Sumerians' choice.[1] We are fortunate to know quite a lot about this region because it holds 70 percent of the world's petroleum reserves, which has prompted intensive study by oil prospectors and geologists. During the Ice Age, sea levels around the world were almost 400 feet below current levels. Even as recently as 12,000 years ago global sea levels were so low that rising seawaters were only just entering the shallow basin of the Arabian Sea. At that time, the river system of the Tigris and Euphrates flowed through the deepest part of the Persian Gulf, down what geologists call the Ur-Shatt River. The

Mesopotamian delta did not exist. Submerged sand dunes under the northern gulf and oxygen isotope readings from deep-sea cores offer strong evidence of the extreme aridity of the region.

Between 13,000 B.C.E. and 4000 B.C.E. sea levels rose significantly as ice sheets melted. Meteorologists suggest that there was increased rainfall in the Near East in this era and botanists point to increased plant life. By 5000 B.C.E. a large marine estuary formed where the Euphrates River exists today. Then, over the next two millennia, the vast estuary filled in with silt. The water table remained high, however. As windblown dust drifted in from the Arabian Peninsula, sea levels stabilized and the silt and accumulating dust choked the estuaries so that large swampy areas formed.

This gives us a good picture of what the Sumerians found when they arrived at the land that was to be their home: a patchwork of desert, semiarid plains, lush estuaries, and riverbanks not unlike what is there today. This was the raw agricultural material with which the newcomers would work. It was certainly not a well-watered, temperate environment similar to, say, the Central Valley of California today, but the Sumerians would go on to build Earth's first great cities there and create the first irrigated agricultural plots from drained marshlands. Sumerian scribes tell us of their trees and orchards, well-watered meadows, bountiful fields, fertile soil—a land of milk and honey.

The Sumerians, however, took no credit for the miraculous way their harsh environment was transformed. Instead, they said that Enlil—a god of Heaven and Earth who had descended to this planet from another—"made people lie down in peaceful pastures like cattle and supplied Sumer with water, bringing joyful abundance."[2] They speak of other gods as well, such as Ea (Enki), Enlil's brother. As linguistic scholar Zecharia Sitchin notes of Enki in his first book, *The 12th Planet:*

> His arrival on Earth is associated in Sumerian texts with a time when the waters of the Persian Gulf reached inland much farther

than nowadays, turning the southern part of the country into marshlands. Ea (the name meant literally "house-water"), who was a master engineer, planned and supervised the construction of canals, the diking of the rivers, and the draining of the marshlands.[3]

Of course, modern scholars tell us that these are only myths. Before we look more deeply into what the Sumerians say about their own history, we need to examine the historical context of modern scholarship related to the Sumerian culture.

As noted briefly in chapter 1, by the middle of the eighteenth century Western scholars, historians, and many laypeople in general no longer accepted the Old Testament as representing true history. In fact, it had been relegated to the status of folklore and "tribal legend." At that point in time Europeans and Americans attributed the beginnings of their civilizations to Greece and Rome, which was about as far back as history went, demonstrating how quickly and thoroughly actual history can be lost.

The accepted view began to change, however, at the end of the eighteenth century, when Napoleon ventured into Egypt with his army and a team of scholars. When reports of the wonders of the Nile made their way to Europe, suddenly the ancient Egypt of the Bible became real.

In the early decades of the nineteenth century, as French scholars were beginning to piece together the puzzle of ancient Egypt, various archaeologists and explorers began poking around the decaying Ottoman Empire in the Middle East. Strange dusty mounds littered the barren landscape. Could they be the forgotten cities of biblical Assyria? French archaeologist Paul Émile Botta decided to excavate a mound in northern Mesopotamia near the ancient town of Mosul. His excavations proved it to be the ruins of Dur Sharru Kin, the home of King Sargon II.

English archaeologist Austen Henry Layard selected a site about 10 miles downriver, where in 1843 he unearthed Nineveh, the capital of Assyria according to the Bible. Nineveh proved to be full of treasures, but scholars realized that it existed rather late in the biblical chronology; it had fallen to Babylon in 612 B.C.E.: "And he will stretch out his hand against the north, and destroy Assyria; and he will make Nineveh a desolation, a dry waste like the desert." (Zephaniah 2:13)

Babylon itself was discovered in the early twentieth century. The biblical accounts came to life when the great ziggurat the Tower of Babel was revealed. The ancient city was a fortress, with surrounding walls that were wide enough to allow 10 chariots to gallop side by side upon them. Excavations found that it was exactly as the Bible and ancient Greek and Roman historians had depicted it: a vast complex of palaces and temples where wondrous hanging gardens were once situated.

Layard's find ignited a renewed interest in the Bible as a valid historical document. He later discovered the royal library of the Assyrian king Ashburnipal, which contained 25,000 clay tablets. As several generations of scholars labored to decipher these cuneiform tablets and those retrieved by other archaeologists in the mid-1800s, they kept running across postscripts, almost disclaimers, stating that the tablets had been transcribed from earlier records, though which records and from where could not be determined. Long before the actual ruins of the Sumerian civilization were unearthed, scholars came across references in the Babylonian and Assyrian tablets to the ancient language of Shumerian (which was not familiar to modern linguists) and to unusual names that belonged to no identifiable peoples or language.

After Layard's discovery of Nineveh, most people thought that it and Babylon existed as far back in recorded history as it was possible for us to go. Yet scholars became convinced that there was a more ancient predecessor to the Assyrian and Babylonian civilizations. In a curious turnabout, historians who had dismissed the Bible turned to it as the source for the next discovery.

Genesis pointed to two possibilities: Akkad and the land of

Shinar: "And in the beginning of his Kingdom: Babel and Erech and Akkad"; (Genesis 10:10) "And it came about as they journeyed east, that they found a plain in the land of Shinar and settled there." (Genesis 11:2) When the ruins of ancient Akkad were uncovered and revealed that it had preceded Babylon by 2,000 years, it seemed clear that it was the trunk and Babylonia and Assyria were branches. That seemed to settle it: Civilization dated back 3,500 years to ancient Akkad.

The case was not quite closed, however. As scholars studied the statues, obelisks, and tablets of Akkad, they discovered exactly what they had gleaned after examining the Assyrian and Babylonian artifacts: evidence that it had been preceded by an even earlier civilization. The trunk, after all, had to have roots.

The historical stage was set for another brilliant British archaeologist to take the spotlight. C. Leonard Wooley began excavations in southern Mesopotamia in 1922. Over the course of 12 seasons he unearthed the remains of another biblical city, Ur of the Chaldees, the birthplace of Abraham, and retrieved clay cylinders written in cuneiform. Scholars soon realized they were the originals that the Akkadian and Babylonian scribes had studied and copied.[4] It was now clear that the "plain of Shinar" from which the Bible tells us "the men set about to erect a tower reaching to heaven" was Mesopotamia.

The discovery of Sumer captured the world's imagination. Wooley's excavations were carefully followed and reported by the media. He found walls enclosing the palaces, temples, and ziggurats of the Sumerian cities. The pathway from myth to history had been a long, dusty, intricate, winding maze.

Here we should keep one very important fact in mind: Until its remains were actually discovered, Sumer was believed to be a myth, a product of imagination. It is astounding that what turned out to be the cradle of Western civilization had been dismissed as a mere folktale until its discovery. If nothing else, it is a lesson for modern scholars to be less hasty with their assumptions and less sure of their claims regarding what is true and what is false in ancient history. New discoveries are made every year and they often challenge—and then change—the old assumptions and models.

Further "myths" of the Bible that referred to a number of legendary ancient cities and peoples were slowly proved to be factual history. As exciting as the new discoveries were, they also opened up deeper mysteries, controversies, and challenges: Who were the Sumerians who built dams and canals and walled cities according to plans that would subsequently be handed down for thousands of years, ultimately to those who established Babylonia? They called themselves the black-headed people. When scholars eventually deciphered their cuneiform script, their accounts of how their civilization was brought into being seemed like science fiction mixed with very practical human knowledge:

> When the royal scepter was coming down from heaven, the august crown and the royal throne being already down from heaven he [the king] regularly performed to perfection . . . laid the brick of those cities in pure spots. These cities, which had been named by names, and had been allotted half-bushel baskets, dredged the canals, which were blocked with purplish wind-borne clay, and they carried water. Their cleaning of the smaller canals established abundant growth.[5]

These descriptions and instructions come from what has been referred to as the "First Farmer's Almanac": "Keep a sharp eye on the opening of dikes, ditches and mounds [so that] when you flood the field the water will not rise too high in it." With strict attention to detail the instructions go on: "Let the pickax wielder eradicate the ox hooves for you [after weeding and] smooth them out . . . [These are] the instructions of Ninurta, the son of Enlil."[6]

The black-headed people did not claim to have invented any of the fundamentals of their remarkable civilization. In repeated writings the Sumerians claimed that "gods" came to earth and taught them everything after having dredged the swamplands and built the cities. Scholars of the twentieth century deemed these accounts to be myth as readily as late-eighteenth-century scholars deemed that the cities of Ur and Nineveh were myth. A curious transformation had occurred regarding such cities: While they themselves could no longer be considered mere legend, the historical accounts of the people who created those first cities could only be considered cultural folktales!

The Sumerian accounts repeatedly refer to both the primary gods such as Enlil, Enki, Ninurta, and Ninhursig and the lower-ranking working gods, the Anunnaki, among which they counted a pickax god, a brick-mold god, a metalsmith god, and so on. But such distinctions do cause some confusion regarding what the Sumerians considered to be gods. Clearly, they were not gods as we think of them. They are depicted much more as humans who perform specific tasks or give exact instructions on how to perform them (as in the preceding quote from the "First Farmer's Almanac"). Even though the Anunnaki operated as what we would consider supervisors or mentors, the Sumerians referred to these beings as gods.

Modern scholars have relegated these beings to the mythological or religious realm of a Sumerian pantheon. They dispute the Sumerians' own descriptions of them as real, flesh-and-blood people who came to Earth to create and mentor them. And who are we to believe: the Sumerians themselves, who revolutionized the world, left a vast archaeological record of their accomplishments, and sought no credit for these accomplishments, or modern academics whose worldview descends from one that formerly denied the very existence of the Sumerians and now will not permit them such a history? Either the Sumerian gods were advanced human advisers and teachers, as claimed in their cuneiform writing, or they were the creations of an ancient imagination.

What does the evidence support? Aside from the fact that scholars do not know the place of origin of the Sumerians or the roots of their language, which leaves open the possibility of the truth of the Sumerian accounts, let us turn for clues to the accomplishments of this ancient civilization: They built the first cities, which were unlike anything human beings had ever designed or constructed. A large workforce had to be organized and fed to accomplish this feat. As noted earlier, agriculture on a scale large enough to feed the whole population required the development of an intricate system of irrigation and flood control. The Sumerians were also responsible for the first appearance of the ox-drawn plow, mentioned in the ancient "First Farmer's Almanac."

The cities, a dozen in all, were carefully planned. The initial task was to build an elevated mound for each to protect it from floods. Then buildings were constructed using standardized bricks made of clay that had been reinforced with chopped reeds and straw, set in molds, and baked in kilns. Typical houses were either one or two stories high, sturdy, and built close together, with narrow lanes running between rows of these structures.

It is notable that the mode of construction the Sumerians used required the advent of two significant innovations: the kiln and the standardization of building materials. The invention of the kiln also made it possible to smelt and alloy metals, two more processes to add to an amazing string of innovations in a very compressed period of time.

Another accomplishment to add to the list is the invention of writing, for we would know little of the Sumerians if they had not inscribed all kinds of facts and records on their ingenious clay tablets. Seals were also invented for the purpose of stamping their clay tablets, a form of movable type much like the rubber stamps we use today.[7]

Now, we must recall again what the Sumerian world looked like: There were no trees, no stones, and no metals in the surrounding environment, making the region an unlikely choice for settlement of any kind, let alone for establishment of a culture with grandiose aspirations. The builders and occupants of the cities needed fuel for their brick kilns and to heat their homes in the winter; they needed raw ore to smelt and more fuel for the smelting process.

How did the Sumerians get around these limitations? They used naturally occurring petroleum products such as the bitumen and asphalt that bubbled to the surface of the earth in that area. They discovered—or were shown—that these materials could also be used to seal and caulk cracks and to build roads.

Before the Sumerians there were no bakers, harpists, carpenters, metalsmiths, jewelers, artists, engineers, mathematicians, bureaucrats, or scribes. All these innovations appeared for the first time in their cities between 3700 B.C.E. and 3000 B.C.E. In addition to irrigation, agriculture, kilns, and writing, they also invented the wheel, the chariot, bronze, sailboats, mathematics, the harp, astrology, schools, and the idea of trades and professions. In short, they invented nearly the entire foundation of all future civilizations—all in one fell swoop.

Civilization after the Sumerians was based on five basic components: agriculture, cities, metallurgy, specialization, and social stratification. The Sumerians must have possessed some very special genes because they seem to have come out of nowhere to perform miracles—at least on technological matters—when compared with their contemporaries and the sum total of human prehistory.

The Sumerian epoch of innovation was not only without precedence; nor has it ever been duplicated. Greece and Rome added very little to the basic technical framework that was handed down from Sumer through Babylonia and Assyria. Up to the sixteenth century Western Europe contributed very little in the way of revolutionary inventions. The ox- or horse-drawn plow was still used in Europe and America as well as the rest of the world right up until the twentieth century, almost 5,000 years after it was invented.

Ancient Greece, Rome, and the rest of Europe relied on the basic cereal crops that originated in and around the Fertile Crescent. We still grow hybrids of those same crops. The techniques of process metallurgy and the seven basic Old World metals remained unchanged after the fall of Greece and Rome; the eighth metal was not discovered until 1,000 years later.

But the real problem surrounding all of these impressive accomplishments, so radically advanced in relation to the circumstances of the rest of Earth's population at that time, is that there is no traceable, step-by-step path leading to them from the hunter-gatherer way of life. Science has not explained the Sumerians' sudden, unprecedented explosion of development. But science could not be forthcoming when, as the Sumerians themselves asserted, these developments were instituted by an already advanced civilization—the genesis race.

SEVEN

Egypt:
Mysteries in the Desert

Around the same time that the cities of Sumer grew, another curious civilization began building a ziggurat and then a great pyramid along the Nile River. But as with Sumer, the glory that was once ancient Egypt eventually disappeared like some enchanted mirage. The purpose of the pyramids and temples was forgotten as the desert winds swept sand over and around them for century upon century. The pharaohs, who, garbed in their royal costumes, had ruled over the land of the Sphinx for three millennia, were long gone, faded like exotic dreams. In time the sands covered their tombs with their many treasures, leaving only the head of the Sphinx exposed to the sun god, Ra.

An unlikely hero brought the grandeur and mystery of this forgotten land to light. By the end of the eighteenth century Napoleon Bonaparte was struggling with his ambitions and the limited opportunities to exalt his own reputation in Europe. Though he had been educated at a military school, he actually considered himself as much a rational scientist as a general: "If I had not become commander-in-chief of the army, I would have launched myself into the study of the exact sciences. . . . And since I have always had success in my great undertakings, I would have become a highly distinguished scientist."[1]

The diminutive French leader aspired to follow in the path of Alexander the Great, who had conquered Egypt in ages past. How better to realize his goals than to organize a military campaign and set off for the land along the Nile? Conquering Egypt and the surrounding lands, however, was not all that Napoleon had on his mind. He wanted to study ancient Egypt. To this end he organized a team of 167 scholars, mostly scientists, as part of the military operation, selecting a group of the best minds in France and swearing them to secrecy. Those who agreed to go on the expedition were told neither the end destination nor the objectives.

While Napoleon was leading his army through a series of battles, many of the scholars were dispatched to various parts of Egypt to study everything from flora and fauna to artifacts. Surveyors, mathematicians, and cartographers were part of the team that made a series of key discoveries about the Great Pyramid.[2] After carefully surveying and measuring the monument, the scientists realized it was perfectly aligned to true north, which automatically squared it with the other points of the compass and made it an accurate reference and triangulation point.

Research continued from that time to today has proved that the Great Pyramid is essentially a scale model of Earth and a geodesic marker of the center of Earth's landmass. The ratio of the pyramid's height to its perimeter equals the ratio of Earth's radius to its circumference. The colossal monument elegantly squares the circle and incorporates *pi* in numerous features.

In addition to initiating these discoveries, Napoleon himself was profoundly affected by his encounter with the Great Pyramid. On August 12, 1799, Napoleon told his men to leave him alone in the King's Chamber, as Alexander the Great had done millennia before. The general was said to have been very pale and impressed when he came out. When an aide asked him in a jocular tone if he had witnessed anything mysterious, Bonaparte replied abruptly that he had no comment, adding in a gentler voice that he never wanted the incident mentioned again. Many years later, when he was emperor,

Napoleon continued to refuse to speak of his time in the pyramid, merely hinting that he had received some presage of his destiny. At St. Helena, just before his death, he seemed on the verge of confiding this experience to the French historian (and his memoirist) Emmanuel de Las Cases, but instead shook his head, saying, "No, what's the use? You would never believe me."[3]

Napoleon's expedition ignited an interest in ancient Egypt that has inspired generations to try to solve its mysteries. His team produced 26 large-format *(grand monde)* volumes of scholarly work. Incredibly, that was only the beginning of Egyptology. The amount of intellectual effort that has been poured into studying Egyptian antiquities since then is staggering. There are some 10,000 listed archaeological sites in Egypt and millions of artifacts have been recovered and cataloged over the course of several hundred years of excavations. They all attest to a grand civilization equal to if not surpassing that of Sumer. In fact, after wars broke out between the two cultures, Sumer was consumed within a few thousand years as the events in the Bible continued to unfold.

Enough books and papers have been published on every single aspect of ancient Egypt to fill entire libraries, but the debate over who built the Great Pyramid—and how and why—rages on to this day. Egyptologists insist that it was built around 3500 B.C.E., during the reign of Cheops, to serve as a tomb. Slaves and farmers supposedly used primitive methods, including wooden sleds, ramps, and ropes. There is no definitive proof of this construction scenario, however. The only thing that can be studied is the monument itself, which produces these pieces of information:

- Every detail of its precise architecture seems to have been meticulously planned.
- The structure embodies geodesic alignments and measurements and mathematical ratios.
- The structure is made of solid stone, unlike many other later pyramids that were constructed with masonry fill and an outer layer of cut stone.

- The pyramid covers roughly 13 acres.
- It comprises approximately 2.5 million stone blocks weighing from 1 to 70 tons each with an overall weight of 6 million tons.
- Although the majority of blocks in the pyramid are in the 1- to 3-ton range, there are many blocks weighing 5, 10, 20, and even 40 tons. The heaviest single block is 75 tons.[4]

The Great Pyramid that has been studied and that appears to us today does not represent the original finished construction. As physicist John Zajac explains, "While the bulk of the pyramid's core was constructed of 4,000- to 40,000-pound blocks of soft limestone, the outer layer of the pyramid was made of a beautifully bright, protective layer of polished stone. These 'casing stones' are missing today."[5] There were 144,000 of these casing stones made of polished white limestone, similar to marble in hardness and durability. The average weight of each stone was 20 tons. It has been said that a thirteenth-century earthquake loosened the stones and the pyramid was quickly ransacked, with thieves taking the precut stones to finish their palaces and mosques. This version of how the casing stones disappeared, however, has never been confirmed, and neither archaeologists nor historians have delved any deeper into the mystery.

The greatest remaining mystery, however, is how and why massive Egyptian monuments like the Great Pyramid and the Sphinx were constructed. One aspect of the enigma surrounding the construction of both the Great Pyramid and the Sphinx is the fact that the Egyptians neither described nor depicted in any of their hieroglyphic texts or art how or why they built these structures. Yet these people are known for having left copious records, in one form or another, of every aspect of their lives: In tombs and temples, on vases and bas-reliefs, elaborate scenes reveal everything from the representation of the habits of their daily lives to their conceptions of the gods in the heavens. So why are there no records, descriptions, or explanations related to these two monuments? A second aspect of the mystery of the monuments stems from the fact that the ancient people who Egyptologists claim built the Great Pyramid lived in a society based on labor-intensive agriculture. With irrigation to maintain, animals to feed, and fields to tend, it seems odd that they would divert valuable human resources to a massive building project, and even if they did have a pool of laborers available for construction of the pyramid, it could never have been very large.

Regarding the construction of the monument, how did the Egyptians acquire the sophisticated architectural principles and advanced engineering concepts necessary to plan and execute such a major undertaking? According to Zajac: "The cornerstones have balls and sockets built into them," which were positioned at the corners to allow the pyramid to move freely should there be an earthquake. Zajec believes that the building found in the Great Pyramid and Sphinx is so sophisticated in some respects that we could not duplicate it even with the technology we have today. Who, then, could have built this precision-engineered monument and how did they manage to construct what has remained the world's largest man-made stone structure?

Could the Great Pyramid have been built as the Egyptologists claim—with slaves and farmers using some combination of wooden sleds, ramps, and ropes to muscle the stones into place? Could it have been accomplished without the use of metal tools, dray animals, or wheeled vehicles (none of which were known or used at that time)? A 1-ton block of stone is roughly equivalent to the weight of a medium-sized car or an adult elephant. Cutting even these smaller blocks away from the matrix rock and dressing them for transport would itself have been a considerable task—one that is difficult enough today with the use of explosives and jackhammers. While it may have been possible to free the building blocks from matrix rock at the quarry site and dress them for transport with the dolerite hammers and sedges that archaeologists say the ancient Egyptians regularly used, it must have been a slow, tedious process indeed. And while it would have been possible to haul the 1.5- to 2.5-ton blocks from the quarry to the site with wooden sleds and rope, again, the method would have been extremely arduous, time-consuming, and dangerous, as would ferrying these stones to the site by raft down the Nile, and using a ramp to bring stones into position in the upper tiers of the pyramid as the construction advanced. But even if the smaller stones were moved in any of these ways, the blocks weighing over 40 tons could not have been transported by any of these methods. In fact, no studies or simulations address the transport of these larger stones.

In our modern construction we never use materials with the size and mass of many of the stones found in the monuments of the ancient Egyptians, and anything that does have substantial mass is transported on high-strength steel wheels. For example, a 200-ton autoclave was moved 750 miles over U.S. roads on a 112-wheel rig powered by two large diesel tractors. NASA had to build a special crane in order to lift its space shuttle weighing 430 tons. And a New York engineering company uses a huge hydraulic crane with a maximum load capacity of 500 tons to lift smaller cranes to the tops of buildings under construction. Without these sophisticated means of transport at their disposal, it seems the task of constructing the Great Pyramid, with its massive building materials, would be impossible.

If the modern archaeological community wants to prove that the ancient Egyptians built the Great Pyramid using specific primitive techniques, devices, and labor, it is necessary that in their tests scientists duplicate exactly the materials and conditions that they suggest the ancients used. For example, a test might consist of cutting, dressing, and transporting from quarry to building site one 70-ton block of stone using the exact methods and materials—ropes and wooden sleds—that Egyptologists claim were used by ancient builders. Once at the building site, the stone block should be hoisted up a ramp set at a 30-degree angle, to match the slope of the sides of the Great Pyramid, for a distance equal to the length of one side of the pyramid. Overall, the ramp must rise a total of 300 feet from the ground.

This test represents a minimalist version of the enormous challenge the ancient builders faced, but before the Egyptologists' theory of how such monuments were built can be universally accepted, it must prove successful in meeting this challenge.

It is interesting to note that in 1995 an expert team—led by archaeologist Mark Lehner, master stonemason Roger Hopkins, and the late Aly el Gasab, one of Egypt's foremost specialists in moving heavy statues—attempted to demonstrate how the ancient Egyptians quarried and transported the heavy stones. They decided to make a 35-ton replica of an obelisk using what they believed were the same methods employed by the ancients. (A 35-ton obelisk is less than one tenth of the weight of the heaviest Egyptian obelisks.)[6]

The team started out by attempting to quarry a block of granite using the same type of dolerite hammers that the ancients are said to have used. The work progressed so slowly, however, that they gave up on the hammers in favor of bulldozers and other machinery, which made short work of quarrying the obelisk. The team's very abandonment of ancient methods seems to prove that even an obelisk weighing less than one half of the heaviest block of stone in the pyramid cannot be quarried, dressed, and moved in any efficient manner using primitive means.

The team still wanted to prove, however, that the obelisk could be raised using a system like the one conjectured to have been used by the ancients. This involved lowering the obelisk into a slanted trench while holding it in place with variously positioned ropes, all pulled taut. More than 100 men gathered by the team managed to hoist it only about halfway to the upright position. They were later able to raise a 2-ton obelisk, but, as the Egyptian quarry owner asserted in an interview, they should not have bothered with anything less than 100 tons if they wanted to prove that their theories had merit.

After a five-year hiatus the team regrouped for a second attempt at raising the obelisk after it had been moved into place using modern machinery. This time they did succeed in bringing the 35-ton obelisk upright, but because they had not attempted to cut or dress the obelisk or carve its surface beforehand, as the ancients would have done, it was not a strict duplication of the task accomplished thousands of years ago.

It is humbling to imagine that somehow the ancient Egyptians cut, dressed, and moved not just one but several million such pieces of stone to create the Great Pyramid. How many could they place in a day, a month, or a year? If they placed five finished stones per day, every single day of the year, it would have taken more than 500 years to complete the monument. Even if they had placed an inconceivable 100 blocks a day, the pyramid would have taken nearly 70 years to complete.

If the Great Pyramid was built as a tomb for the pharaoh, as has been surmised, would the pharaoh reigning at the time of the beginning of its construction have been thinking about the burial of future pharaohs? Perhaps he planned to have his own body mummified and stored for placement in the pyramid upon its completion. That no mummy has ever been found in the Great Pyramid does cast some doubt on the supposition that the massive construction was intended as a tomb. The generally accepted theory for all the pyramids in Egypt is that they were constructed as monuments to the pharaohs' greatness and that their chambers were filled with all manner of treasures and necessities for the pharaoh's afterlife. But no such treasure has been found in the Great Pyramid.

Perhaps the real treasure of the Great Pyramid lies in its geodesic alignment and the fact that *pi* is found in various ratios used in the stone structure by the architects who designed it. The pyramid's height is to its base perimeter as a circle's radius is to its circumference: Twice the length of one side of its base divided by its height is equal to the value of *pi*. Perhaps it is these that point to who, how, and why the Great Pyramid was built. If the gods built it, they did so for a reason, one that we have forgotten with the passage of time. One obvious message of the Great Pyramid is its very embodiment of its builders' knowledge—their sophisticated grasp of the size and shape of the earth and the principles of architecture and mathematics that could be recognized only by a culture (such as ours) that might share some of this awareness.

The ruins of ancient Egypt are some of the keys to understanding human history and the intervention of a more advanced race in our past. The mysteries of the Great Pyramid, though well known, remain unsolved; Egyptologists are still unable to explain how the ancient Egyptians could have constructed such a structure with their rudimentary mathematical knowledge, basic engineering skills, and primitive tools.

As we will see in later chapters, similar massive structures have been found in China, Peru, and Mexico—three of those places where ancient civilizations suddenly blossomed and flourished, and three of the places that point to the intervention of a genesis race.

EIGHT

The Indus Valley:
The Water People

Just as in what was once Sumer and in Egypt, ruins scattered across a vast region of India and Pakistan display an unexpected sophistication if we consider that the original structures were built when most of Earth's peoples were still living in mud- or thatched-roof huts. More than the other five primary civilizations on the planet, however, the one that emerged abruptly in this part of the world remains "lost" because its language has resisted translation.

According to anthropologists, the Indus Valley was home to the largest of the newly emerged ancient urban civilizations. Located in what is today southeastern Pakistan and western India, the Harappan civilization appears to have blossomed abruptly in an extraordinarily sophisticated form sometime around 3000 B.C.E. to 2500 B.C.E. As established by archaeologists, the Harappans built half a dozen major cities of brick and stone, complete with sewer systems, orderly streets, and public and private baths. Their racially mixed society—as depicted in their statuary and other artwork—eventually extended 1,000 miles from its point of origin and included at least 1,500 separate settlements.[1]

We do not know who built this sophisticated urban society. Tablets with inscriptions have been discovered but they have yet to be deciphered. Compared to that of ancient Egypt, the Harappan culture was discovered rather late—by Western archaeologists in the 1920s. Most of its extensive ruins, including major cities, remains to be excavated.

When Harappan cities such as Mohenjo Daro were first discovered, scholars assumed they would be much like those of Mesopotamia. They found no evidence of armies, however. Clearly, this industrious civilization had managed to spread across an area larger than France without using force. Another interesting feature that separates this ancient civilization from others, such as those in Egypt and Peru, was its lack of temples, palaces, colossal architecture, and monumental displays of wealth, indicating that it was a relatively egalitarian society.[2]

The Harappans built their cities according to models that we still use today. The streets were straight and laid out in a rectangular grid pattern. Like the Sumerians, they used bricks (made out of baked earth and wood) as their primary building material. These bricks—standardized in a length-to-width-to-height ratio of 4:2:1—were a signature of Harappan construction. As indicated by coins, tokens, and seals, they also used standard weights throughout the broad expanse of their civilization.

The long-deserted Harappan city of Dholavira—discovered in 1967 in the state of Gujarat, India—can lay claim to several firsts: the first billboard, the first sewage system, and the first baths. It is a curious irony of human history that the sophistication exhibited by Dholavira's city planning and engineering more than 4,000 years ago surpasses that of their modern-day counterparts in much of Pakistan and India. What was the message on the ancient billboard that once looked down on this great stone city but has long since been toppled? No one knows because the script has yet to be deciphered.

The Harappan community of Mohenjo Daro, home to 50,000 residents, was located on the bank of the Indus River. It comprised houses, a granary, baths, an assembly hall, and a tower—all made out of bricks. The streets were 8 to 10 feet wide on average and the city was divided into two parts.

On the upper level was the Citadel, which included an elaborate tank called the Great Bath. The Great Bath was 40 feet long and 8 feet deep—a large public facility by any standards. Constructed of fine-quality brickwork and drains, it was made watertight by the use of two layers of brick, lime cement, and bitumen as a sealant. The bath included a shallow section for children and was surrounded by a veranda. A giant granary, a large residential building, and several aisled assembly halls were also on this upper level.

To the east of the Citadel was the lower city, consisting of houses, potter's sheds and kilns, dyer's vats, and metalworking and bead-making shops. Like the Sumerians, the people of Harappan society had to deal with periodic massive flooding of the river and thus seem to have had an excellent working knowledge of irrigation and flood-control techniques. In addition, their houses had indoor plumbing and many had private baths. There is every indication that the Harappans were as sanitation-minded as modern Americans.

It has been learned from excavations that tax collectors used standardized weights to assay goods, potters turned out standard-ized designs, and the elite carried customized soapstone seals embossed with Indus script and animal designs, using them to stamp trade goods. "They also had a tremendous craft technology, if not the best craft technology in the Bronze Age," claims Jim Shaffer, of Case Western Reserve University. "In city after city, the Indus peo-ple built deep, brick-lined wells, smelted and cast copper and bronze, and made jewelry."[3]

Ancient Sumerian texts tell of trading in the third millennium B.C.E. with two seafaring civilizations, referred to as Makkan and Meluha, in the vicinity of India. These accounts are fascinating in their descriptions of trade—which appeared to have included copper by the tons—conducted with sophisticated financial arrangements. The Sumerian tablets describe Meluha as an aquatic culture in which water and bathing played a key role, which causes us to recall the Harappan public baths. That these two civilizations had contact is borne out by the fact that Indus Valley objects have been found buried with Mesopotamians.

The same questions generated by the other ancient civilizations birthed in the same era can be asked of the Harappan culture: Why do we find this sudden explosion of sophisticated knowledge and what is its origin? Archaeologists and anthropologists have claimed that prior to the blossoming of Harappan society, people had lived in the Indus Valley for thousands of years in small primitive villages, but why are artifacts and records documenting this fact missing?

Ultimately, the sophistication that suddenly blossomed in Dholavira and Mohenjo Daro spread westward for 1,000 miles—perhaps even farther. A recent discovery off the coast of eastern India indicates that India's ancient civilizations may have been even more widespread than previously understood. There have always been legends of lost cities submerged beneath the seas of Poompuhur on the Coromandel coast. But in the year 2000, while conducting a routine survey, India's National Institute of Oceanography found 20 anomalous traces in a 5-mile area of these waters.

The National Institute of Oceanography called in author Graham Hancock to conduct a series of exploratory dives, and Hancock was astonished to find conclusive evidence of human settlements—an "archaeological smoking gun," as he termed it. The reason is obvious: The ruins lie 80 feet below the surface—a level that has not been above the water for at least 11,000 years.

As we will see in later chapters, this recent discovery of an underwater city is similar to those made in South America, where local legendary accounts attribute the creation of their fantastic cities and the invention of civilization to "gods" with human characteristics who brought their knowledge from afar.

NINE

Mysterious Civilization X: The Chinese Pyramids

It is well known that China's civilization is ancient and that over time its people have created wonders such as the Great Wall, superb porcelain, and exquisite silk. Unlike Egypt, however, the land of the ancient dragon is not very well known for its pyramids—yet there are about 100 of them located in a 70-mile radius of the city of Xian on the central plains southwest of Beijing.

The pyramids remained unknown to the outside world during the years of the Cultural Revolution, when China was closed to foreigners, and even though the country is open to visitors today, access to the area where the pyramids are found is normally restricted because the Chinese government has established its space program in the region. In 1994, however, a German writer by the name of Hartwig Hausdorf managed to visit and photograph some of the restricted regions in China and was lucky enough to travel to the Xian, or Qin Chuan, province of central China, where he found pyramids as significant as those in Egypt. Hausdorf wrote a book about his adventures titled *The Chinese Roswell: UFO Encounters in the Far East from Ancient Times to the Present.*[1]

During his stay, Hausdorf investigated six of the pyramids, taking photographs of them and shooting 18 minutes of video footage. When he got home and reviewed the tapes, he realized that there were at least 100 more pyramids in the background. Many of these structures were in poor condition, which is not surprising because they are made of landfill and clay instead of stone. Most are from 100 to 300 feet in height, though Hausdorf estimated the Great White Pyramid to be 1,000 feet tall. (This may be an exaggeration due to the flatness of the surrounding land.) The German researcher—who has written several other books about his expedition to China—is convinced that an extraterrestrial race built the pyramids.

The area that Hausdorf explored is not the only region in China where pyramids exist. Chinese archaeologists recently announced that they had discovered a pyramid-shaped structure in the Inner Mongolia Autonomous Region in northern China. The three-story stone pyramid is located on a mountain ridge about .5 mile north of Sijazi Township. The bottom course of stone is more than 100 feet long and 50 feet wide. Seven tombs and the ruins of an altar along with pottery shards were found inside the building.

Chinese archaeologist Wang Shiping realized that one of the newly discovered pyramids is located at the exact geographical "navel" of the country.[2] We have seen this same geodesic orientation at Giza. In fact, if we follow latitude 30° north from Giza through Pakistan and India to the Yellow River, we will have traced a path through the locations of three of Earth's first ancient civilizations: Egypt, the Indus Valley, and China.

The fact that there are mysterious pyramids in China came as a surprise to many people. As far as is known, the Chinese government has not conducted any officially acknowledged archaeological investigation into these structures. This seems strange in light of how proud the Chinese are of their long heritage. The pyramids, however, have not been entirely unknown to the American government. During World War II the Chinese allowed U.S. photoreconnaissance planes to fly over much of China. Pictures of pyramids scattered in the country's central plains were taken during these missions but, for security reasons, were never revealed to the public.[3]

In *The Chinese Roswell* Hausdorf tells the story of two Australian traders who were traveling through the wide-open plains of central China 100 years ago. The pair discovered the pyramids and went to a local monastery to inquire about their origin and age, and there the monastery's custodian told them they were very old—the monastery's records went back 5,000 years and the pyramids preceded the monastic habit of record keeping! The custodian also told them that the pyramids belonged to an age when the old emperors ruled China. These emperors were said to have stressed the fact that they did not originate on Earth; they were descendants of the "sons of heaven, who roared down to this planet on their fiery metallic dragons," much like the first "divine rulers" of Sumer.

Hausdorf claims that the Chinese government has blocked his attempts to continue his investigations. He is convinced that it is trying to hide something, and he points to two items that he contends support his claim: The government has planted fast-growing pine trees on the sides of the pyramids to obscure the actual shape and it will not allow any excavations of the structures.

The area around Xian, where Hausdorf found the pyramids, is famous for being the location of the terra-cotta warriors that guard the burial tomb of the legendary first emperor of China. Ancient texts say that the tomb of Qin Shi Huangdi—located in a pyramidal mound—contains a model of the Chinese empire with flowing rivers of mercury and has a ceiling that is covered with jewels arranged as the constellations in the sky. Because the same texts allude to the existence of the clay warriors, they seem to be trustworthy.

The burial mound is 150 feet tall. According to Chinese historian Sima Qian, beneath the outer mound is a 140-foot step pyramid built in five terraces. Qian's text claims that 700,000 workers labored on the structure. The floor was made out of molten bronze, upon which the sarcophagus was laid. The tomb remains largely unexcavated because several attempts have shown high concentrations of toxic mercury, which would make archaeological work hazardous.[4]

Most historians had relegated the Xia—the lost race who created this ancient civilization—to the realm of myth and legend. As with many of Earth's first civilizations, however, the archaeological record has proved them wrong. According to Chinese tradition, the Xia built their settlements near rivers, lakes, and streams, much as the Sumerians and Harappans had. The philosopher Feng Hu Tzu, who addressed the issue of tools used by the Xia, stated, "In the Age of Yu, weapons were made of bronze for building canals and houses. . . ."[5]

The Great Yu referred to by Tzu was known as the regulator of the waters and builder of canals who dredged the Yellow River after a great flood, just as Enki dredged the Tigris River. He traveled tirelessly for 13 years, draining the land of water, just as the Sumerian gods had. One Chinese tradition claims that "but for Yu we should all be fishes." The myths of the deluge hero Yu hearken back to the post–Ice Age epoch when the glaciers and vast ice sheets were melting and creating vast, roaring rivers and huge lakes across the northern hemisphere. The Yellow River that Yu tamed is known as "China's sorrow" because it has caused terrible and deadly floods throughout history, just as has the Tigris River.

There is an amazing convergence between the Chinese and Sumerian accounts, which, as we will see, also agree with those of the ancient Mexican and Peruvian civilizations. Wherever we find civilizations with pyramids and the beginnings of irrigation agriculture, we find accounts of "gods" descending to Earth to teach humans how to live a civilized life. Like the mythology of these other cultures, Chinese mythology begins with a creator of the universe—in this instance, Pangu—followed by a succession of sage emperors and cultural heroes who came down to Earth to teach the ancient Chinese how to clothe themselves, grow plants, and pursue language and architecture.

Another similarity can be found in the dragon, which was regarded as a deified serpent. This clan emblem found at Xia sites is also a motif commonly found in Mesopotamia. The dragon was also the symbol of the perfect man, the son of Heaven, the emperor.

Yet another meeting of the myths of these cultures is found in the origin of humans. According to Chinese myth, human beings are made of yellow earth and mud, an account that finds echoes in chapter 2 of Genesis and in the myth of Sumer: "O mother! The creature you are going to name has come into being. Give it the image of gods. Mix the mud of the bottomless pit. Make his arms and legs. O mother! Announce the newborn's destiny: That is man!"[6] Ancient Chinese legends also recount a great flood in which eight people—the same number as in Genesis—survive the deluge in a boat.

Although all these similarities are intriguing, there is no doubt the ancient civilization that built the pyramidal structures in China is more enigmatic and unknown than the other five civilizations that emerged so suddenly across the world. Because of this it is perhaps wise to be skeptical of stories that have emerged from the area and, much as you would for any such account anywhere, to be thorough in tracking down source materials to verify them. For instance, a widely circulated story of extraterrestrial intervention in China—one that both Erich von Däniken (author of *Chariots of the Gods?*) and Hausdorf refer to in their work—remains highly controversial and difficult to confirm given the Chinese reluctance to officially acknowledge or investigate inexplicable events. I myself could not satisfactorily verify it, and the fact that it is said to have occurred a generation ago makes the process of corroboration even more difficult.

Briefly, it involves the supposed 1938 discovery of strange skeletons in a remote area of China bordering Tibet. The skeletons, which were said to have unnaturally thin bodies and large, overdeveloped heads, did not resemble any human racial group. Along with the skeletons was found a stone disk bearing a grooved spiral of characters that Dr. Tsum Um Nui, a respected Chinese archaeologist, determined to be a kind of recording. Apparently the Peking Academy of Prehistory forbade him to reveal the conclusions of his research.

In 1965, the story continues, 716 more disks were found in the same cave complex where the original was discovered and eventually the Peking Academy allowed the professor and his four colleagues to publish their report, entitled "The Grooved Script Concerning Spaceships Which, as Recorded on the Discs, Landed on Earth 12,000 Years Ago."

The disks were said to tell of an ill-fated space probe sent to earth by the inhabitants of another planet. The probe ran into trouble over the Bayan Kara Ula mountain range and was forced to land. The survivors of the accident tried unsuccessfully to communicate their plight and their peaceful intentions to the local inhabitants, the Han tribe, who lived in nearby caves.

Along with misreading the intentions of the marooned aliens, it is likely the Han would have been frightened by the survivors' appearance. Some of the Dropas (the name the aliens supposedly gave themselves) were hunted down and killed until, eventually, the Han realized they were harmless. The Dropas explained their difficulty: They had come down from the clouds and because there was no way to repair their ship, they could not return home.

Archaeologists have continued to study the caves, finding crude pictures of the sun, the moon, unidentifiable stars, and Earth inscribed on the walls, with pea-sized dots connecting these representations. The disks and the cave drawings were supposedly dated at roughly 12,000 years old. The area around the caves where the disks were said to have been found is still inhabited by two tribes, though anthropologists have had trouble identifying them; they are quite small and frail and appear to be neither Chinese nor Tibetan.

Now, while the story of these discoveries in Bayan Kara Ula is intriguing, is it true? Oddly, the disks no longer seem to exist—but in my search for answers I did come across some documentation with viable sources that, while not related directly to the disk account, is very interesting in its own right. It is a report from Reuters in Beijing dated June 6, 2002, and bore the title "Tunnels, Pipes, Tower, from 'ET Launch Site' Found in China." The article noted that a team of Chinese scientists was heading out to a remote area to investigate "a mystery pyramid that local legend says is a launch tower left by aliens from space." The article went on to describe the site as containing a 180-foot-tall pyramid and "rusty iron scraps, pipes, and unusually shaped stones" dubbed "ET relics."

Soon after the publication of this report an investigative article by Jo Lusby and Abby Wan was published in *City Weekend,* a biweekly English-language publication printed in Beijing. It began:

> On the south bank of a saltwater lake sits a metallic pyramid said to be between 50 and 60 meters tall. In front of the structure lie three caves, each with triangular openings. The two smaller caves have collapsed, but the largest central cave is still passable. Inside, on the ground, lies a 40-cm length of pipe, sliced in half. Another red-brown pipe is sunk into the earth, only its lip visible above the ground.
>
> Outside the cave, half-pipes, scraps of metal, and strangely shaped stones are scattered along the southern bank of the lake. Some pipes run into the water; it is unknown what may lurk in the salty depths.[7]

The site described in the article is in an extremely remote corner of Quinghai province. The "ET relics" were first reported to the Chinese authorities by a team of U.S. scientists hunting for dinosaur fossils in 1998. The site was ignored until a Chinese journalist got wind of the report, after which he and a group of colleagues decided to view the evidence firsthand. The journalist, Ye, claims, "We just stuck to the facts . . . we tried simply to describe the site as we saw it." Ye filed six reports detailing his observations, each of which was published in the newspaper *Henan Dahe Bao.*

The real mystery of this structure discovered in a desolate, barren desert next to a salt lake was noted after the rocks and metal samples from the site were analyzed. According to the official

Qinhua News Agency, "results of preliminary rock and metal analysis show the pipes are 30 percent ferric oxide with a high content of silicon dioxide and calcium oxide; 8 percent of the sample's makeup was categorized as unidentifiable."

The engineer who conducted the studies said the levels of silicon dioxide and calcium oxide point to the pipes having been on the mountainside for a long time—at least 5,000 years. Iron smelting, however, dates back only 2,000 years.

The origins of the findings at the site in Quinghai province remain unresolved. Up until now few people have been aware of the pyramids dotting the country's landscape, and the underground complex hidden beneath Emperor Qin Shi Huangdi's burial mound has yet to be entered. But as the people and government become more interested in uncovering the truth of its long history and in sharing that truth, we may soon be on the threshold of knowing a great deal more about a culture that, like others in the world, seemingly reached beyond its means and knowledge to create great pyramids whose remains we can still see today.

TEN

Links Between Ancient Mexico and Peru: The Mystery of the Jaguar People

THE LOST TRIBE

Historians usually mention the four earliest civilizations on Earth as being those of Mesopotamia, Egypt, India, and China, each of which is said to have sprung up in the valley of a great river system between 3700 B.C.E. and 1500 B.C.E. The civilizations of the Americas are seldom included in this grouping, even though some began as far back in history as their Asian counterparts.

A little-known people living on the gulf coast jungle of Mexico millennia ago organized a highly sophisticated and stratified society, which included building complex ceremonial sites. Known as the Olmecs, their culture was the earliest civilization in ancient Mexico. Carbon dating of charcoal found at sites such as La Venta and San Lorenzo indicates the Olmecs occupied these areas from about 1500 B.C.E. to 400 B.C.E.

In the 1940s archaeologist Matthew Sterling made some mind-jarring discoveries at La Venta. Upon arrival at the site, his team noticed a large chunk of stone protruding from the ground at the center of an enclosed area. The rock, tilting forward, was covered with unusual carvings. When they dug it out of the earth they found a stele measuring 14 feet high by 7 feet wide and about 12 inches thick. Their excitement soon turned to extreme puzzlement, however, for the two tall men depicted on the stele could never have been in Mexico 4,000 years ago!

The figures, extremely realistic in their representation, were dressed in elaborate robes and wore European-style shoes with curled toes. One had been defaced but the other was clearly a Caucasian male with a high-bridged nose and a beard. As far as is known, however, there were no Caucasians in Mexico prior to the conquistadors. Who carved these monuments and who served as the models? And how had the 20-ton stele been hauled there from the basalt quarry 60 miles away?[1]

But the stele is not the only puzzling discovery at La Venta. A large mound with a fluted shape provides an enigmatic parallel to the ziggurat that was the focus of communal religious ceremonies in Sumer. More than 100 feet high, it is believed to have been part of a huge ceremonial center that included a step pyramid. The original overall complex at La Venta was 4,000 feet long and 2,000 feet wide.

Another Olmec site, San Lorenzo, was not excavated until 1966, when archaeologist Michael Coe and his team made a number of startling discoveries. During their digs they unearthed what are certainly among the strangest artifacts in the world: the Olmec heads. Five in number, they are massive pieces of carved basalt that appear to have been deliberately buried in a specific alignment.[2] The heads range in weight from 5 to almost 20 tons, stand 6 to 10 feet tall, and the largest has a circumference of more than 20 feet. With the nearest basalt quarry being 63 miles away, how were these massive sculptures dragged to the burial site? Indeed, why were they carved in the first place—and why were they buried if they were intended as monuments? Archaeologists remain stumped.

But the central mystery of the heads is their appearance: Their features are unmistakably Negroid, yet according to anthropologists, there were no Africans in pre-Columbian Mexico during the time of the Olmecs!

In his excavations Coe also discovered a sophisticated drainage system of carved, basalt-lined ditches and an elaborate network of channels and sluices, all of which still functioned once they were cleared of accumulated debris. Coe's team, however, could not comprehend the system's purpose. The Olmecs had labored intensively in this region of dense jungle; it gradually became clear that the San Lorenzo site was only one of many. Remains unearthed in some of the hills nearby were also undoubtedly from this forgotten civilization.

Along with the creation of the heads, stele, and waterworks, the Olmecs engaged in massive earth moving and curious burial practices. The main pyramid at La Venta, about 300,000 cubic feet in volume, was part of a site covering an area of some 3 square miles that included platforms, plazas, and several smaller pyramids. To create the graves, an estimated 15,000 cubic feet of earth had been scooped out of the ground to make a deep pit. Then the floor of the pit was covered with serpentine blocks and the graves themselves were lined with small blue tiles or were paved with mosaics.

While the graves at La Venta contained several large heads, pieces of jade jewelry, and other artifacts, the vast majority of Olmec artifacts are sculptures: figurines, decorated stone steles, votive axes, and altars. Some of these were polished to a mirrorlike sheen and all demonstrate well-developed skills in sculptural design and carving techniques with a level of sophistication very advanced in comparison to the primitive artwork generally associated with early agrarian cultures. Both the basalt and jade often used by the Olmecs are difficult materials to work with. Basalt is a hard volcanic rock and jade is a very hard mineral rated at 7 on the hardness scale that places diamonds at 10. It takes time, great skill, and the right tools to create an intricate piece of art from such materials. The Olmecs did not have metal tools so we are left to wonder how they crafted such pieces and where they learned their techniques.

For reasons unknown, all of the Olmec sites seem to have been abruptly abandoned. Most of the jewelry and other artifacts show signs of having been defaced or partially mutilated. No one really knows who the Olmecs were, why they built massive monuments in the jungles of Mexico, why they carved gigantic heads, or why they suddenly disappeared. We do not even know what they called themselves. The name Olmec was derived from the Aztec Olman, which means "rubber." Unlike the later Aztec and Mayan civilizations, we have no Olmec myths or legends to turn to for clues or answers. There were no remaining Olmecs to tell their stories when the conquistadors arrived, and the inhabitants the Spaniards did come upon—those who archaeologists claim have always inhabited Mexico—did not resemble the various races depicted in the art that was found. In fact, it is very curious that the natives who met Cortés are depicted nowhere in Olmec artwork. How did an entire civilization vanish and where did its people go?

It is tedious work to dig up and document artifacts, inventory and catalog pottery shards, and carefully pick through the ruins of buildings and monuments. But piecing it all together, making historical sense of the story the artifacts tell, is the real challenge in the end. When we read anthropological accounts describing the Olmec culture, religion, and social structure we have to keep one thing in mind: All are based on speculation, conjecture, and hypothesis. The descriptions are plausible reconstructions founded on educated guesses that are often made to conform to preexisting archaeological and anthropological models.

In 1996 the National Gallery of Art in Washington, D.C., presented an exhibition titled "Olmec Art of Ancient Mexico," the first comprehensive survey of Olmec artifacts to appear in the United States. The exhibition was covered by *Time* magazine:

> They built large settlements, established elaborate trade routes
> and developed religious iconography and rituals, including cer-

emonial ball games, blood-letting and human sacrifice, that were adapted by all Mesoamerican civilizations to follow.

And then about 300 B.C., their civilization vanished. No one knows why. But they left behind some of the finest artworks ever produced in ancient America.[3]

When the Olmec sites were first discovered, there was a great debate about where they fit in the scheme of development. The argument was eventually resolved and it is now generally agreed that the Olmec civilization is the "mother culture" that gave birth to civilization in Mesoamerica. But does this assertion square with its high degree of artistic achievement and other accomplishments?

In a seed culture we would not expect to find a complex, highly stratified social organization that produces monolithic monuments and advanced works of art. Where, then, are the developmental precursors to the culture that produced the artifacts found at the Olmec sites? The problem inherent in labeling the Olmecs a mother culture—indeed, the issue we run into everywhere that we find the sudden appearance of civilization, whether in Sumer, Egypt, India, or Mexico—is summed up in the *Time* article:

> [B]ut archaeologists don't know what transformed a society of farmers into the class-based social structures of the Olmec, with their leaders and commoners, bosses and laborers, artisans and priests . . . while many of the experts have plenty of theories about the Olmec origins, social structure and religion, few of these ideas are universally accepted.[4]

So the mysteries remain—and scientists do not even hazard guesses about some of them. The massive Olmec heads that could not have been moved by the means at the Olmecs' disposal, the monuments' faces that mirror the features of people who lived nearly half a world away, the sudden appearance and disappearance of an entire civilization—these inexplicable facts perhaps point to a hole in our own conceptual framework, to our lack of some key data and the overall vision to put together the puzzle.

The evidence may point to the possibility that the Olmec civilization arrived on the gulf coast of Mexico in an advanced state. Contrary to the speculation of archaeologists that the different racial types depicted in Olmec art represent that culture's interaction with foreign cultures, perhaps Olmec society comprised these diverse races that separately represented the precursors of the Olmec civilization. And perhaps, as we will see, these Olmec precursors acquired their civilizations from a genesis race.

CONNECTIONS TO PRE-INCA CIVILIZATION

In the Andean highlands and along the coast of central and northern Peru, traces of a civilization have been found whose monuments, artifacts, and development pattern are strikingly similar to those of the Olmecs. And like the Olmecs, this ancient South American civilization disappeared without leaving any written records behind. One of these sites—Chavin de Huantar in north-central Peru—has even been dated to the same period ascribed to the Olmec culture: 1500 B.C.E. to 300 B.C.E.

Situated at nearly 11,000 feet in the upper Monsa River drainage between the Cordillera Blanca and the Cordillera Oriental, in a magnificent setting, a complex of terraces and squares is surrounded by structures dressed in stones that are ornamented with zoomorphic iconography. A U-shaped mound frames a 140-foot plaza centered on the axis of this monument and a sunken, 70-foot circular court lined with cut-stone blocks sits in the middle of the complex.

One of the most interesting artifacts found at this site is the Tello Obelisk, a 13-foot-tall piece of white granite decorated with intricate carvings. Now housed in the National Museum in Lima, the obelisk, a slightly tapered quadrangle with a perimeter of 3 feet at its base, was probably set in the center of the sunken court.

The nearest source of white granite is 10 miles away in mountainous terrain. The type of granite used is crystalline, very dense and hard, almost chisel resistant, yet the finished product was highly polished and very precisely cut. The early Peruvians lacked metal tools, so similar questions arise as with the Olmec monuments: How did they remove the obelisk from the quarry and transport it to the site, and with what tools did the sculptor carve the intricate bas-relief?

And a now familiar puzzle is presented regarding the emergence of the sophisticated culture that created the obelisk and its site. According to Carlos G. Elera, of the Department of Research, National Museum of Peru:

> The "Chavin" culture, which is renowned for the magnificent carved stone stele found at the Andean highland center of Chavin de Huantar, has been seen as a "mother culture" or source of formalized ceremonialism and monumental architecture in the Andes as [have] the Olmecs in Mesoamerica.[5]

Mr. Elera went on to describe a site he had studied in 1990 along the north coast of Peru, where—according to some archaeologists—the earliest monumental architecture in the Americas has been found: "The investigation has yielded unprecedented new data regarding the origin and development of ceremonial centers during the Formative Period on the Peruvian North Coast."[6] Mr. Elera believes the north coast developed at about the same time or even earlier than Chavin de Huantar, making this area the site of the first complex societies in the Americas.

Residential populations at these first coastal centers are estimated to have been about 30 times greater—from 1,000 to 3,000 people—than in earlier hunter-gatherer villages of the region. The evidence of social complexity dates back about 4,700 years. At the same time, evidence is found of the intensified use of domesticated plants and increasing trade between different regions. Grand-scale architectural complexes emerged between 2700 B.C.E. and 1800 B.C.E., corresponding to the building of ziggurats in Sumer and the step pyramid at Saqqara in Egypt.

More than 50 rivers flow through the north coastal region to the Pacific from the western Andean cordillera. They transect an otherwise arid desert terrain, forming linear oases. Although the surrounding desert—known as the Atacama—is one of the driest in the world, the river oases make it a habitable environment. In addition, the Peruvian coast is one of the richest fisheries in the world. There are seven principal valleys in the region and 24 complexes have been at least partially excavated and researched there.

These early monuments were far more than simple mounds of dirt and gravel. Site plans closely resemble those of the Olmec complexes: large mounds at one end, a step pyramid at the other, and a courtyard in the middle of the complex. The walls of the platforms featured modeled and painted friezes and the outer platform walls were constructed with monolithic basaltic blocks cut in an angular shape, set in adobe mortar, coated with plaster, and occasionally painted.

The Aspero complex is one of the earliest and largest original settlements, with 500,000 cubic feet of cultural deposits. Far from a small-scale, primitive complex, it covers an area of 26 acres and includes six truncated pyramids arranged among 17 mounds. The biggest, Huaca del los Idolos, measures 130 feet by 95 feet, is 35 feet high, and was once topped with summit rooms and courts. The Huaca del los Sacrificios is similar in size, with rooms that are about 30 square feet and stone walls that are more than 3 feet thick and 7 feet tall.

Another massive complex, El Pariso, is located about 1 mile from the mouth of the Chilon River adjacent to the floodplain. It contains the region's largest monuments. The complex is made up of 13 mounds arranged over a 120-acre area. A nuclear group of seven mounds forms a U shape, with the largest mounds on the arms framing a plaza. The courtyard is approximately 15 acres. The site's two largest structures run parallel to each other, 1,200 feet in length and 545 feet apart, and all of the site's structures are uniformly oriented slightly east of north (as they are at Olmec and Mayan sites), perpendicular to the summer solstice sunrise in 1500 B.C.E.

While they acknowledge the sudden growth of civilization in the region—'With no local precedent there is a relatively sudden appearance of massive monuments, at a time corresponding to sea level stabilization around 3000 B.C."[7]—scientists cannot agree on the cause of this abrupt genesis of culture.

Once again, we must look at the estimated amount of labor available to complete such sizeable complexes and the time it took to build them. It has been estimated that the Initial Period pyramid complexes on Peru's north coast in Lurin, Rumac, and Chilon represent over 12 million person-days of work. Based on a workforce of 50 people working every day, building such monuments would require 700 years—an astonishing proposition implying a dedication of effort spanning more than 40 generations. It is unlikely that more labor would be available in such a small overall population that included women, children, and the elderly as well as those whose major responsibilities centered on food production, irrigation projects, food distribution, and other tasks related to agriculture.

As with the Great Pyramid and the Olmec heads, the handling of colossal blocks of stone with primitive tools and methods presents a seemingly impossible challenge, and once again these factors point to the extraordinary scope of the effort required to build such complexes and monuments.

SHARED MYSTERIES

The Chavin and other ancient cultures of coastal Peru and the Olmec civilization share much more than the construction of their monumental complexes. Similarities can be seen in various artifacts of the two civilizations as well. Both the Chavin and Olmec cultures depict zoomorphic figures—especially avian and feline—in their iconography, carvings, and art. The Chavin are known as a jaguar-worshipping culture, as are the Olmecs. In addition, both groups carved curious head statuary, some with downturned lips, and are the only cultures to display these features.

Perhaps the most enigmatic parallel between the two civilizations is their sudden appearance from obscure origins, followed by urbanization, stratification, and specialization coincident with the building of sizeable monuments. It is the monuments such as the colossal Olmec heads and the Tello Obelisk that usually divert attention from the most fundamental question: Where did these civilizations originate?

The unresolved issue with the Chavin and other coastal cultures is the same as the unresolved issue with the Olmec culture: We lack evidence of the incremental steps in their development, an understanding of how they learned to meet the Herculean challenges of building monolithic monuments and how they acquired sophisticated social concepts and artistic skills. The following scenario of the development of culture is drawn from theories accepted by anthropologists.

A small tribe composed of a group of hunter-gatherer nuclear families, probably on the urging of a charismatic chief and his allied shaman, decides to settle down and change its seminomadic way of life by focusing on growing specific crops. The chief is convinced that they should build massive monuments for reasons that are unclear. A brief period of intense discovery and rapid change takes place and their society begins to realize the value—the necessity, in fact—of task specialization and of mobilizing and organizing their workforce.

It is an easy evolution to describe but a difficult process to understand. Where is the motivation behind this effort? We can easily envision the stages of social and technical development that occur when a people move from a hunter-gatherer culture to one that is agriculture-based and finally to a full civilization because we have read accounts of these transitions and are at the far side of the process ourselves. But for the hunter-gatherers at the beginning of the process, there are no precedents, no precursors to copy, nothing from which to borrow. What they would have needed is more manpower and more time—neither of which they had, as is borne out in the archaeological record—or outside help, an external source of input, the help of an advanced race that already had such knowledge.

ELEVEN

Clash of Civilizations

YUCATÁN EMPIRES

When Cortés sailed to the shores of the Yucatán Peninsula in 1519, he had no idea what kind of strange, enchanted, and dangerous land he was about to conquer. A hurricane had forced him off his chosen route, but if his voyage had been one of folly up to that point, his luck was about to turn. Lady Fortune surely smiled on Hernán Cortés as she had on few mortals up to that time.

Cortés and the other conquistadors were highly motivated and it is not hard to understand why in retrospect. History usually focuses on the exotic societies that the Spaniards found in the "New World," but it is important to remember what was going on in the Old World at that time. The plague had been sweeping through Europe repeatedly for several hundred years, with another epidemic erupting in the early 1500s. Parts of Spain, especially Andalusia, had suffered recurring famine.

Europe was by no means very civilized at that point in history, despite the Europeans' illusions to the contrary. The Age of Enlightenment had not yet begun and superstition and illiteracy were the norm. Europeans had a poor grasp of geography; the general population still believed the world was flat and that the sun revolved around it. In fact, the Mayan calendar—devised thousands of years earlier—was more accurate than the one the Spanish captains used. Throughout the continent the Church was extremely powerful and intolerant of heretical ideas and other religions and the Inquisition had been making certain that none of these flourished.

Spain was ruled by a monarchy and the Spanish aristocrats wielded tremendous wealth and power. There was little, if any, social mobility. Men like Cortés were fated to remain low- to mid-level military officers their whole careers. He and the other conquistadors sailed to the New World to seek the wealth and notoriety that they could not access in their country. Once there, they had to respect the Church's agenda, which focused on the conversion of the natives to Christianity, but this came second on their list after the acquisition of gold and power.

As Cortés surveyed the land and tried to gather as much information as he could, he had no idea that the ruins of ancient civilizations surrounded him. He was unaware that the Aztec city of Tenochtitlán—toward which he and his men would soon march—rivaled the cities of Europe.

The Aztecs were known to be fierce, war-hardened warriors who had conquered and subjugated many northern tribes during their rise to dominance. Montezuma, the Aztec king at the time of Cortés's landing, who had known almost nothing but success, was about to be thrust into a situation so tangled and full of irony that it is still difficult to believe it actually happened.

At the time of these events the Olmecs had been gone for almost two millennia and the jungle had already reclaimed the ruins of their mysterious monuments. The natives that Cortés met when he first put ashore were descendants of the Maya. Their ancestors had built another vast civilization that stretched from the Yucatán south and west into Guatemala and Honduras. But it too had vanished in about 800 C.E., leaving behind a population of subsistence farmers living in thatched-roof huts.

If the captain could have gone back in time and witnessed the Mayan civilization at its peak 500 years earlier, he would have been astonished to find the area bustling with activity: Roads paved with limestone cement led to large ceremonial sites; priests performed rituals on the summits of pyramids; sculptors chiseled glyphs into stone; plasterers applied lime stucco to the walls of various buildings; artists decorated the pyramids with brightly colored feathered serpents and geometric patterns. On the whole, the culture would have appeared to be more concerned with aesthetics than with monoliths. The Maya built their centers on human dimensions. Cortés might have been curious about the crosses carved on the pyramids—the cross, it seemed, was a universal symbol, rather than representative of Christianity alone. After questioning the *caciques* (priests), the captain would have learned that the intricate Mayan calendar consisted of a Long Count divided into five cycles—the Five Suns or Five Ages of Man—with each cycle lasting about 5,000 years. According to Mayan reckoning, Cortés arrived in the time of the Fifth Sun, the last age of man. The priests would have told him that the world was 80 million years old, and that they had calculated that Earth revolved around the Sun in 365 days.[1]

The priest's knowledge of astronomy and command of mathematics would have surprised Cortés. Mayan astronomers had charted the movements of the Moon, Mercury, Mars, Jupiter, and Venus. Their base-20 system of math included the concept of zero, which they discovered 700 years prior to its discovery in Europe.

When asked about their origins, the priest would have said that after Kukulkan created Heaven and Earth, he realized that he had no one to praise him and glorify the creation, so he made the animals. After listening to them, he realized that their praise was not adequate, so he tried to make people. In his first attempt he used clay, but it dissolved in the rain and the creatures could not multiply. Next he tried wood, but that was not quite equal to the task either. He finally fashioned the first Maya out of milled corn. A page from the Popul Vuh tells the story. (The Popul Vuh was the sacred book of the Quiché Maya containing their mythology, cosmogony, traditions, and history. Handed down orally, it was first committed to writing in the middle of the sixteenth century.)

The wooden people scatter into the forest
Their faces are crushed
They are turned into monkeys
And that is why monkeys look like humans
They are what is left of what came before
An experiment in human design.[2]

Kukulkan, the Mayan name for the feathered serpent called Quetzalcoatl by the Aztecs, is similar to the dragon in China—a symbol of the perfect man, the emperor, and the creator of all beings. But exactly who is this creator? The Maya and Aztecs agree on the following account: "A white man with strong formation of body, broad forehead, large eyes, and a flowing beard. He was dressed in a long white robe reaching to his feet. He condemned sacrifice, except of fruits and flowers, and was known as the god of peace.[3]

According to the myths, this mysterious man, accompanied by 19 assistants, came from across the sea in a boat that moved by itself. They all lived among the ancient Maya for 10 years, during which time he taught the people how to use fire, cook, and build houses and instructed couples to live together as husband and wife. In a clear echo of the accounts in Sumer, this "god" is a man from an advanced society who brings the gifts of civilization to these people of the New World. Scholars dismiss such stories as allegorical myths of cultural heroes and believe they are not to be taken as actual accounts of real events. They have made this pronouncement before, however, and have been proved wrong.

We know that Cortés would have been amazed by the sophistication of the ancient Mayan civilization because of his reaction to what he found when he reached Tenochtitlán, the main city of the Aztecs. He wrote in a letter to the king of Spain:

The great city of Temixtitan is built on the salt lake, and no matter by what road you travel, there are two leagues from the

> main body of the city to the mainland. There are four artificial
> causeways leading into it, and each is as wide as two cavalry
> lances. The city is as big as Seville or Cordoba. The main streets
> are very straight. Some of these are on the land, but the smaller
> ones are half on the land [and] half canals where they paddle
> their canoes. All the streets have openings, and some of them
> are very wide . . . there are bridges made of long wide beams
> joined together very firmly and so well made that on some of
> them ten horsemen may ride abreast.[4]

Cortés was obviously impressed by the beauty, wealth, and precise civil engineering displayed by the Aztec capital. However, he
was still compelled to ransack and destroy it. The myth that has
been handed down in Western folktales is that he and his small army
of 600 men, by the grace of God, defeated an empire—but that is
not how it happened. The Aztecs had made many enemies during
their reign and they exacted heavy tributes from vanquished tribes.
As Cortés marched to Tenochtitlán to confront Montezuma, he was
met by large armies of tribes that were hostile to the Aztecs and that
had been mobilized for battle He managed to make alliances with
some of them and he learned as much as he could about Montezuma
from his enemies. By the time the Spaniards reached the Aztec city,
they had acquired a formidable army.

But the terrible irony that allowed them to conquer the Aztecs
was Montezuma's belief that Cortés might be the returning god
Quetzalcoatl. According to Aztec lore, after the feathered serpent
planted the seeds of civilization, he and his entourage climbed in
their "boat" and left, promising to return in the year One Reed—
exactly the year Cortés arrived. For the Aztecs, this occurrence
would have been akin to a flying saucer with the message "Second
Coming" emblazoned across the hull suddenly appearing out of the
clouds, landing in Washington, D.C., and opening to reveal its first
occupant, who looks just like Jesus.

Montezuma was stricken with anxiety and confusion. His first strategy was to try to bribe Cortés to stop, turn around, and depart the land. He sent the captain lavish gifts as the army approached the city, but that only whet the Spaniard's avaricious appetite for the empire's riches. The Aztec ruler never truly understood the reality of the situation, and the rest is history.[5]

Cortés and his men roughly matched the description of Quetzalcoatl that had been handed down for many generations. Perhaps this can give us some clues to help solve the mysteries of the Olmecs and their curious carved heads and figures on the stele. The stele figures and altar figures created by Olmec artisans are Caucasian in appearance; the Olmec heads bear Negroid features; and many Olmec figurines depict people with Asian facial features. Perhaps these artifacts commemorated Quetzalcoatl and his retinue.

The reference to Quetzalcoatl finally making people out of corn parallels the gods' creation of Adam and the placement of the first man in the garden to cultivate it. Both stories distinguish the beginning of agriculture and the separation of the new human from his human-prototype ancestors. The Old Testament refers geographically to the Fertile Crescent and Palestine, while the Popul Vuh is concerned with Mexico, but the events each text describes occurred at about the same time.

Maverick archaeologist Scotty MacNeish has traced the origin of corn to the central highlands of Mexico, where it was grown as a crop as early as 7000 B.C.E. Wheat *(emmer)* was being grown in Jericho and Jarmo at the same time. Advanced civilizations suddenly appeared concurrently in Sumer and along the gulf coast of Mexico around 3700 B.C.E. These are the roots of the first two distinct civilizations that developed half a world apart.

What other similarities do we find? In both cases, the people of these civilizations do not claim credit for having invented agriculture or civilization; they attribute these developments to the intervention of an outside party. In both cases they tell of humans being created by "gods" who experimented with a series of prototypes before creating modern human beings. In both cases the people tell of a remnant population having survived a great flood. As we will see, the Incas of Peru told very similar stories about their origins.

PEOPLE OF THE SUN

The Incan empire was contemporaneous with the Aztec and suffered a similar fate. When the Spaniards arrived, the empire stretched for 2,500 miles—including what are today southern Ecuador, all of Peru, all of Bolivia, and the northern half of Chile. Much of the empire was in the Andean highlands, with Cuzco at the center of the kingdom. The Incas built some 20,000 miles of roads and a sophisticated system of irrigation canals to water their carefully terraced agricultural plots.

Incan society was tightly organized. At the head was the supreme Inca, a direct descendant of the sun. The supreme Inca's rule was absolute: He was the head of state, commander of the armies, and authority for all taxes and laws. In short, he was "the source from which everything flows" and his title was passed on from one generation to the next so that the noble lineage remained pure and genetically intact. According to the Incan creation account, the creator Viracocha sent out two of his children—Manco Capak and Mama Oello—"to gather the natives into communities, and teach them the arts of civilized life."[6] These two children, brother and sister, became husband and wife so that they could maintain the purity of the creator's bloodline. The supreme Inca had to carry forward this tradition by marrying his blood sister. Though he kept concubines, only the offspring of his sister could produce the next supreme Inca. The title was passed down from the father to the eldest son of the Inca queen. It was all a carefully controlled genetic operation, for the queen was selected from the best of the supreme Inca's sisters.

Members of the Incan nobility were also descendants of the sun. All of the highest positions in the society, including the priests, military officers, and court and government officials, were of the same noble caste.[7]

Like the Aztecs to the north, the Incas had conquered many tribes on the bloodstained road to building an empire. The Incas placed a high value on gold but it was not a monetary value. To them gold was the sweat of Inti, the sun, and was used reverently in their art and architecture.

This was all part of the background that set the stage for a bizarre clash of civilizations in the year 1529. Incan gold was a siren song to explorer and conquistador Francisco Pizarro, who had been born in poverty, and lured him to play the same role in Peru that Cortés had in Mexico. Like Cortés, Pizzaro seemed to have providence on his side.

Not long before the Spaniards arrived, the Incan Huayana Capac wanted to split his empire in two, giving his two sons, Atahualpa and Huascar, an equal share to rule. It proved to be a fateful decision. Neither brother wanted to divide the empire and share rule, so a civil war broke out between them. Atahualpa emerged the winner and ascended the throne. But the fraternal feud and resulting civil war had weakened the relatively stable empire at a most inauspicious moment in its history. The Incan empire soon went the way of the Aztecs before it.

A SIMILAR ORIGIN

The Incas believed their capital city of Cuzco was the "navel of the world" and average citizens considered themselves children of the sun. But the sun god, Inti, was actually ranked below Viracocha, the creator and teacher of the arts of civilization. In comparing Incan origins with those of the Aztecs and the Sumerians, we may wonder whether Viracocha was an immaterial god living in an inaccessible heaven or—like Quetzocoatl and the Anunnaki—a human living among the people.

The story of how the Incan world came into being aligns with the biblical account of Genesis:

The world was created by Viracocha near Lake Titicaca. After the great deluge or the receding of chaotic floodwaters, Viracocha descended to earth and created plants, animals and men on the empty land; he built the city of Tiahuanaco and appointed four world rulers.[8]

Can we better define the identity of Viracocha? The chronicles, or oral records, of the Incas describe the citizens of Tiahuanaco as the Viracochas, who "were fair-skinned and wore long white robes." Viracocha is also described in the singular as "a man with fair skin, a white beard, attired in a long robe and sandals, carrying a staff, with a cougar lying at his feet."[9]

Though there are different accounts, they all agree that Viracocha built Tiahuanaco, brought culture to the people, and then—just like Quetzalcoatl—set off and promised to return one day.[10]

The Incan origin account is revealing:

A long time ago, when the world was filled with savages, misery, and poverty, a brother and sister—a married couple—Manco Capak and Mama Oello [Viracocha's children] left Lake Titicaca. Inti, the sun god, had sent them to refine the surrounding peoples, and gave them a golden stick for testing the land for cultivation and then settling in a suitable place.

Having found such a place, they had to found the state, teach the people to live proper lives, and advocate the worship of the sun god. The journey took a long time. Eventually, in the Cuzco Valley the golden stick disappeared into the ground, and they could start their mission. Manco Capak taught his people the cultivation and irrigation of land and handicraft, while Mama Oello taught women spinning, weaving, and sewing.[11]

Manco Capak—one of the four world rulers—became the supervisor of the Ursa Major world—that is, "the world of the north horizon."[12] Interestingly, the description of the golden stick given to Manco Capak and Mama Oello is like that of a kind of soil-sampling instrument.[13]

Here we are confronted by the same set of themes we encountered in Sumerian and Aztec creation stories. The Incas did not claim to have invented their civilization but instead attributed it to a god and his children, who long ago lived among them and taught them many skills. All of these accounts suggest that these visitors were physical beings with superior knowledge and power—like the "sons of God" and the Nephilim in Genesis. There are an astonishing number of coincidences to be merely the result of happenstance.

As in other cultures among Earth's first civilizations, we find pyramids and monolithic structures in those of South America. The ancient temple complex of Machu Picchu is thought to be an Incan ruin. Its location—perched on a forbidding ridge in the Andes Mountains northwest of Cuzco—causes us to wonder, as we have in other instances, just how the Incas could have transported the 10- to 15- ton blocks of stone used to build it. While the Incas did build an elaborate road system with stones of much smaller size, they had no wheeled vehicles and archaeologists admit once again to being unable to understand the process or techniques used.[14]

We run into similar questions at Sacsayhuaman, another Incan site. There, 100-ton blocks of stone were cut from the matrix rock, chiseled into strange yet exact polygonal shapes, and fitted together to last, it seems, until the end of time. How did the Incas accomplish these enormous tasks?

The Viracochas of legend come to mind. The Egyptian sun god Ra comes to mind, along with all the "children of the sun" living along the Nile, in the jungles of Mexico, and in the highlands of Peru. The gods, it seems, built these structures within these first civilizations, perhaps to remind us that they were here and that they are coming back as they promised they would.

TWELVE

Lake Titicaca: Viracocha's Home Base

Lake Titicaca, on the border between Peru and Bolivia, is the spiritual home of South America and many myths have arisen from its waters. One claims that the lake is where Viracocha created the first people. Another holds that Viracocha and his children rose up out of the lake to begin their work of civilizing the people. They all agree that Viracocha lived at Lake Titicaca.

Situated at an altitude of 12,500 feet and measuring 120 miles long and 40 miles wide, Lake Titicaca is the highest navigable lake in the world. Strangely, the lake's shoreline is strewn with millions of fossilized seashells. You would not expect to find ancient examples of marine life stranded at such an elevation, but geologists theorize that Titicaca was thrust up from the sea during a period of uplift that created the South American continent about 100 million years ago. It is hard to imagine the mighty force that pushed the lake from sea level to more than 2 miles above the coast, into the rarified Andean air, but the evidence is unmistakable. The several marine species that the lake still supports are further evidence of its oceanic origin.

The lake sits in the Altiplano, the largest drainage basin in South America, formed where the two mountain chains of the Andes are farthest apart. During the Pleistocene epoch the lake covered most of the basin, an area 500 miles from north to south and 70 miles east to west, and the water level was high above Titicaca's present-day surface. It receded from those peak levels and has fluctuated about 250 feet during the modern era.

The ruins of the Incan city of Tiahuanaco are situated 12 miles south of the lake and about 100 feet above the current shoreline. Unfortunately, we can only imagine what this site looked like during its glory days. From the monolithic ruins and other evidence researchers have pieced together, it seems it was an enchanting place. The entire complex was aligned to the cardinal points and faced the rising sun on the equinox. An artificial canal surrounded the civic center of city. The most significant structure, the Akapana, consisted of seven terraces rising to 50 feet, with each measuring 600 feet per side, the size of two football fields. The terrace walls were constructed of precision-joined masonry that needed no mortar and the top-level terrace was covered with green gravel and crowned with buildings. A sunken court measuring roughly 150 feet on each side was set into the upper terrace. Internal cut-stone channels are thought to have provided drainage to the structure, but their purpose is debated.

A second massive platform mound, the Kalasaya—a 390-by-360-foot construction with a sunken central court—is located next to the Akapana. It was a step pyramid in the ziggurat mold, an earthen mound faced with large andesite blocks that was so impressive that the Spaniards made visits simply to gawk and wonder. However, after the time of the Conquest, the Kalasaya began to be used as a quarry and 90 percent of the original facing stones have since been removed. The most easily transported stones were ransacked and used to build a nearby church and bridge. Sitting in front of the Kalasaya was an additional sunken court.

Not much of the city remains except for the ruins of a tantalizing collection of monolithic structures: the Gateway of the Sun, the entrance to the Kalasaya; the stairway and sunken courtyard; several anthropomorphic statues (resembling the Alantes statues at Tula in northern Mexico); and a variety of smaller artifacts.

The Tiahuanaco builders had to travel about 50 miles to obtain the andesite they used from natural volcanic formations. Sandstone quarried about 10 miles from the site was also used. How did they manipulate and haul huge blocks over those distances? If the ancient tribes of Peru did build Tiahuanaco and other sites such as Machu Picchu and Sacsayhuaman using primitive tools—as archaeologists claim—then their methods should be easy to duplicate.

Similar to chapter 7's proposed simulation of stonework necessary for the construction of the Great Pyramid, a satisfactory test of possible methods used to build Peruvian antiquities would consist of quarrying a 60-ton block—much smaller than the largest stones at Tiahuanco—from the quarry 50 miles away and transporting it to Tiahuanaco using the exact same methods proposed by archaeologists. Once at the site, the block must be lifted, perhaps to the height of the lintel of the Gateway of the Sun, and moved into place. Given the results of much less challenging tasks in the past, it seems all but impossible for this to be accomplished.

Independent researchers have long questioned both the orthodox view that the Incas built Tiahuanaco and the recent date ascribed to the site's construction. What are we to make of the monstrous construction blocks (one is estimated to weigh more than 400 tons) located 200 meters southwest of the Kalasaya? These megaliths are part of a site known as Puma Punka. There are several theories about what role this site played in the overall complex. Orthodox scientists believe that the blocks were hauled to the site and were never actually used, but Peruvian scholar Arthur Posnansky, who studied the site for 50 years, found during his excavations conclusive evidence that Puma Punka was a pier. After decades of research, Posnansky became convinced that Tiahuanaco had been built as a port when the lake level was much higher.[1]

In fact, many features of Tiahuanaco indicate that it was a port. "Vast harbor constructions, piers and dykes (and even dumped cargoes of quarried stone at points beneath the old waterline), leave no doubt that this must have been the case," author Graham Hancock noted in his excellent book *Fingerprints of the Gods.*[2]

Posnansky estimated that Tiahuanaco served as a port 17,000 years ago, basing this figure on the celestial alignment of the site. We can correlate it with the results of a geologically based climate study of Lake Titicaca that were presented in a January 25, 2001, press release from Stanford University and in the January 26, 2001, issue of *Science.*[3] According to the study—which was the first to take deep core samples from the bottom of the lake—tropical South America has experienced alternating cycles of heavy rainfall and drought over the past 25,000 years, which have caused the level of Lake Titicaca alternately to overflow and to recede. The report said, "Lake Titicaca was a deep, fresh and continuously overflowing lake during the last glacial state, signifying that the Altiplano of Bolivia and Peru were much wetter than today."[4]

Then, about 15,000 years ago the Altiplano underwent a big change. A long dry era began that lasted for 2,000 years and the lake level dropped significantly. A wet period followed between 13,000 and 11,000 years ago. Several more alternating wet and dry cycles occurred after that era until an extremely dry period took place between 5,000 and 6,000 years ago, "during which Titicaca fell some 250 feet below its present-day level."[5]

We can see that Posnansky's estimate is not far off: The lake was at its highest levels at the end of the Ice Age 15,000 years ago, when it was really more of an inland sea. At 500 miles long, it would have needed a port. When the lake plunged to its lowest level, about 5,000 years ago, Tiahuanaco would have ceased being a port because it would have been more than 20 miles from the shoreline.

Modern science has presented a rather confusing picture of Tiahuanaco's past. Archaeologists initially asserted that the Incas built it in the fifteenth century but changed this view as more evidence was gathered. Now some scientists believe that a culture called the Tiwanuko built the city and created its civilization some time around 1000 B.C.E.; others say that it was built 3,000 years ago.

But 3,000 years ago the lake would have been recovering from major drought, putting Tiahuanaco even farther from the shoreline than it is today. Why would its builders have positioned the city so far from the lake's shore? Even its construction would have been more difficult without the ability to ferry huge stone blocks to the site. After the last drought cycle 5,000 to 4,500 years ago, Titicaca began rising again; the southern portion has overflowed its banks numerous times but the lake has never come close to its peak levels.

Archaeologists believe that the civilization that built Tiahuanaco collapsed sometime between 800 C.E. and 1000 C.E. and that the city and immediate area were virtually abandoned. If this is true, it is an odd coincidence that the Mayan civilization also collapsed in this same time period. It appears that the populations of both civilizations dispersed and never reorganized. Large-scale monument building and agriculture were never reactivated.

The legends of the local tribes say that prior to their existence there was a previous civilization that died away due to a mysterious catastrophe. According to this myth, a comet or asteroid appeared between the constellations of Orion and the Bull around the same time. Rocks have been found that bear depictions of the comet. Many researchers visiting the incredible ruins of Tiahuanaco note that they look as though they were destroyed by some large cataclysmic event.[6]

But the mysteries continue: Along with the myth that credits Viracocha with building and inhabiting Tiahuanco and Viracocha's children with teaching primitive tribes the ways of civilization, there is a legend that has been told by the people living around Lake Titicaca since the time of the Spanish Conquest some 500 years ago. It has been passed down from generation to generation and claims that there is an ancient sunken city in Titicaca's depths. A recent discovery as reported by the BBC, "Archaeologists Probe Lake of Mystery," just may prove this to be an accurate historical record:

> La Paz, Bolivia, Aug. 24—A stone anchor and animal bones were among the artifacts scientists said they found beneath South America's Lake Titicaca in what is thought to be a giant 1,000-year-old temple.
>
> After 18 days of diving below the clear waters of Titicaca, scientists said Tuesday that they had discovered a 660-foot-long, 160-foot-wide temple, a terrace for crops, a pre-Incan road, and a 2,600-foot containing wall. [7]

The submerged site is located 66 feet below the surface. This large temple complex had to have been built when the lake level was much lower than it is today. The site was above the lake for several thousand years but then the new wet cycle, which continues today, overwhelmed it.

Other findings have mystified scientists. As the divers were discovering the ruins beneath Lake Titicaca, another archaeological team was busy excavating the Island of the Sun and the Island of the Moon, two of the 41 islands that rise from the lake's clear waters. They exclaimed that the ruins they had uncovered there would rival Machu Picchu in tourist interest in the future.

But with such variances in water level, how did the ancient peoples who built these monuments and centers survive? In modern times, the Altiplano is subject to prolonged and severe droughts punctuated by seasons of disastrously heavy rains that cause flooding. The air is thin and does not retain much moisture or heat. Daily temperatures show wide fluctuations and frosts can occur any time of year, making agriculture a constant struggle. Hail and winds also impact crops and only highly adapted, hardy, short-season tubers and grains can be grown. Agronomists say that just 20 percent of the Andean food crops are grown above 10,000 feet today.[8] Much as the area around the Tigris River was in ancient times, Lake Titicaca today seems a harsh, forbidding place around which to build a civilization.

Thousands of years ago, however, when the lake was the size of an inland sea, it would have created a microclimate that was likely somewhat milder. Over the years various scientists and other observers noticed a series of odd ridges on the ground whenever the lake level dropped. Studies of the newly exposed ground revealed that in fact the rippled patterns were the remains of raised fields. Some 35,000 acres of fossilized raised fields have been identified so far—enough acreage to support a population of 100,000 to 120,000 at the Tiahuanaco urban site and about 300,000 total in three surrounding villages.[9]

Raised-field agriculture is extremely efficient, but on such a scale it is also labor- and management-intensive. Such extensive acreage under cultivation would have required many workers and large volumes of water. Archaeologists have identified a complex irrigation system surrounding Tiahuanaco—including wetlands, dikes, aqueducts, causeways, and canals—that was used to store and deliver water to a sophisticated agricultural complex. By 500 C.E. the landscape surrounding portions of the lake was largely man-made.

Scientists have shown that raised-field technology employing elevated platforms of earth surrounded by ditches and canals is an ingenious design. The planting platforms consist of earth dug from the ditches, creating an enriched soil structure (an ancient precursor of the modern-day French biodynamic intensive method of raised-bed plantings). The permanent platforms of closely spaced rows increase yields and reduce competition from weeds, and the sediment from the canal is high in nitrogen, an essential component of fertilizer.

Agronomists reconstructed some of these plots and the resultant crops produced higher yields than conventional modern-day practices. Raised fields have also proved to be natural heat conservers. Experiments have shown that this type of agriculture can reduce crop damage from 100 percent to only 10 percent mortality. The entire agro-hydrologic scheme shows a high degree of plant and soil science knowledge as well as an excellent command of engineering principles. How could such a complex system be discovered and developed by people just beginning to use agriculture?[10]

The fossilized raised fields exposed as the water level drops, along with the newly discovered temple complex, prove that people were living in the area near Titicaca both at a time when the lake's level was well below what it is today and at a much later date, when they experienced the floods that submerged their temples and fields.

Another mystery surrounding these ancient people relates to the myth of Mama Oello walking the countryside, periodically testing the soil with her golden rod. Recent research has shed new light on this old account. According to agronomists, the ancients developed methods for detoxifying the few species that will grow at this high elevation: "[A]stonishingly sophisticated analyses of the chemical compositions of many poisonous high altitude plants and tubers had been undertaken by somebody in this region in the furthest antiquity."[11] It seems that this pre-Incan race of people could detoxify noxious plants and turn them into "nutritious vegetables, harmless and edible."

Like corn, the potato originated in this part of the world, flourishing near Lake Titicaca, and was exported to the Old World after the Conquest. The potato plant, however, is a member of the nightshade family, which is generally poisonous—and at high altitudes its tuber also contains toxic alkaloids. It seems that pre-Incan people likely determined that potatoes would survive the high altitude only to discover that most of these tubers proved to be toxic.

They solved this problem by freeze-drying the potato into a powder, a practice still followed today by local farmers, who claim that they can store their potatoes for up to 6 years in this form. But scientists have discovered that coincidentally the freeze-drying process removes the tuber's harmful alkaloids. Did the ancient predecessors of these farmers discover this accidentally?

These discoveries individually and collectively attest to a level of technology far beyond that of primitive tribes and make it clear that Lake Titicaca was inhabited by a pre-Incan advanced civilization.

The myths that tell of the gods or Viracocha (the genesis race) teaching the arts of architecture, agriculture, and astronomy to the primitive local people seem to be borne out by the findings of archaeologists, agronomists, and geologists who have long searched for answers here. As we will see in the next chapter, the sophisticated knowledge of the Maya suggests connections to beings far superior in their knowledge.

THIRTEEN

Masters of Time and Place

GEODESIC MYSTERIES

If you were to find the 90th meridian north on the globe and run your finger along it, starting from the polar circle, you would trace a line through Canada and Lake Superior to the mouth of the Mississippi River, across the Gulf of Mexico to the Yucatán, and straight into the heart of what was once the Mayan civilization. Continuing through Mexico and Guatemala, this line connects many of the principal Mayan sites—evidence of their geodesic alignment.

For quite some time researchers have been documenting the astronomical alignments of ancient archaeological and megalithic stone sites all over the world. But discovery of their geodesic alignment has been more recent. *Geodesy* refers to the theory and practice of surveying to determine the position of specific points on Earth's surface. It is distinguished from plane surveying in that it deals with areas whose dimensions are so great that the curvature of the Earth must be taken into account. Geometric geodesy involves the creation of a mathematical model of Earth, while physical geodesy studies Earth's gravity field. Geodesic studies are referred to in many practical fields of endeavor, including mineral resource location, reduction of the effects of natural hazards, cartography, and study of Earth's propagation of gravitational and electromagnetic energy. The discovery of the precise alignment of Mayan sites along the 90th parallel is significant because it demonstrates that the Maya were aware of Earth's curvature and knew the advanced formulas used in geodesy.

A specific branch of geodesy, *archaeogeodesy,* encompasses study of the positioning of prehistoric monuments and other ancient artifacts with respect to geodynamic phenomena, as well as the possible representation by such monuments of particular features of Earth. The science of archaeogeodesy received a big boost in the eighteenth century, when Napoleon Bonaparte's team of scholars investigated the properties of the Great Pyramid of Giza.

One of the group's primary tasks involved surveying areas of Egypt and drawing up detailed maps of the country. After the surveyors discovered that the Great Pyramid was perfectly aligned to true north, they decided to use the meridian passing through its apex as the baseline for all other measurements and orientations. When their first maps were completed, the team was surprised to find that the Great Pyramid's meridian cut the Nile delta neatly in half and that, if extended, the diagonals running from the apex to its northeastern and northwestern corners formed a triangle that encompassed the entire delta area.[1]

They also discovered that the Great Pyramid was set almost precisely on the intersection of latitude 30° north and longitude 30° east, with a nominal error factor. These computations and configurations meant that the Great Pyramid served as an accurate geodesic marker. Since that time, many geodesic and astronomical orientations and alignments have been discovered at and between ancient sites all over the globe.

The ancient Mayan civilization covered an area that included southern Mexico, Guatemala, Belize, and northern Honduras. A detailed analysis of the region in relation to the landmass of North and South America reveals a striking fact: The area of Mayan civilization lies almost precisely in the center of this enormous geographical mass.

A survey shows that the longitude 90° west bisects this geographical area almost in half, and that the latitude 20° north extends through the Yucatán, while the latitude 15° north runs through southern Guatemala. Orienting from the intersection of latitude 15° north and longitude 90° west, this geographical area extends north on the 90th meridian to Devon Island, Canada (at latitude 75° north, roughly the uppermost reach of North America) and south to Tierra del Fuego (at latitude 55° south, roughly the southernmost reach of South America). The east–west area extends from longitude 150° west (using the Pacific Ocean island of Tahiti as a marker) to longitude 30° west (using the Azores Islands in the Atlantic Ocean as a marker). This is a very important geodesic configuration. (See fig. 2.)

Another key feature of Mayan geodesy lies in the precise alignment—with negligible deviation—of many of the major Mayan so-called ceremonial centers along the north-south axis of the 90th meridian. A list of important Mayan sites located along this meridian includes Dzibilchaltún, Uxmal, Sayil, Xpujil, Becán, Chicaná, Calakmul, Uaxactún, and Tikal. It would be difficult to plan such a precise orientation without detailed geographical and geophysical knowledge. In modern geodesic analysis it would be achieved by surveying two points, called stations, many miles apart. The latitude and longitude of each would then be determined by astronomical means, and exact global-positioning coordinates would be derived. The precise placement of the Mayan sites indicates that they were surveyed and triangulated, implying knowledge of the spherical shape of Earth as well as of its landmass and oceans. (See fig. 3.)

Frans Blom, the well-known Danish archaeologist, surveyed the Mayan site of Uaxactún in 1924 and recognized that the eastern-most plaza, Group E, probably functioned as a solar observatory.[2] The cardinally aligned Group E is situated on an elevated artificial platform 200 meters by 100 meters. An elongated terrace mound on the eastern edge is topped by three west-facing structures. Fifty meters to the west is pyramid E-VII, a structure that appears not to have supported any building. As viewed from E-VII, the three

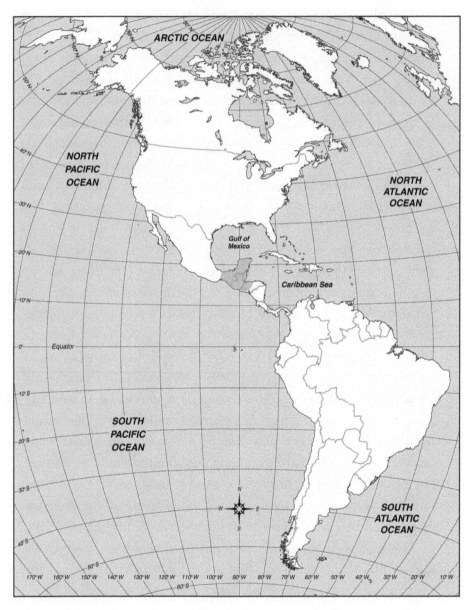

Fig. 2. The shaded area in Central America designates the region of the
Mayan civilization, which was located precisely in the center of the western
hemisphere's North American/South American landmass—
an important geodesic configuration.

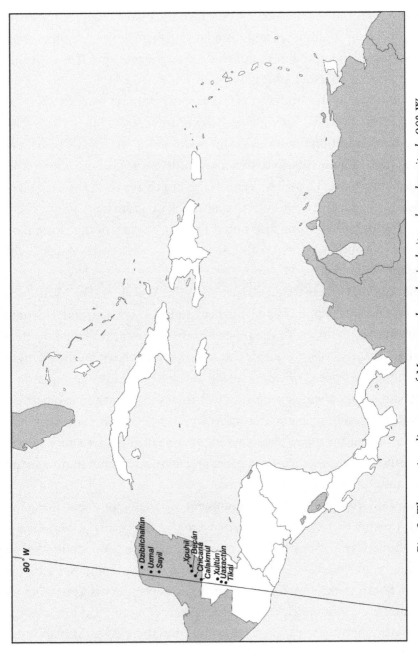

Fig. 3. The precise alignment of Mayan archaeological sites along longitude 90° W

eastern mounds and their structures mark the extremes and mid-point of the rising position of the sun relative to the horizon. In 1989 Anthony Aveni and Horst Hartung made accurate measurements of the alignments and found a satisfactory fit with these three positions, leading them to conclude that pyramid E-VII was probably used as a solstice observatory.

But while the findings of archaeoastronomy, such as these at Uaxactún, serve to demonstrate that our ancestors knew more than we have traditionally given them credit for, it is difficult to believe that the monuments and step pyramids were nothing more than celestial clocks. This view seems to be indicative of the Western tendency to reduce everything to a mechanistic model.

Aveni and Hartung also noted that the alignment of Group E on a north–south axis points almost exactly to the center of Tikal, the heart of the ancient Mayan realm.[3] Other researchers have reported that out of 19 sites found elsewhere in the Mayan realm, 13 of them resembled Group E. While further studies by Aveni and Hartung concluded that none of the other Group E complexes could be classified as actual observatories and that they may have fulfilled a more symbolic purpose, this conclusion doesn't take into account their geodesic alignment. It seems logical to assume that the geometrical patterns resulting from the interfaces between different axes had some useful purpose. The exact alignment of these structures along a principal meridian could suggest an engineering plan that included an aerial orientation and function.

With this geographical alignment of many of their sites, the Maya appear to have achieved what the Egyptians accomplished with the Great Pyramid: They created a massive geodesic marker in what is the "navel," or geographic center, of the landmass of North and South America—a feat requiring a sophisticated command of accurate astronomical, mathematical, and geographical knowledge.

Although Western science has traditionally viewed Mayan pyramids and other structures as being ceremonial sites, the odd antenna-like structures referred to as roof combs at Palenque, Tikal, and elsewhere might have served a very different function, as might the platforms, or terraces, and the pyramids themselves. Before we can conclude what that purpose might have been, we must take note of the long-running enigma of the Mayan road system, or *sacbeob*.

Why would the Maya, who had no dray animals or wheeled vehicles, bother to build paved roads through the jungle when a relatively narrow, primitive path would have served the needs of those traveling on foot?[4] It seems to us a difficult enough job for the Incas to build stone roads throughout their empire, but the Maya took even greater pains by leveling their roads and then covering them with lime cement, a task requiring a tremendous amount of labor and maintenance in a jungle environment. Many of these roads connected sites such as Uaxactun with pyramids and were laid out in straight lines. If our ancestors' teachers did in fact come from the cosmos, it makes sense that they would create geodesic markers to guide their comings and goings from Earth and to act as landing platforms for their spacecraft. A 60-mile line along a north–south axis paved with lime cement and painted white would have been clearly visible to an approaching spacecraft. We already know that the Great Pyramid can be seen from outside Earth's atmosphere, providing a readable target to vehicles flying in from outer space. This thesis points both to a very practical purpose for these monumental structures and to a possible source of the advanced skills necessary to build them.

One principal area of geodesic study is devoted to determining where to position radio transmitters, which involves the study of the propagation of electromagnetic waves. The careful alignment of ancient sites, however, indicates that this aspect of the science may not be as modern as we presume. Archaeogeodesy reveals that ancient peoples may have used their knowledge of energy fields and geometric alignments to harness Earth's electromagnetic or gravitational properties. We might ask if, in addition to guiding incoming space flights, ancient monuments might have been part of a grid used to transmit energy in ways we do not yet understand. The sophisticated mathematical knowledge demonstrated by Earth's first civilizations lends credence to this notion.

ANCIENT MATH WIZARDS

The science of mathematics accurately reflects a civilization's ability to reduce objects and events to abstract symbols. Surprising though it may seem to us today, most cultures throughout human history lacked this ability. One of the most important features of advanced mathematics and an important innovation in human thought is the concept of zero—of something that represents nothing, which takes abstraction to its highest and most paradoxical level.

The concept of zero was independently developed by three cultures: East Indian, Mayan, and Babylonian. Most ancient (and many not-so-ancient) cultures could barely get past counting on their fingers and toes. Some had no concept of numbers at all, while others had only a very rudimentary system in which a sizeable number of objects, people, or activities was simply referred to as "many."

It is curious that the concept of zero, and thus of the place system, did not occur to the Romans (known for being excellent engineers) or Greeks (known for their mastery of geometry). We need only try to manipulate large numbers using the cumbersome Roman numeral system to understand the importance of this concept. In the Roman system, which has no zero, letters are used to represent numbers. The obvious disadvantage in such a system is that numbers representing large quantities become quite long and increasingly complex. The Greek system is just as unwieldy. In fact, as important as we consider these two civilizations to have been in shaping our current culture, we do not use their basic math systems.

We have, however, borrowed many features of the far more ancient Mayan and Sumerian numerical systems, each of which was ingeniously integrated with its culture's astronomical charts and calendars. Both the Sumerians (who followed a base-60 system) and the Maya invented the system of ordered position on a lateral string—which we still use today, referring to it as place value, or place notation. In this system, the position of a numeral is crucial; for example, the difference between 1 and 1,000,000 is the difference between being poor and being rich. The Maya (who used a base-20 system) were the first to conceive of a systematic use of a symbol for zero in the place-value system, which was used to indicate the absence of units in any of the ordered positions. They were at least seven centuries ahead of Europe in this development.

The Mayan numerical system was the essence of simplicity and elegance, consisting of only two symbols compared to our nine. A dot represented 1 and a bar 5.

In our place-value or decimal system a number increases by the power of ten (1; 10; 100; 1,000; etc.) with the addition of zero and/or a movement of the decimal point laterally to the right. Thus the number 1 becomes 10 as a zero is added and the decimal point moves to the right of zero. In much the same way, numbers in the Mayan vigesimal system increased by the power of 20 (1; 20; 400; 8,000; etc.) though the Maya worked vertically, with the lowest number place located at the bottom of the column. They multiplied a dot or bar by 20 in an upward orientation depending upon where it was in relation to the bottom number or lowest place value. Therefore, at the lowest unit level a dot is 1 and a bar is 5; raised up one level, these are multiplied by 20, then by 400, and then 8000, and so on (versus our 10; 100; 1,000; and so on). With this system Mayan merchants could easily place a vertical row of pebbles on the ground or draw a row of dots or lines to represent small or large numbers.

The Sumerian base-60, or sexagesimal, system was a powerful one because 60 can be divided by 2, 3, 4, 5, 6, 10, 12, 15, 20, and 30, thus making it easy to create fractions. We still use base-60 to keep track of time, dividing hours into 60 minutes and minutes into 60 seconds, and to calculate angles in our 360-degree circle (180 degrees = a half circle; 120 degrees = a third of a circle; 60 degrees = a sixth of a circle; and so on).

While the 360-degree circle has long been an established fact for us, the Sumerians 5,000 years ago attributed their knowledge of the concept to their gods. And this was not the only mathematical knowledge they received. Eleanor Robson, a teacher at the Oriental Institute at Oxford University, writes the following about the Sumerians' sophisticated system of math and their desire that it be passed on within their culture:

> Our best evidence is from the 18th-century (B.C.) Nippur, where multiplication and reciprocal [division] tables, tables of squares and square roots, of cubes and cube roots, and tables of metrological units and their sexagesimal counterparts can all be firmly placed in the elementary curriculum for trainee scribes.[5]

Cuneiform tablets show that the Sumerians were performing complicated math using angles and square roots thousands of years before Pythagoras, who may simply have rediscovered their work. In truth, many of the inventions and philosophical concepts we attribute to the Greeks and Romans actually originated in Sumer and Babylonia. Greek and Roman philosophers and scientists often made oblique references to "ancient sources" of information, seldom naming them because in some instances they may not have known their names.

We are left to wonder why the Maya and Sumerians were leaps and bounds ahead of the rest of the ancient world in their understanding of numbers, formulas, and astronomical data. And once again, we are left to wonder how they acquired such knowledge so hard on the heels of the Stone Age. Only an advanced race that already had such knowledge could have taught them, which is, as we shall see in the next chapter, what the ancients themselves tell us.

FOURTEEN

The First Divine Rulers: Myth or History?

What is myth? According to the American Heritage Dictionary a myth is:

1. A traditional, typically ancient story dealing with supernatural beings, ancestors, or heroes that serves as a fundamental worldview of a people
2. A fiction or half-truth
3. A fictitious story, person, or thing[1]

From the perspective of these widely accepted definitions, it is clear that myths are to be separated from facts and distinguished from real historical accounts and accurate records. It is also obvious that dismissing as "myth" an account that someone has related as true is the same as suggesting the teller either is lying or is unable to discern the difference between fact and fiction. But those who readily designate accounts as myth may have a particular worldview that will not permit certain accounts to exist as historical fact.

The existence of ancient Sumer was thought to be a myth for centuries until it was discovered and excavated and found to be the cradle of civilization. The Great Flood is called a myth, and yet this "mythic" account—of humanity being all but wiped out by a great deluge—is found in more than 200 cultures all over the world. How could so many different peoples tell the same story?

We find that three of Earth's primary ancient civilizations share common themes in their creation myths. In each case, gods descended from the heavens to create human beings and to give humanity the gifts of civilization. After creating humans in their image, the gods then instructed the embryonic race on how to live and left behind a theocracy based on the idea that the king was descended from the gods or had been appointed by the gods.

Garcilasso de la Vega, son of a Spanish conquistador and an Incan princess, asked his uncle, an aging Inca, to tell him the story of his people's origins, including how Lake Titicaca became the source of their civilization. His uncle responded:

> . . . all this region which you see was covered with forests and thickets, and people lived like brute beasts without religion nor government, nor towns, nor houses, without cultivating the land nor covering their bodies . . . [Viracocha] sent a son and daughter to give them precepts and laws by which to live as reasonable and civilized men, and to teach them to dwell in houses and towns, to cultivate maize and other crops, to breed flocks, and to use the fruits of the earth as rational beings . . .[2]

No disembodied gods, angels, or spiritual forces could have done that. Viracocha is always described as a man who stayed with the people and taught the arts of civilization, much as the gods clothed Adam and Eve in the Garden of Eden and sent them out to cultivate the land.[3] Moving north from Peru to Mexico, we find that the Aztecs and Maya held a similar belief. Quetzalcoatl (Kukulkan)—a white, bearded man with a long cape and an entourage who came "on a boat without oars"—brought them the gifts of civilization.

The Sumerians tell the same basic story. Our modern Western civilization is an offshoot of the ancient Sumerian civilization, via the branch of ancient Greece and Rome. The Sumerian accounts should have special interest for us because, as scholar Zecharia Sitchin states in his book *The 12th Planet,* "There is also no doubt that the 'olden gods' were the gods of Sumer; records and tales and genealogies and histories of gods older than those pertaining to the gods of Sumer have not been found anywhere."[4] Sitchin is a linguist who is adept in many ancient languages, including Hebrew and Sumerian. He has translated more than 6,000 Sumerian cuneiform tablets, and according to his translations of the Sumerian accounts:

> These were no mere local deities. They were national gods— indeed they were international gods. Some of them were present and active on Earth before there were Men. Indeed, the very existence of Man was deemed to have been the deliberate creative enterprise on the part of these gods.[5]

In the Sumerian Enuma Elish we find this:

> For Quingu's part in the war he was made to provide blood for the creation of man. . . . He divided the Anunaki and placed 300 to guard the sky, and 600 to dwell in heaven and earth. He had them create Babylon, building Esagalia temple and a high ziggurat.[6]

Sitchin makes the point that all of the accounts of the gods who intervened in human affairs agree that these gods were human. We find the Sumerian god Enki traveling from place to place, carrying out a variety of duties and appointing various overseers:

> Enki appointed over each of these a god or a goddess. He then went to place the brick-god Kabta in charge of the pickaxe and the brick-mold. Enki laid the foundations, built the houses and put them under the charge of Mushdamma—the great builder Enlil.[7]

Are Kabta, Enki, and Enlil spirits, or are they humans in charge of supervising workers on massive projects? We must keep in mind that the Sumerians attributed the building of their civilization to these beings, an echo of which is found in biblical accounts of gods and angels coming down to Earth to intervene in and direct the affairs of human beings with their great—even frightening—powers that could enable them to destroy entire cities. Skeptics and most scientists consider them to be myths. Even believers and biblical scholars shy away from taking these accounts literally.

The biblical gods, angels, and "sons of God"; the Sumerian Anunnaki; the Mesoamerican Quetzalcoatl; and the Incan Viracocha were all human. Anthropologists and mythologists explain them as universal archetypes and the stories of their actions as archetypal patterns. But it seems that only those first civilizations of Earth, those that built stone monuments and cities, those that were so advanced in the areas of agriculture, technology, and mathematics, have stories of an intervening party—human in appearance—that created people and then brought them the knowledge necessary for civilization, including that of law and trans-tribal political unity.

By contrast, the indigenous people of North America lived in the same fashion from the time when the ancient Maya were building their temples and watching the sky to the time when the Europeans met them 2,000 years later. They did not build roads or monumental structures; in their stories they had no Viracocha or Quetzalcoatl, no humanlike beings who gave them civilization.

Perhaps modern scholars bring to bear their own cultural biases and preconceptions in their interpretations of the ancient stories of the Sumerians and the Maya. Of course, not all myths can or should be taken literally, but it has proved productive to look for the kernels of truth in them, for the possibility that they may recount some historical fact. Many lost cities and ancient artifacts would still be buried if someone had not taken such a leap.

And what of the descriptions of these human yet otherworldly visitors, the references to how they arrived and what they did once here? We might dismiss them as not at all accurate in their description of the arrival of a superior race from elsewhere in the cosmos. But if indeed the progenitors of humankind were from an advanced civilization, our human ancestors certainly would have lacked any but the most rudimentary ways of describing their arrival and their skills and technology. We know this from our own civilization's contact with primitive tribes around the world. There were no horses in what are now North, Central, and South America when Cortés landed on the shores of Mexico. So when his cavalry mounted the horses they had brought with them, the native people who first beheld them later described horse and rider as a single beast, a monster, part giant dog and part human. Similarly, the natives of the North American tribes called guns "fire sticks" when they first encountered them. We known these descriptions to be inaccurate—yet, however simply, they do describe something of the truth.

Another example of this different, yet truthful, perspective is the "cargo cult." During World War II the United States maintained a base in Melanesia on Vanuatu Island, which received cargo loads of supplies at intervals. The natives saw these being delivered, then watched the strange rituals performed by people who wore clothing that made them all look alike. After observing these details, they tried to invoke the gods to bring them cargo. They established their own mock air base and set up a control tower and radio antenna (a vine strung between poles). They dressed in an approximation of U.S. Army uniforms and marched in drill formations. During their ritual the chiefs uttered the phrases they'd heard the white men speak, such as "Roger . . . over and out . . . you have landing clearance . . . come in." Then they waited for the food and clothing to arrive.

The Old Testament Book of Ezekiel has often been quoted to support the thesis that ancient astronauts visited Earth. The verses cited are usually those that tell of Ezekiel seeing in the heavens "wheels within wheels," which are said to be references to the visitors' spacecraft. But there are other passages that can be seen as support: In his first vision of the wheels Ezekiel saw four creatures who "had the likeness of a man." (Ezekiel 1:5) Ezekiel 1:26 is even more descriptive: "[A]bove the expanse that was over their heads there was something resembling a throne, like lapis lazuli in appearance; and on that which resembled a throne, high up, was a figure with the appearance of a man."

Of another vision, Ezekiel says this:

> Then I looked, and behold, a likeness as the appearance of a man; from His loins and downward there was the appearance of fire, and from His loins and upward the appearance of brightness, like the appearance of glowing metal. And He stretched out the form of a hand and caught me by a lock of my head; And the spirit lifted me up. (Ezekiel 8:2,3)

Now that we have jet aircraft, space modules, and knowledge about electromagnetism, can we fail to see what he struggled to convey? He was grabbed and raised up by an unknown force. It is interesting to note that people who claim to have been abducted by UFOs describe a similar experience: A beam of energy paralyzes them, and then they find themselves floating up to the craft. Perhaps it was some kind of invisible electromagnetic force that raised Ezekiel—a force that he could describe only by using the word *hand* in conjunction with the word *spirit*.

How might we understand what he is seeing, based on his description? It could be that from his vantage point on the ground, Ezekiel is looking into a spacecraft and seeing a man standing at a console of sorts. The interior of the craft glows, as does the exterior. He can see the man to the waist and then his body disappears—perhaps behind a control panel covered with lights (which would give it "the appearance of fire"). The description of "glowing metal" surrounding the man matches descriptions given today by those who have shared their accounts of UFO encounters.

Ezekiel's descriptions continue: He refers to the wheels in the sky rushing like "a storm wind" and like "a great cloud with fire flashing and a bright light around it." (Ezekiel 1:4) It is easy to see how this might be the description of a vehicle in the sky approaching at great speed. The workmanship of the "wheel" was "like sparkling beryl" (Ezekiel 1:16)—a vivid way of describing a very smooth, shiny, metallic surface. And "As for the rims they were lofty and awesome, and the rims of all four of them were full of eyes round about." (Ezekiel 1:18) From these words we can see a circular metallic object with a row of lighted holes (round "eyes"). He goes on to describe what could be a power source: "In the midst of the living beings there was something that looked like burning coals of fire, like torches darting back and forth among the living beings. The fire was bright, and lightning was flashing from the fire." (Ezekiel 1:13) "Fire," "burning coals," and "lightning" are all that the prophet had in his vocabulary to describe light that did not come from the sun, moon, and stars. He sees an intense light that intermittently erupts with lightninglike pulses. What might be its source?

His whole account is riveting. Indeed, he might well be the best single witness testifying to the actual nature of the "gods" and their level of advanced technology. Interestingly, there are many similar accounts from India telling of *vimanas,* cigar-shaped craft that soared through Earth's skies in the distant past.

Ezekiel's encounter took place by the river Chebar, actually a shipping canal built by the Sumerians that was connected to the Euphrates and flowed close to the confluence of the Tigris. It is an account that would not have surprised the "black heads," who left many stories of the gods taking off and landing. The Sumerians described "the house for descending from heaven" as having been made by the gods themselves (they "had fashioned its parts"). Additionally, "Its cornice was like copper."[8] With a seeming confusion of terms, these ancestors of ours were obviously struggling to describe something out of their range of experience. Still, they have managed to communicate that the object was metallic and soared up into and down from the heavens—seemingly crucial details.

But not only the phenomena of light and metal are described in the accounts of the Sumerians and Ezekiel. Returning to the Old Testament, Ezekiel tells of "the man clothed in linen . . . with a writing case at his loins" who is one of six men appointed by the Lord to be executioners of the city, "each with his destroying weapon in his hand." (Ezekiel 9:2) It was the man in linen who was sent to put "a mark on the foreheads of the men who sigh and groan over all the abominations which are being committed in its midst." (Ezekiel 9:4) Ezekiel is quite clear: The beings are men.

THE GIVING OF LAWS

According to the accounts from Earth's original civilizations, after the gods created human beings, they gave them agriculture and then they gave them rules and regulations by which to live. This progression is mirrored in Genesis. In chapter 24 the gods begin giving the Jews their laws: "And if the man takes the life of any human being, he shall surely be put to death" (Genesis 24:17); "Six years you shall sow your fields, and six years you shall prune your vineyard and gather in its crop, but during the seventh year the land shall have a sabbath rest, a sabbath to the Lord." (Genesis 25:3,4) The first cited verse contains the law that forms the basis of a civilized society—it is harsh and uncompromising, but establishes a moral code and points to the value of life. The latter verse offers sound agricultural planning: Letting fields lie fallow is necessary to restore the fertility of the land. That is one of the legacies early civilizations in the Middle East left behind. Many millions of acres of once productive farmland are now infertile or have even been turned into desert due to poor agricultural practices.

The chronicle of civilization is a story of abrupt changes in human society. It is a dramatic tale that demarcates the Old Time and the New Time, with many twists and turns in between. As civilization advanced, men experienced many conflicts, wars, and conquests. In the Old Time there had been no organized body of laws, no decrees, and few regulations; in the New Time laws were created by a "divine" power with the authority to enact and enforce them.

In Genesis 3 the gods issue Adam the agricultural covenant. Some time later, in the Book of Exodus, they instruct Moses and give him laws. Between the two events there was time for humankind's steps of development: Agricultural man replaced primitive man, and then civilized man replaced agricultural man. With civilization must come complex social organization and a system of laws, which must go hand in hand.

On the whole, the Sumerian and biblical accounts agree: "Enlil also selected the kings who were to rule over Mankind, not as sovereigns but as servants of the god entrusted with the administration of the divine laws of justice."[9]

In time, then, Earth's first advanced civilizations suddenly had divine kings from heaven sitting on earthly thrones. The appearance of these earliest civilizations was accompanied by a radical social transformation from a simple egalitarian system to, eventually, a complex pyramidal system with a divine king at the apex. We may wonder why a race that had been egalitarian for millennia would suddenly exalt members of the tribe to a godly status, and why so many of the first and later civilizations followed this same path of social development.

The civilization of the Incas of Peru, like that of the Aztecs of Mexico, developed later than the ancient cultures, but their imperial forms of social organization had obviously been handed down for many generations. The ruling Inca was considered a direct descendant of the sun. He and his wife, who was also his blood sister, were considered to be in a direct genealogical line that led back to the gods, the brother and sister Manco Capac and Mama Oello, whom Viracocha had sent to earth "to gather the natives into communities and teach them the arts of civilized life."[10] Incan culture did not condone incest in the society in general. The reason the royal Inca family was permitted to intermarry and have children was to ensure the purity of noble blood.

Like the Incas, the Chinese, the Mesoamericans, and the Egyptians all believed that their rulers were descendants of the sun god. The Egyptians viewed the pharaoh as an incarnation of divinity who, like the royal Incas, had absolute authority. His commands were unquestioningly obeyed and carried out. Why would the Incas and the Egyptians share the same veneration and belief about their ruler, and why would both cultures link divinity to the sun?[11] Could mythic archetypes, rather than the real impetus of outside intervention, have been at the root of all these societal developments, from the acquisition of laws to the institution of hierarchical social organization, including the reign of a divine king?

MYTH OR REALITY?

If we accept the genius of Sumerian innovation in mathematics and agriculture, in their ability to build great monuments, invent the wheel, and know the planets in the solar system, can we dismiss their own history of their creation and acquisition of this genius? We may ask the same question relative to the Aztecs, Incas, Egyptians, and Olmecs.

We have seen the elements in the emerging pattern: stories of gods descending from the heavens to create humans, the rise of agriculture and civilization, the building of immense monuments, the development of arts and sciences, the institution of laws, and the reorganization of society, with a king to rule over all. Could all of this be the product of myth? In the predominantly Judeo-Christian West, anthropologists and historians dismiss Quetzalcoatl, Enki, Ra, and Viracocha as myth, yet largely accept as a historical figure a man who was born of a divine father, performed miracles, offered teachings, gave new laws, and rose to heaven after his death: Jesus of Nazareth.

FIFTEEN

The Evolutionary Status Quo?

DOES DARWINISM PLAY A ROLE?

For 2 million years people of all races and ethnic groups lived in close association with nature as hunter-gatherers using primitive tools. In essence, humanity reached a kind of stasis in the middle to late Paleolithic period, when primitive people had spread around the globe to every continent except Antarctica. This global homogeneity is evidenced by excavation of Paleolithic sites all over the world. Almost all cultures and tribes were living in the exact same way: They hunted, fished, and gathered plants; learned to make fire; built simple shelters; produced tools; and sewed clothes made of animal hides or plant materials. Food consisted of wild plants, fruits, nuts, fish, and meat. Prior to 10,000 B.C.E. no group leaped far ahead of the bulk of humanity on Earth. This kind of even development is what evolutionary theory predicts for any species, including *Homo sapiens.*

These Stone Age people traveled in seminomadic groups through established territory, occasionally using caves, pit houses, and temporary structures for shelter. Their first tools were made of stone and then bone. Stone scrapers were used for working hides and wood. Bone needles, barbed harpoons, and spear throwers became fairly sophisticated about 15,000 years ago. The early Stone Age, however, accounts for the largest part of the Paleolithic period, which lasted for millions of years.

There was very little innovation after humans conquered the management of fire and invented bone tools and weapons. The progression from early Stone Age implements to those that were more developed took hundreds of thousands of years. The same is true for the development of social organization and the ability to formulate and synthesize abstract ideas from a variety of experiences. For a very long time humans made little of what we would define as progress.

Cultural evolutionists—those who apply Darwinian theory to the development of human culture—contend that civilization should have been the next step for all peoples—but civilization did not arise within each of the world's various cultures as a natural progression. Instead it aggressively spread from a few roots to overtake less technically inclined groups. We can trace the civilization that now exists in most of the world to Western Europe, where it was channeled through Greece and Rome from the source civilizations in Egypt and Mesopotamia.

We know that 20,000 years ago all people up to that time— approximately 100,000 generations—were hunter-gatherers living in simple egalitarian tribal units. By comparison, only 500 generations in total have depended on agriculture, and only 10 generations have lived in industrial civilization. The majority of cultures were still made up of hunter-gatherers 3,000 years ago, and a significant portion of the world's population still did not practice agriculture or live in civilization in the fifteenth century C.E. It is important to note that 99.99 percent of our genetic heritage dates from the pre-Neolithic era. In essence, our genes were formed before the development of agriculture, which led to certain biological, social, and cultural consequences.

What specific changes brought us to civilization? Four principle developments can be credited: agriculture, the wheel, writing, and metallurgy. In each case a considerable amount of conceptual work—the development of the brain, of consciousness—was invested in the discovery process. This conceptual work is the all-important precursor to development of any technology and is the component of the process that is almost never considered or analyzed by scholars, archaeologists, and anthropologists.

There is simply is no way to understand cultural evolution without first considering the occurrences that changed human consciousness (the brain) roughly 40,000 years ago, 10,000 years ago, and 6,000 years ago. Mostly, we've considered the developments at these three specific points without attempting to account for the mental leaps that allowed for these developments—in much the same way that Darwinists fail to consider the importance of intermediate steps in the development of flowering plants from nonflowering plants.

Describing an innovation after the fact often does not shed any light on the process that led to it. Robert Fellner's analysis is an exception to the rule. In his excellent paper "The Problems and Prospects of Cultural Evolution" (part 2), he addresses the underlying issue:

> While introducing the Darwinist school of cultural evolution I mentioned internal differences within it; indeed, these quite divergent views can only be unified under one heading because they all rest on the assumption that the mechanisms of Darwinian evolution—independent variation, natural selection, and resulting differential reproduction—are concepts of explanatory power in examining cultural development (Dunnell 1980; Rindos 1985). This assumption must be seriously questioned.[1]

This is the crux of the problem we experience in trying to understand our own historical development by looking through the lens of Darwinism. It cannot account for the leap from a primitive way of life to civilization in such a compressed time period. Nor can it identify why these leaps were made within only a few groups, why all humans did not make them simultaneously. The Darwinian mechanisms cannot account for this kind of radical "evolutionary" divergence. As Fellner says:

> Concepts, like genes in biology, are the basic unit which lie behind any observable cultural change. We cannot, after all, construct a new tool without having first imagined it; for indeed, while chance events may, in rare cases, lead to the discovery of unknown tool types, their recognition and subsequent exploitation demand nearly as much thought as if no "outside" stimulus had occurred.[2]

This is a critical point. Typically, attempts to describe major advancements in technology and cultural development allude somewhat to the role of accident or chance. The belief that accident plays a major role in such discoveries amounts to Darwinism applied to human history. But this reliance on cultural Darwinism presents one of the major stumbling blocks to our understanding of history's enigmas and anomalies.

These represent information that does not fit into generally accepted theoretical models. If data do not make sense when applied to a model, either the model is changed to allow for this information or the data are ignored or somehow explained away or made to conform to the model. Within the framework of accepted theoretical models, science cannot explain why specific peoples began diverging radically from the rest of human culture at certain intervals, especially around 4000 B.C.E., a time when the culture of Mesopotamia was vastly different from that of the rest of the world. In 3000 B.C.E. the cultures of the Indus Valley, Egypt, and Peru diverged from the way of life most common at the time. By 1500 B.C.E. these cultures and the remainder of humankind experienced completely disparate development patterns. The homogeneity of humankind was a thing of the past.

If we examine the status of development of the rest of the world around 3500 B.C.E., we find that from northern Europe south to South Africa (excluding Egypt), east to most of China, Southeast Asia, Australia, and new Guinea, and west to North America and South America (except for Peru), humans were essentially living as human beings had lived for tens of thousands of years. They were either still hunter-gatherers or just beginning to engage in primitive agricultural experiments.

This long period of relative stability in no way predicted the agricultural revolution that had begun in 7000 B.C.E. Once birthed, agriculture spread north slowly from the Near East, as did the inventions of the Sumerians. True large-scale, controlled-irrigation agriculture did not originate separately in Europe or Africa; nor did metallurgy or the invention of the wheel. The source was clearly the Middle East, stretching from the Dead Sea to the Fertile Crescent region of Mesopotamia.

A similar trajectory was followed in Mesoamerica and Peru. Developments occurred in a localized geographic area and spread very slowly from there. From 3000 B.C.E. to 1500 B.C.E. the Olmecs of Mexico and the Chavin and north-coastal cultures of Peru had developed irrigation agriculture;[3] it is thought that in China rice began to be cultivated; and in the Indus Valley an extensive civilization emerged. The fact that these areas produced major food crops (they are still the world's principal crops) seems a significant coincidence. Russian agronomist and geneticist Nikolai Vasilov, who conducted extensive studies of the origins of agriculture, pointed to three of these sites as primary agricultural centers: the Middle East, China, and Mesoamerica. It is in these same areas that so many other technical advancements—mathematics, civil engineering, astronomy, and so on—had their origins.

Darwinism, however, cannot explain this series of developments. How is it that humans departed not only from the hunter-gatherer norm for their own species, but also from primate norms—from those animals who differ from us by only a genetic fraction? In truth, we deviated from primates only slightly for millions of years. Then something happened. Perhaps the premise that an advanced civilization had a hand in the development of Earth's early human cultures can provide an explanation.

If the theory of evolution can be applied to social development, as some scientists have suggested, then all human cultures around the world would have birthed civilizations at nearly the same time, as evolution does not allow for any radical differences to exist within a species. Because there is virtually no genetic variance among human groups—certainly none that confers any significant difference in intelligence or technical genius—there is no genetic or evolutionary basis for the Sumerians suddenly to grow so far beyond people in other parts of the world.

What of the theory that cultures develop slowly, in piecemeal fashion over long periods of time? As applied to the development of Earth's first civilizations, the theory might play out like this: A group of seven hunter-gatherers are standing in a field. One of them, a smart fellow they all trust, has proposed the idea that they start a civilization. He turns to one and says, "You're going to be the farmer"; and to another says, "You will be the stonemason"; and to a third says, "You will be the accountant." To a fourth he states, "You are the metallurgist"; to a fifth he says, "You will make a fine architect"; and to a sixth he says, "You will be the scribe because you are patient and have a steady hand. I want you to make notations and keep records after I teach you how to perform what I have invented and called writing. You see, I have made up all the plans." Of course, all would greet his ideas enthusiastically at first, and then scratch their heads. What is a stonemason, what is a metallurgist, what is an accountant? Every trade or profession requires a body of knowledge, a systemized set of principles and practices that have been accumulated through generations of trial and error and that must be learned and put into practice anew over a long period of time.

If the development of civilization requires time, then, how did Sumerian, Egyptian, and Harappan culture defy this theory, growing so quickly and exhibiting full-blown knowledge of trades and professions when these civilizations themselves were just beginning? A group of untrained men could not have undertaken the task of laying out and building such constructions as the Great Pyramid and the cities of Mohenjo Daro and Tiahuanaco. We need only look to the common wheel and plow to see how slowly skills and implements develop in most cultures: After the wheel and plow were invented, there were almost no changes in agricultural methods for more than 4,000 years—and their use continues today in some parts of the world. By contrast, in a rather short period of time 5,000 years ago, the creative bonanza included the invention of the wheel, writing, mathematical systems, architectural and engineering methods, and the selection and cultivation of principal food crops that still feed the world today.

What of the theory that humans have an innate urge to become civilized—that is, to create a complex and stratified society with highly developed technology, aesthetics, and systems of law and government? Let us move forward 5,500 years from the beginnings of civilization in Mesopotamia. If this theory were to be borne out in fact, we should surely expect to find that the rest of humanity had followed the path of the development of Earth's first civilized cultures. And certainly by the sixteenth century C.E. we would see a more homogenous distribution of "civilized" humans.

But that was not the case. There are libraries of personal journals, diaries, and various recorded eyewitness accounts from the colonial period showing that most human cultures in the world had not followed the path of civilization as it developed in ancient times, and those that had, such as the Aztec and Incan cultures, had not developed in the way that the world's most powerful cultures—Western European cultures—had. European colonialists applied the terms *savages* and *heathens* to the indigenous peoples they encountered, who in some cases lived more primitively than they. Certainly there was no indication that the Europeans, who believed they brought civilization to these peoples, were in fact superior in any area except technology, and they certainly demonstrated no moral supremacy.

The following historical accounts are not intended to imply that the contact between European civilization and the largely "uncivilized" world was an encounter between a superior race and inferior races. They are presented to contradict the theory that humanity shows a universal impulse toward civilization as I have defined it throughout this book, and to suggest that the impulse for such civilization actually arose from an outside source acting upon Mesopotamia, Egypt, and other ancient cultures.

AUSTRALIAN ABORIGINES: LIVING IN DREAMTIME

There is some controversy among various European countries over who actually "discovered" the continent of Australia. A series of French maps based on Portuguese originals from the mid-sixteenth century show a large landmass named Java de Granda, and a French navigator by the name of De Gonneville asserted in 1504 that he had discovered Australia. But the first European whose claim to having sighted and landed on Australia can be substantiated was a Dutch sea captain named Willem Janszoon.

Europeans may have thought they were discovering a new land, and it was certainly new to them, but they actually arrived about 40,000 years after it had first been discovered. There is no doubt that the Aborigines were Australia's first people. Said to have migrated from Asia to Australia across land bridges roughly 40,000 years ago (though this time frame is disputed), when sea levels were lower, they have been living on the Australian continent ever since.

After the last Ice Age the sea level rose and the ocean reclaimed the land bridges, isolating the Aborigines from the rest of humanity for about 39,000 years. They carried on the same traditions and ways of life of the genus *Homo sapiens* in other parts of the world; they were hunter-gatherers as had been their kin across Europe, Asia, Africa, and North and South America.

In 1770 England's Captain Cook sailed to Australia. When he returned to his country he gave favorable reports of the area around Botany Bay, which convinced the British government to attempt to colonize it. Cook's first account tells of skirting the coast near Port Hacking and noticing a small group of indigenous people who walked briskly along the shore. Apparently they did not realize the "blessings" that the strangers poised in the ship along their coastline were bringing them from distant, civilized lands:

> The natives used many threatening gestures and brandished their weapons; particularly two, made a very singular appearance, for their faces seemed to have been dusted with white powder, and their bodies painted with broad streaks of the same color, which passing obliquely over their breasts and backs, looked not unlike the cross-belts worn by our soldiers; the same kind of streaks were also drawn down their legs and thighs like broad garters; each of these men held in his hand the weapon like a cimeter . . .[4]

Cook and his men could have been time travelers visiting the Paleolithic period. If they had been and had visited their own Europe 7,000 years earlier, they would have found themselves confronted by a very similar welcoming committee.

> The place where the ship had anchored was abreast a small village . . . we saw an old woman, followed by three children, come out of the wood; she was loaded with firewood, and each of the children carried its little burden . . . she kindled a fire. We thought it remarkable that of all of the people we had yet seen, not one had the least appearance of clothing, the old woman herself being destitute of even a fig leaf . . .[5]

Cook found the Aborigines to be excellent hunters and fishermen as well as deadly accurate foes with their 10-foot-long spears.

They were also fierce and intrepid. The two warriors who first met them showed no sign of retreat as they threatened Cook's party of forty: "I could not but admit their courage; and being very unwilling that hostilities should commence I ordered the boat to lie upon her oars . . ."[6]

To show the natives his goodwill and at the same time induce them to friendliness, Cook parleyed sign language with them for about a half hour and then had his sailors row close enough to toss nails, beads, and other tokens to the skeptical Aborigines on the beach. When he waved, they waved back, which led him to believe that he had earned a degree of their trust. He decided to put the boat ashore—but he had misread their signals. The Aborigine warriors rushed them and Cook felt compelled to fire his musket between the attackers:

> Upon the report, the youngest dropped a bundle of lances upon the rock but recollecting himself in an instant, he snatched them up again with great haste. A stone was then thrown at us, upon which I ordered a musket to be fired with small shot, which struck the eldest one upon the legs, and he immediately ran to one of the houses, which was distant about 100 yards. I now hoped our contest was over.[7]

But the fray was not over. The wounded man returned to hurl another stone and then his comrade threw a lance. Cook ordered a third round of buckshot and the fracas finally ended with Cook's landing party leaving more trinkets on the beach and retreating to their ship. It is an amazing, action-packed account that reveals how much Cook had at stake. He had sailed around the world to discover new lands only to be confronted by hostile natives. The Aborigines, for their part, had as much or more to worry about: They did not know what they were up against or where these strangers came from.

The account is all the more fascinating when we realize that it actually documents an encounter between humanity's ancient past, the Aborigines, and a new branch on the tree of civilization that had been planted in Mesopotamia so long ago. Although Captain James Cook could have traced all the way back to ancient Sumer and Egypt, via the Greek and Roman empires, the civilization he was so proud to represent, in reality he was familiar with only its latest incarnation—his culture. The ruins of the earlier civilizations had not yet been discovered at the time of his voyages. This reveals an ironic hallmark of Western civilization: We very quickly forget our past, our true history, as we press ever forward, blazing new trails.

Cook may not have been able to trace his civilization back to its roots in Sumer and Jericho, but the Aborigines knew their past. They knew that they had lived on their land a very long time—they saw the straight line stretching far back in their past; their lives had remained the same for countless generations. To them, both the present and the past were virtually identical: Dreamtime. They were one with the land. They understood its plants and animals in exquisite detail and held knowledge of it that had been hard won over the course of many millennia. The Aborigines were a Stone Age people. They lived in temporary shelters made of tree boughs and bark. Their tools and weapons were made of stone or wood. They had invented an ingenious device, the boomerang, but also used the standard spear, club, and stone ax. The women used a digging stick for getting at roots, grubs, and insects and the men were master hunters, using nets and gigs to catch fish.

While Cook wondered at their extremely primitive state and subsequent generations of European settlers would consider them an inferior race, they were, in fact, in the mainstream of human cultural evolution. Had the incredible developments not occurred in the Fertile Crescent from 5000 B.C.E. to 3000 B.C.E., Cook and his crew would likely have been little different. Though the colonizers wondered why the Aborigines hadn't evolved a civilization, the natives of Australia were actually the norm. Instead the Europeans might have asked why they themselves had deviated so far from humanity's evolutionary baseline.

The outcome of the Aborigines' encounter with Western civilization was tragic, repeating a scene that had already played out in North America and South America, and that would be repeated elsewhere with similar results.

NEW GUINEA: THE LAND THAT TIME FORGOT

Lying north of Australia, New Guinea is the second largest island in the world, 1,500 miles long and 500 miles wide. It is still relatively unknown to the West and was virtually unknown in any detail until the early part of the twentieth century. Botanists are still finding new plant species in its dense rain forests. Isolated and mysterious, the land is ribbed by forbidding mountains with snowcapped peaks that surround high grassland basins.

The sheer variety of its people makes New Guinea a complex country. The native population is composed of nearly 1,000 tribes who speak more than 700 distinct languages—a number that represents almost 45 percent of the world's languages overall. The tribes are divided into three major racial groups: Negritos, Papuari, and Melanesians. The Negritos, who resemble the Pygmy tribes of the Upper Congo in Africa, live in the highlands and have little contact with the Papuari and the Melanesians. Their traditional costume includes elaborate feathered headdresses and they pierce their noses with bone ornaments.

Various European explorers had sailed around the island, mapping it, by the seventeenth century. While a few brave expeditions ventured close to the shore, it was not until Britain took a serious interest in colonizing Australia that New Guinea received significant attention. Voyages of exploration multiplied in the nineteenth century but few of these landed on the island and those that did came to regret it rather quickly, for the indigenous population was extremely fierce.

It was not until the final decade of the nineteenth century that a number of expeditions landed and began to explore New Guinea.

What they encountered shocked them. As recorded by some of the early explorers of the island, the natives were "warlike and cannibal in character" and regarded "setting foot on their special territory a hostile act." These were not the only obstacles that the first explorers had to contend with. They also found a paralyzing climate of extreme humidity and swampy rain forests that hummed and crawled with ravenous mosquitoes and leeches.

What was bad for them has been a boon to modern anthropologists, providing the opportunity to examine ancient human cultures that had obviously lived in the same locale, undisturbed by outside influences, for many generations. In the early twentieth century the native people of the island were living a step beyond the Australian Aborigines of the seventeenth century in terms of cultural development: They were hunter-gatherers and simple horticulturalists, cultivating a few wild plants, including yams, coconuts, and taro, but not yet domesticating them. They did have domesticated pigs but also hunted wild ones, and the coastal inhabitants caught fish with hooks and spears. There was no indication, however, that they were simply trailing behind in their development of a civilization; even in the twentieth century, they were living as they always had.

THE AMERICAS

There were an estimated 50 to 90 million people in North and South America in the sixteenth century when Europeans made contact (the total world population at the time was roughly 400 million) and the portrait of the New World's cultural makeup was complex. Mexico had already seen many advanced civilizations rise and fall. The Aztecs ruled in the fifteenth and early sixteenth centuries, when Cortés arrived. The Olmec, Mayan, and Toltec civilizations were already in ruins by that time. Peru had also seen a succession of civilizations flourish and perish from 3000 B.C.E. to 1500 C.E., when the Incas came to power.

However, the majority of tribes that were spread across the vast South American continent including present-day Paraguay, Venezuela, and the entire length of the coast, as well as the whole of the Amazon basin, were simple hunter-gatherers. There were also many primitive tribes in Central America and isolated areas of Mexico, though the tribes in Mexico generally practiced maize culture in addition to hunting and gathering.

North of present-day Mexico there were about 10 million people. While most of the tribes—there were hundreds of separate cultures speaking dozens of distinct languages—were living as their ancestors had at the time of European contact and settlement, the cultivation of corn, beans, and squash had spread from Mexico north to the Pueblo people of the American Southwest. On the plains of North America the tribes hunted buffalo, lived in tepees, wore clothing made of buffalo hides, and hunted with bows and arrows. The tribes of the eastern woodland cultures built longhouses, hunted deer and rabbits and made clothing from their hides, and gathered berries and nuts. The tribes of the Northwest built wooden lodges, fished for salmon and trout, and carved totem poles. In the Far West and in the intermountain regions across California, Nevada, and Utah, peoples lived in wickiups, gathered acorns and pine nuts, and, along the coast and near rivers, streams, and lakes, fished and collected shellfish. All of these cultures were complex, made up of specific practices and beliefs, but each followed the way of life of its ancestors, which had been the same for thousands of years.

THE AMAZON: CHILDREN OF THE RAIN FOREST

"The Brazilian Indian agency Funia has launched an expedition to search for isolated tribes living in the Amazon jungle and map their territory."[8] This headline, though it might seem outdated, was reported by the BBC News on March 27, 2001.

We live in a world of incongruities and radical discontinuity. While technologically advanced nations send probes to Mars and bioengineer new species of plants, small groups of people on our planet still manage to live in the Stone Age—a dichotomy that we might do best to preserve, for the extinction of the tribes that have inhabited the Amazon region for countless generations most often goes hand in hand with the loss of the rain forest and their other traditional ecosystems.

There were more than 500 different tribes in the area that is now Brazil when the Portuguese landed there in 1500. The estimates of the population at that time range from a few million to 10 million. In the twentieth century alone, however, 87 Amazon tribes vanished from Earth. Today there are only about 320,000 indigenous people living in the region in 170 tribes. Continuing an unbroken line that stretches back thousands of generations, they carry on the traditions and ways of life of their Paleolithic ancestors. Like the Aborigines of Australia, they have survived for eons by acquiring an intimate knowledge of the plants, animals, rivers, and climatic patterns that make up their world and environment.

If the promise of Funia official Manoela Mescia Costa is kept, perhaps their way of life can continue for generations to come: "This is not about entering into contact with them; they have been isolated and should remain that way."[9]

AFRICA: THE DARK CONTINENT

The African continent is a vast, complex mosaic of peoples, religions, and traditions. Africa contains some 3,000 different tribal units that are grouped into larger affiliations based on language, customs, and geography. For the most part the continent is divided at the Sahara Desert. Northern Africa belongs more to the Mediterranean world and the primary religion there today is Islam. Historically, influences from the advanced ancient civilization of Egypt spread southward to touch some areas of the continent along the coasts. Some of the cultures of sub-Saharan, tropical Africa are Pygmy, Bantu, Negrito, and !Kung (Bushmen).

During the centuries when Europeans were exploring and colonizing the New World, they also invaded Africa, where they found tall, fierce warriors in the Zulu and the Masai, who tended cattle not to kill and eat the meat but to periodically drink the animals' blood, and the !Kung and Hottentots, who lived in the southernmost part of the continent.

The African tribes that had migrated from the north and penetrated into southern Africa 1,000 years before the arrival of the Europeans found that other emigrants had preceded them. But unlike the very dark-skinned people who were natives of the south, these older emigrants had skin with a yellowish tinge. They were very small, slight people with an average height of nearly 5 feet, and they spoke an unusual language comprising clicking sounds. The newcomers from the north found the tribe—whom they called Bushmen—to be skilled hunters and very knowledgeable about which plants to gather and eat.

These northern and southern tribes coexisted peacefully for centuries, until white colonists arrived and began shooting and driving away the wild game they depended upon. In retaliation the Bushmen raided the white settlers' livestock—and soon the colonists and the natives were at war. In 1802 a famine struck that turned the tribes against each other. These twin conflicts decimated the Bushmen, and the tribe's surviving members fled to the remote areas of the Kalahari Desert.

There they learned to obtain water from the roots of several plants and from the desert itself by sucking it up from the sands through hollow reeds. They also learned to identify 300 different types of plants by look, smell, feeling, texture, and taste. The Bushmen continued hunting; the members of the few scattered tribes that remain, like the !Kung, are stealthy, peerless hunters. They can sneak up on a grazing herd undetected and send poison arrows into the hearts of their prey.

The Hadzabe tribe, who live along the remote shores of Lake Eyashi, are typical hunter-gatherers leading a primitive, nomadic life. Because they are constantly on the move, they have no need for permanent shelter. During the rainy season they seek shelter in caves. While the men go hunting, the women look for wild fruits and roots. They live as 100,000 generations of their ancestors lived—as all of our ancestors once lived.

TIME FOR A NEW THEORY

Many of the native peoples whom Europeans encountered around the world either perished in war or were enslaved or died from starvation and diseases brought to their homes by the colonists. Western civilization has been contacting indigenous cultures all over the globe for 500 years and the outcome has always been the same: The native tribes lose; their way of life is undone.

Almost without exception these cultures have not embraced Western civilization with open arms. Given the treatment—and disrespect—they have received at the hands of Europeans, we cannot wonder why. The invading explorers and colonists believed they were emissaries from a superior civilization, that the natives in each case of contact were backward savages. This attitude was used to justify harsh, often brutal treatment. The irony, of course, is that the seemingly alien, "savage" way of life was the very kind of existence followed by the Europeans' near ancestors before the arrival of some external influence that altered their course.

These cultures are important for many reasons, not the least of which is that they provide us with an invaluable glimpse into our own past and reveal the dramatic contrast between those cultures that first—and rapidly—developed astounding civilizations millennia ago and those that existed across the vast majority of the planet at the same time. As these surviving primitive cultures illustrate, and contrary to accepted theory, without external intervention or contact we have no internal need to alter our ways of life toward civilization.

So the few ancient, fast-growing civilizations—the advanced nature of which we have archaeological proof—do not fit our theoretical models. Perhaps, then, it is time to change the model. Who or what lit a fire under these cultures? Perhaps now is the time to take as truth the explanations of our ancient ancestors: These cultures were contacted and stimulated by an advanced race; the cultures in the rest of the world were not.

If we look at a map of the world and think back to the Ice Age, it is possible to guess at why these specific cultures might have been chosen. There were abundant water and extremely fertile alluvial plains in Mesopotamia, Egypt, China, and the Indus Valley. The gulf coast of Mexico was fertile and wet. The climate in these places had warmed—and all that was needed was technical know-how in order for them to blossom.

SIXTEEN

Ancient Enigmas: The Domestication of Plants and Dogs

THE ENIGMA OF PLANT DOMESTICATION

Agriculture and civilization go hand in hand. Together they represent a 180-degree departure from the human norm, which was the hunter-gatherer form of social organization and subsistence. According to author Jack Challem, "What we are—and were—can be deduced from paleontological data (mostly bones and coprolites) and the observed habits of hunter-gatherer tribes that survived into the twentieth century."[1] Hominids, protohumans, *Homo sapiens neanderthalis*—all the ancestors of modern humans—survived for millions of years by living in relative harmony with nature, gathering plants and hunting in nomadic or seminomadic tribes.

The seeds of grains and legumes, which have been a staple of the Western diet since the onset of the agricultural revolution, were not part of the diets of our ancient ancestors. In fact, they have been consumed by humans for only a small fraction of the time that humanlike species or humans have existed. Agriculture has existed for only about 10,000 years and civilization for half that span. From a mathematical perspective, humankind has actually spent about

99.99 percent of its time in the primitive, pre-agricultural state. Indeed, a large portion of the world's population did not convert to agriculture or embrace civilization until the last millennium, and many primitive cultures did so only after contact with external civilizations. Agriculture and civilization are experiments still being tested in the crucible of long-term survivability.

All of this points to the probability that agriculture and civilization were concentrated for some time in those sites where civilization first appeared. Examining history and trying to determine the exact origins of agriculture and the various food crops is thus an integral part of ascertaining whether the theory of outside intervention is accurate. What is immediately apparent from any survey of the origin of principal crops is that that they are associated with four of the primary ancient civilizations: Mexico; Peru; and the Fertile Crescent, where corn, potatoes, and wheat originated; and China, where perhaps rice originated. Many secondary crops, such as barley, soybeans, lentils, peas, beans, peppers, squash, cocoa, cotton, and alfalfa (used as animal forage), also came from these four centers of civilization.

The first pertinent question to ask is why hunter-gatherers turned to agriculture. The long-standing theory had been that there were survival benefits from agriculture and that because it brought specialization and the division of labor, it ultimately created more leisure time. But recent studies have shown that theory to be inaccurate. The !Kung of the Kalahari still maintain a hunter-gatherer way of life and studies have found that they are not and never have been nutritionally deprived, they spend less rather than more time procuring food, and they have known about plants and have consciously chosen not to grow them.

Why, then, would some hunter-gatherers voluntarily commit to growing plants and to completely changing their tribe's way of life without any assurance that doing so would improve their chances for survival? Four main theories have been proposed and all are based on the idea that the switch to agriculture was a necessity and not a choice:

1. Some anthropologists believe that a climate change in the Near East led to drought and desiccation, which brought people together in oases, thus prompting the need for increased food production and a less nomadic way of life.
2. Another school believes that simply an increasing population was the driving force.
3. Some scientists suggest that fishing villages had an abundance of food, which led to a more sedentary life and experimentation with agriculture.
4. It has been offered that people and plants developed a symbiotic relationship of sorts: People artificially selected plant species to grow and became dependent on them for food, and the plants became dependent on people for propagation.

None of these proposals has received universal acceptance and none can be proved. Further, none addresses why agriculture first appeared in locations that were far apart geographically and why it developed in conjunction with the sudden appearance of advanced civilization.

As discussed in chapter 15, the theory of evolution as it has been applied to the origins of agriculture and civilization is predicated on the assumption that there is an inevitable, universal pattern of humankind's development from hunter-gatherer to agriculturist to civilized being. But the historical record does substantiate this assumption. Agriculture and civilization spread from the first points of their development to other areas at different times and in an uneven distribution pattern. Further, the natural mechanisms that motivated humans to create agriculture and civilization have not been clearly delineated or justified in terms of the primary evolutionary mechanisms of mutation and adaptation. In fact, agriculture and civilization almost completely go against generally accepted Darwinian mechanisms. If we examine the record, we find that human culture as a whole did not develop in a slow, gradual, and incremental process of transformation from the primitive to the complex. Instead what we find is an explosion of development, a quantum leap compressed into a mere fraction of humanity's existence as a species, a radically changed way of being, and an entirely new survival strategy based on the human engineering of plants and animals undreamed of by those of the Paleolithic period.

All of the mechanisms of agriculture are based on artificial processes: Humans select the plants and animals they want to grow or domesticate because these species meet specific requirements. The basic distinction between domesticated plants and animals and their wild ancestors is that they are selected and developed by humans because they are or could be adapted to the conditions and care that people maintain for them. The labor that humans invest in this results in an ongoing, multigenerational commitment that is predicated on a high level of continuous planning, intent, and control over nature that had never been exhibited during humankind's long prehistoric existence.

That situation creates a chain of consequences for domesticated plants, animals, and humans. Like all other animals, we are absolutely dependent on plants, for only plants can convert solar energy, via photosynthesis, into usable nutrients to form the base of the food chain. The Bible tells us, "All flesh is grass." Even the animal protein consumed by meat eaters ultimately comes from plants because the animals humans routinely eat are vegetarians.

There are about 250,000 species of flowering plants in the world, of which we use 10 as crops to provide the bulk of human food. Interestingly, many of these 10 species are from just two plant families, the grass family (Gramineae)—which includes cereals such as wheat, corn, oats, barley, and rice—and the bean family (Leguminosae)—which have been among the major crop plants in the world since the onset of agriculture. While a bitter controversy has been raging between advocates of genetically modified organisms (GMOs) and opponents of GMOs, our history of genetically tampering with plants and animals stretches back thousands of years to some of these first crops, albeit the methods once used were far more traditional than those used today. Over time we have radically changed many plants and animals—so much so that they are now less like their wild ancestors and more like separate, unrelated species. Today, wild grains and fruit look very different from their commercially grown counterparts, and they taste nothing like the commercial varieties. Indeed, it is often impossible to even find the original ancestor of a modern crop.[2] How did we get here?

The primary process that humankind has used to domesticate plants and animals is selective breeding, which is actually a process of hereditary reorganization. According to the accepted hypotheses, we have selected specific characteristics that appealed to us. But artificial selection is entirely different from natural selection. Natural selection creates stabilized biological systems that ensure the development of a normal wild phenotype, an organism that contains a broad diversity of properties that preadapt it to a wide variety of environmental conditions, thus ensuring survival of the species. Artificial selection does just the opposite. It breaks down precisely those stabilized systems, thereby creating gene combinations that cannot survive in nature.

In order to make a plant species palatable, high in nutritional quality, easy to harvest, able to survive cultivation, and adaptable to competition with other plants, we usually alter the plant significantly from its natural habits. Farmers do not want tall spindly plants, so plant geneticists have selected and bred for dwarf mutations. Branches usually do not add to yield, so farmers have selected for non-branching varieties. Nature wants the seed heads to break apart easily for the most thorough seed dispersal, but delicate seed heads can affect everything from efficiency of harvest and processing to ease of shipping and shelf life, so we have selected for more resilient fruits, grains, and vegetable. Toxins are normally present in plants to fight off pests, but we have bred out the toxins to make plants edible or tasty, then we spray them with pesticides to protect them as they grow. In short, we make plants unfit, using the anti-evolutionary process of artificial selection.

Embarking on this process, of course, takes time. It does not occur in one or even dozens of seasons. The first step is to look for *sports,* mutations that exhibit desirable characteristics. Then seeds must be selected from the healthiest and most viable plants, to be planted the following year, when the process must be repeated again, and again the year after that, until the desired characteristics appear regularly: a larger seed, a bigger fruit, more leaves, a better flavor, and so forth. All of this is obtained by disciplined observation over an extended time period. Would early humans have known how to conduct this process?

It has been said that when humans domesticated plants, plants in turn domesticated humans. We take for granted the invention of agriculture, but for the world's ancient peoples the change from a nomadic hunter-gatherer life to a sedentary agricultural one was not only a total revolution, it was also a huge gamble whose outcome is yet to be determined. We have "bet the farm," so to speak, on agriculture, which at this stage of development is a highly mechanized, industrial enterprise dependent on artificial input. But even at the time of its inception in that handful of ancient populated areas, the change amounted to a complete upheaval of human existence.

Hunter-gatherers lived in an egalitarian tribal culture that moved around a home territory in search of food. The concepts of private property, acquisitiveness, and personal wealth did not exist. The need to organize a large workforce did not exist. Warfare was small in scale and limited to conflicts with local tribes. All of this changed when people settled down around crops that were grown. Small families or groups within larger peoples marked out fixed territories for themselves. They began to lay plans for these plots of private property, to acquire goods to use, to work in order to earn money to buy what they needed in order to grow crops or keep their personal properties. These selected areas became something to claim, to own, to protect, and to fight for—which eventually led to conflict, disagreements, and, before long, standing armies. And all of this happened in a very compressed time frame relative to humankind's total existence as a species.

Why did humans turn to such radical change? What promise might have been held in such a gamble and such a move away from the wild grains that were free for the taking? It might be offered that the wild versions of wheat, rice, and corn were much smaller than the domesticated versions and were thus extremely difficult to harvest. There would have been no justification for early humans to invest the necessary time and effort into harvesting these grains. But there is no evidence, in fact, showing that our ancestors ever depended on wild grains. Their staple diet consisted of lean-muscle meats, limited fatty organ meats, and wild fruits and vegetables, "but, significantly, not grains, legumes, dairy products, or the very high-fat carcasses of modern domesticated animals."[3] We know that no primate species consumes grass seeds as part of its regular diet and that Paleolithic humans did not before 8000 B.C.E. In fact, we are not and have never been adapted to digesting such grains until they are processed;[4] we lack the enzymes required to derive energy from the type of natural fibers that predominate in wild cereals unless they are milled and cooked.

Our remote ancestors, then, did not eat what they could not digest—and they did not have the technology to make grains digestible and thus edible. This provides no help in understanding how people would suddenly decide to grow what they had never before eaten. Why would they choose to domesticate grasses? How could ancient humans be certain that the endeavor would pay off? And why would they give up the only way of life human beings had ever known for a gamble? These represent vertical leaps in thinking. It is easy to reason back from the facts now that we know about plant genetics and breeding, but it is a serious challenge to begin at the beginning (assuming that is what our ancestors did).

Perhaps the most puzzling aspect of humankind's sudden turn to agriculture and civilization is that there is no evidence of the intermediary steps of widespread farming villages that experimented with plant and animal domestication. A jump from a hunter-gatherer culture to the agricultural life of the Sumerians in the space of several thousand years without any small-scale precedent and without any evidence that the resulting crops would sustain humans seems something of a miraculous leap.

There are several theories that attempt to explain why our ancestors altered their way of life and how they learned the art of agriculture. The dump heap theory is predicated on the notion that chance observation of a garbage pile with plants sprouting amid the refuse spurred our ancestors to change. But such an observation hardly seems sufficient motivation to rapidly and completely change an age-old way of life. Other theories focus on the notion of convenience (plants could be grown right next to the dwelling site); and the idea that an increased familiarity with plants translated, ultimately, into comfort with growing them, which actually supports a slow, rather than rapid, conversion to agriculture; and the connection between religious beliefs and agriculture, which does not seem sufficient for such a wholesale conversion of cultures.

Regardless of why or how humans embarked on the rapid march to civilization, it is the exact points of origin of the ancestors of the world's four principal crops—wheat, corn, rice, and potatoes—that perhaps tells the greatest part of the story, for it is on the foundations of these crops that our first civilizations were built. We might think that science has the answer to where these plants began, but, like everything else involved in the development of these ancient civilizations, the answers are not readily available.

Assumptions, however, can be made: "Climate changes in the Fertile Crescent some 10,000 years ago [led] to the spread of wild cereals, one of which was the predecessor of modern day wheat. Since those times, many genetic changes, brought about both by accident and by design, have led to a very different plant."[5] But this does not mean that the initial plant species of these crops can be identified. "Durum wheat is a hybrid that occurred spontaneously between an as yet unidentified grass and einkorn [a type of wheat]. . . . Bread wheat is the most widely grown wheat species and one of the few crops for which no wild forms have been identified."[6] This wild grass species and the first wheat have not been pinpointed. Wild wheat has a protective husk, while the seeds of domesticated wheat are naked and remain attached to the stem. The former was allegedly transformed into the latter via accidental mutations between einkorn and other wild grasses in the Fertile Crescent. There has been no answer for why our ancestors would have noted this subtle development and acted upon it.

Scientists believe that the Sumerians, the first bread bakers, bred different varieties of wheat and wild grasses by accidental selection; while harvesting, they naturally selected the mutations—however few there were—that exhibited naked seeds firmly attached to the stem (the opposite of wild wheat). Once again we are confronted with the notion that every step leading to civilization was a "miraculous" accident. Thousands of generations of accidental genetic selection are required by nature in order for certain mutations to appear more frequently. Yet the period, time, or location in which such a gradual and very prolonged process might have taken place on Earth is nowhere to be found and there is no explanation for this botanogenetic miracle. It is as if it was a process not of accidental natural selection, but rather of artificial manipulation.[7]

As with wheat, the origins of cultivated rice are uncertain and have been studied and debated for some time. The plant is of such antiquity and has been grown across such a broad area—from India to China and Japan—that the precise time and place of its first development may never be established.

Corn, *Zea mays,* is one of the two principal food crops to have originated in the Americas. Archaeological and geological excavations, supported by radiocarbon dating of ears of corn found in caves, indicate that a type of primitive corn was used as a food in Mexico at least 7,000 years ago and later spread north and south in the Americas. However, no wild forms of corn have been found.

Unlike wheat, corn is a highly specialized plant and is largely unsuited for efficient, natural reproduction. Although the ear has been specially bred for producing high seed yields, the plant has no mechanism for broadcasting its seeds without human intervention. Native Americans gradually transformed whatever the original wild plant was into the plant called maize, a cultigen, or product of artificial culture—a human-made plant!

Finally, we turn to the humble potato, the most important noncereal crop in the world. The potato is in the Solanaceae family and is closely related to tomatoes, peppers, and tobacco. The natives of the Andes Mountains of South America discovered the tuber around Lake Titicaca and somehow—miraculously—determined that it was edible even though both the plant and its tuber are toxic at that elevation. From archaeological records and carbon dating, it has been determined that the potato was being cultivated from about 8000 B.C.E., making it contemporary with domesticated wheat, corn, and rice.

These four crops feed more people in the world than all other crops combined and account for 70 percent of the total cropland in production. The fact that we cannot find the precursors of wheat, corn, or rice seems to suggest that our ancestors had an amazing gift for complex plant breeding with species that they had previously ignored. Interestingly, the astounding success of these three crops, along with the potato, can be recognized in the fact that, though the agricultural revolution has been under way for 10,000 years, humans have not bred any new major food crops. We have to wonder at such innovation in such a short span of time by people who were just emerging from primitive hunter-gatherer cultures.

Yet the records of the early civilizations are quite clear about the origins of crops and agriculture: They were taught by the gods. In Genesis the gods place Adam in the Garden of Eden to cultivate it and throughout the scriptures he regularly instructs the Israelites concerning proper agricultural practices. The first truly agricultural society of Sumer used terms for farmer *(engar)*, plow *(apin)*, and furrow *(absin)* that were not of Sumerian origin but were credited by the Sumerians themselves as coming from Enki and Enlil: "Agriculture and the domestication of animals were gifts given to Mankind by Enlil and Enki, respectively."[8] Enlil first spread cereals "in the hill country" of the Fertile Crescent and made cultivation possible in the mountains by keeping the floodwaters at bay. The name of the mountainous land east of Sumer—which scientists say is the source of many crops—was E.LAM, which means "house where vegetation germinated."

The Mexican civilizations attributed the arrival of corn to Quetzalcoatl and his entourage, who lived with them for a decade. After creating the ancient people from milled corn, he later taught them the arts of cultivation. Similarly, the Peruvians claim that it was Viracocha, a man with the same description as Quetzalcoatl, who gave the people the blessings of agriculture at Lake Titicaca through his daughter Mama Oella. The potato was developed at Lake Titicaca, the site of Tiahuanaco, which many people believe was Earth's first city.

Rice is intimately associated with many Asian cultures and is the basis of their diets and some of their economies. The Kachins, of northern Burma, say that they were sent forth from the center of the Earth after being given seeds of rice to plant in the perfect world in which they were to live. According to the ancient Japanese religion Shinto, the emperor of Japan is the living embodiment of Ninigo-no-mikoto, the god of the rice plant. In India and throughout the Hindu countries it is said that Lord Vishnu caused the Earth to give birth to rice, and the god Indra taught the people how to cultivate it.

In the Judeo-Christian tradition bread is the staff of life, and for Christians becomes either literally or symbolically the body of Christ, the Son of God.

What becomes apparent is that cereal grains and the potato, the foundation of agriculture and life in our age of human civilization as well as in ancient times, have origins that are mysterious and enigmatic, yet there is evidence that, as the ancients tell, the gods did indeed give humans the gift of turning grass into sustenance.

THE MYSTERIOUS ORIGIN OF
"MAN'S BEST FRIEND"

All dogs descend from mutated wolves, the products, assuming the orthodox view, of one of many genetic experiments that humans began in dim antiquity. Wolves were the first wild animals to be bred and turned into a subspecies, supposedly artificially created by humans at the same time as corn and other domesticated plants.

The domestication of wolves *(Canis lupus)* into various dog breeds *(Canis lupus familiaris)* is probably the best example of the long-term genetic manipulation of another species. Wolves were once the most numerous and widespread carnivores on the planet, occupying many ecological niches and preying on many different species, such as rabbits, deer, elk, and bison.

Some dog breeds—for example, German shepherds, akitas, and samoyeds—resemble wolves so much that it is not difficult for us to accept that they are direct descendants of the wild *Canis*. Most people, however, have difficulty believing that *all* dogs are genetic descendants of wolves. It was long thought that different dog breeds had evolved from different canine species, such as coyotes, jackals, and hyenas.[9] But according to the most extensive genetic research into the ancient origins of dogs, "No dog sequence differed from any wolf sequence by more than 12 substitutions, whereas dogs differed from coyotes and jackals by at least 20 substitutions and two insertions. These results clearly support wolf ancestry for dogs."[10]

For a time dogs were thought to be a different species from wolves, but current genetic research has conclusively shown that wolves are the ancestors of "man's best friend." They can even freely interbreed with dogs and produce fertile offspring—though you would never guess by their appearances that a dachshund and a wolf have the same DNA. As with plants, the domestication and breeding of animals are complex processes that are the result of a good deal of time and effort on the part of humans—a dachshund is the product of many thousands of years of human reorganization of the wolf heredity gene pool.

Unfortunately, it is not possible to trace the process of domestication all the way back in an unbroken line,[11] which is why so many questions arise about it. For instance, we see purebred dogs such as salukis depicted in ancient Egyptian and Sumerian artwork. But how did humans achieve purebred dogs more than 5,000 years ago? To begin to answer this question, we must step back in time to the first taming of wolves. In order to breed dogs, our ancestors had to start with the bold idea that they could take a chance on bringing a wolf into the tribe. Of course, the intention would not have been to make a pet of the wolf. In fact, the idea of dogs as pets did not emerge until the nineteenth century. Prior to that, dogs worked for a living and they were known by their purpose: hunting dogs, guard dogs, sheepdogs, and so on.

But we do not know *how* our ancestors tamed wolves and established relationships with them. The process is lost in antiquity and scientists and dog breeders can make only educated guesses. The taming process could not have proceeded easily or quickly, for wolves can only be tamed, not domesticated. While taming is the first step toward domestication, wolves themselves can go no further. Their wild instincts can never be completely eradicated; a wolf can even turn on its master.

Though we don't know the exact process they followed, we can imagine how our ancestors might have proceeded to tame the wolf. They might first have observed wild wolves for many years, learning their pack behaviors. Wolves are social hunters whose packs are organized in a strict hierarchy. Early humans might have noticed the similarity between themselves and wolves as strictly social animals. At some point they might have stolen several pups from the pack (a dangerous gambit) in order to raise them.

The plan might have been to use these pups as the first hunting dogs. But how might they have taught the wolves to cooperate? And if they managed to get the wolves to hunt for them and the wolves killed a deer, how would the humans get the animals to share their food? It is remotely possible that the members of the tribe had adopted the wolves as cubs and had behaved as wolves themselves from their first contact with the animals, imprinting themselves onto the cubs as the alpha pack leaders. But while theoretically possible, this would demand a degree of intelligence that we have never ascribed to Paleolithic humans.

Let's assume that they cleared this hurdle and established a relationship with wolves as the dominant members of the pack; that would be only the beginning. It would be necessary for the wolves to live in close association with humans for a long while until a mutant was born. Not only is it impossible to imagine that any tribe could have managed a large pack for any length of time, but a mutation would have been necessary for the emergence of the first dog as well, for although dogs and wolves are the same at the DNA level, they are very different in terms of hereditary characteristics. Wolves molt; dogs do not. Wolves breed only once a year; dogs can breed at will. Wolves have erect ears; dogs' ears droop or are flattened. Wolves do not have the up-curved tails of dogs. A wolf has several types of fur and twice the jaw crushing power (1,500 pounds per square inch) of a German shepherd because its muzzle is longer and its teeth are larger than those of a dog. The differentiation had to begin somehow and—according to Darwinism and much like wild cereal plants—how else but as a mutation? Wolves had to mutate and be selectively bred to serve humans.

Archaeologists and paleontologists use size to distinguish dogs from wolves among subfossil remains. It is obvious that dogs were bred to be smaller. But how could our ancestors have known that a wolf could mutate into a dog that would have only those wolf traits—smaller size and a loyal, affectionate, and obedient nature— that they desired? Science can once again resort only to the "accidental miracle" theory. Yet how do accidents produce results that are exactly what human beings find most useful and beneficial? With dogs, as with wheat and corn, it seems that accidents have produced the results of intentional design. Despite the fact that wolves in the wild had not produced a subspecies with doglike mutations in the millions of years of their evolution as a distinct species, we are left to assume that they did so spontaneously when humans decided to tame them—and this within the limitation of breeding only once a year.

Another aspect of the mystery is how the first dog eventually gave rise to the world's many dog breeds. If we are to believe that humans were responsible for these further transformations, then we must remember once again that Stone Age humans had no previous experience with any kind of plant or animal breeding.

The earliest known dog in the archaeological record dates back 14,000 years. But the remains that date to that point in time are few and far between. More dogs have been found buried with humans who died about 12,000 years ago, which indicates that by the end of the Ice Age the human–dog relationship was beginning to be established. It was not until 7000 B.C.E. to 6000 B.C.E., however, that this relationship was clearly established in the archaeological record. The bones of dogs become common in campsites of the late Neolithic period.

By about 5000 B.C.E. there is some evidence of populations of dogs that differ from each other. Evidence of salukis, a member of the sight hound family, which includes greyhounds, has been unearthed from Sumerian archaeological sites. The Sumerians kept these dogs for hunting and used their image on seals and carvings. Egyptian art, tomb murals, and statuary also depict salukis, which the Egyptians seem to have revered. The saluki was the royal dog of Egypt and was known as El Hor, "the noble one." Egyptian tombs dating back to 2100 B.C.E. contain the saluki's image, and these dogs were often mummified and buried with their masters. Other breeds portrayed on Egyptian artifacts include mastiffs, pointers, basenjis, terriers, and a dog similar to the pharaoh hound. Other dogs represented in ancient art include the molussus, parent breed of the mastiff and mammoth war dog of Sumer, Babylonia, and Phoenicia; and the kuvaz, still one of the favorite farm dogs of Eastern Europe. How different all of them are from the wolf in appearance, temperament, and skills! It is surprising that their mutations would have survived the rigors of the wolf pack, or that female wolves, who instinctively breed with alpha males, would breed with males who exhibited the genetic mutations that produced such differences.

An even larger conundrum lies in the fact that dogs begin to appear in the Neolithic record only when these various kinds of prized dogs—clearly bred—first appear in the records of the seminal civilizations of Sumer and Egypt. Where did the purebreds come from? The dogs in Neolithic graves are certainly not salukis or basenjis. And how did such purebred dogs—so vastly different from a wolf in appearance—come into existence in the span of only several thousand years?

On the other side of the world, in ancient Mexico, figurines of dogs have been found dating from about 8,000 years ago; fossilized dog remains have been discovered in several excavations; and, in a fascinating and intriguing combination, artifacts have been found in Mesoamerican burial sites that depict dogs on wheeled objects. These are either full-bodied dog figures mounted on four disk wheels attached to wooden axles or dogs whose bodies become sleds of sorts. The mystery of these objects stems from the belief that the ancient civilizations of the Americas did not have knowledge of the wheel. At one time it was thought that these dogs-on-wheels were children's toys, but scholars have since realized that their inclusion in burial sites marks a more serious significance. To ancient Mesoamericans the wheel symbolized the cycle of life, death, and rebirth. Like gold, neither it nor representations of it were used for utilitarian purposes. The dog also had symbolic significance. In Mexico it was a symbol of the night sun, making the dog a valuable companion to the deceased, who, according to Mexican cosmology, had to journey into the nine underworlds in the afterlife.

Similar wheeled religious funerary objects have been found in Mesopotamia and in Egypt, Assyria, Greece, and Rome, where the dog played a very important role in funeral rites as a guide for the deceased through the underworld. Though the origin of "man's best friend" is steeped in mystery, it seems fitting that in ancient times he was revered for accompanying and guiding humans in the hereafter.

MISSING LINKS AND TOO LITTLE TIME

The available genetic, archaeological, and cultural evidence proves that there are a number of missing links between tribal hunter-gatherers and their transformation into agriculturists—and far too little of the time required for the development of the species of grasses cultivated by the world's first civilizations. The same holds true for the development of wolves into the variety of domesticated dogs clearly bred by these cultures.

Dietary studies—and our own experiences—show that even today the human digestive system cannot process the grains that we depend upon until they are thoroughly cooked. In fact, our bodies are still adapting digestively to the lean-muscle meats and leafy greens that 100,000 generations of hunter-gatherers relied upon.

We must then address how our ancestors acquired the advanced agronomic, genetic, and technical knowledge necessary to select and breed certain wild grasses and wolves into food crops and domesticated dogs, respectively. In the Bible the gods—a superior race of humans—intervene to transform Adam into an agriculturalist or tiller of the soil, and throughout the Old Testament these gods give the Israelites specific instructions on how to grow crops.

In fact, none of the ancient peoples who are given credit by scientists for the development of modern crops and domesticated dogs left any records of how they accomplished these feats in such a short period of time—other than to acknowledge the gifts of the intervening gods who had presented them with this knowledge. It is a logical conclusion, given the sophistication of the processes necessary to achieve these genetic feats, that our ancestors received this information from those who already possessed it.

SEVENTEEN

Metallurgy: From the Fire

Metals are nearly as important to our civilization as is agriculture, but explaining how early humans made the connections that led them to identify ore, see its potential usefulness, and acquire it is even more difficult than explaining how they made strides in plant cultivation. In the case of agriculture we at least might assume that early humans had experience with the plant kingdom and some knowledge of how it operated. Metallurgy was entirely new territory. Anthropologists imagine that the discovery of metallurgy was the result of the accidental contact of ore and fire.

We have seen that the picture painted by those who subscribe to Darwinian cultural evolution leads to the conclusion that our civilization was created by a series of accidental discoveries. Could this be the case for the ancients' discovery and use of metal? In his critique of cultural evolution, Robert Fellner reminds us: "All conscious action—and it is consciousness which makes the difference between a culture . . . and a group of animals behaving instinctively—must be based on thought, in other words, concepts."[1] According to Fellner's thought, then, every step of innovation requires thought to address new challenges and problems. It is not sufficient to rely on the notion of accidental discoveries to explain, for instance, the origins of agriculture because true, lasting innovation requires evaluation, analysis, planning, and a long road of trial and error. Just as there is no evidence of the slow development of wild grass seed into domesticated grain, there is no traceable path from the discovery of freely available gold nuggets to process metallurgy.

The first evidence that Stone Age humans used gold is linked to sites that date from around 6000 B.C.E. But gold is a soft, malleable metal that can be worked with simple tools. It can be found in pure nugget form, though even very early gold artifacts such as jewelry, bracelets, and rings are rarely pure; most contain significant silver content. The ancients called this alloy *electrum*.

Copper also seems to have been in use in 6000 B.C.E. Because it is a more practical metal than gold, its role in the development of civilization is more significant; it was the metal first used for tools and weapons. Copper existing in its native form was originally collected and worked, although "[i]n the ancient Near East, the supply of native copper was quickly exhausted, and the miner had to turn to ores."[2]

At first anthropologists asserted that copper had probably been discovered by the chance dropping of malachite ore, which contains copper, into campfires. There is, however, a problem with this hypothesis: Campfire temperatures reach a maximum of 600–650°C, whereas copper reduction from malachite occurs at a minimum of 800°C. In other words, the extraction of copper requires a kiln that can reach this controlled high temperature. It is unlikely, then, if not impossible that Stone Age humans accidentally discovered copper in their campfires. They could not have envisioned its reduction from malachite or sulfide ore (which together hold 90 percent of all copper) until they invented the kiln.

Even if metallurgy initially began as an accidental discovery, the practical application—making, say, the first cast-metal tool—still would have required a long and rigorous thought process involving a number of conceptual steps and a high level of abstract thinking. Our hunter-gatherer ancestors never exhibited such a level of capability. In fact, up to 6,000 years ago they had only just made the connection to use stone and bone for tools and hides for clothing. Yet suddenly, during the Neolithic period, about 5,000 years ago, those few highly developed civilizations appeared, and they included the technical "miracle" of processing metals among their developments—at the same time when people less than 500 miles away were still living primitively. The sophisticated artifacts found in Sumer and Egypt exhibit extraordinary artistic imagination, technical ability, and conceptual strength. By 3000 B.C.E. the arts of jewelry making, painting, and sculpture were already fully developed in Egypt and Mesopotamia.

The ancient use of silver, tin, and bronze presents a picture similar to that of the emergence of copper in these civilizations. Silver, for instance, is harder than gold and is also more rare. Like gold, pure silver was used for ornaments, jewelry, and as a measure of wealth. Galena (silver ore) always contains a small amount of silver. But more than 4,500 years ago in Sumer it was found that if lead was oxidized into a powdery ash, a droplet of silver was left behind. This led to the discovery of the cupellation process, which entails adding bone ash to lead oxide. According to historians, an ancient metalsmith must have realized that these two ingredients could be combined, leading to the absorption of the lead oxide by the ash and the opportunity for a large amount of silver to be separated out and processed. This became the normal mode of silver manufacture from 2500 B.C.E.

The Sumerians also realized—or were told—that if different ores were blended together in the smelting process, a different type of copper could be made—one that flowed more easily, was stronger after forming, and was easy to cast. Thus we can credit them with the creation of the first alloy—bronze—which required far too precise a mix of tin and copper to be merely an accidental discovery. An ax head from 2500 B.C.E. was found to contain 11 percent tin and 89 percent copper. But tin, unlike gold or copper, is not found in nature. It exists in stannic oxide ore, which is hard, heavy, and inert. Smelting is required to separate out the tin, which means that the process to retrieve tin had to precede the creation of bronze—quite an involved and complicated road to walk, and certainly one that would require minds constantly trained on innovation and purposeful experimentation. And because casting is the only way to shape bronze, the Sumerians even fabricated standardized molds to create the ingots they distributed to their cities. Such rigor, creativity, and focus certainly add up to an amazing feat for a people so recently ensconced in the Stone Age. Their creative abilities were apparently so powerful that by 750 B.C.E. the seven metals of antiquity—gold, electrum, copper, silver, tin, bronze, and mercury—are all on record as having been discovered. Mercury was the last to be found, but the other six had been discovered by 2000 B.C.E. After mercury, no additional metal was discovered for nearly 2,000 years, when, in the thirteenth century, Albertus Magnus discovered arsenic. Another 300 years would pass after his find until antimony become the ninth metal to be discovered.

The various civilizations that grew up and flourished in the many years after the rise of the Sumerians had a much easier time of it, for they inherited all the principles, tools, and methods of the people of Sumer—yet no significant discoveries were made for almost three millennia! In *A History of Metals* author L. Aitchison is obviously impressed when he notes that by 3700 B.C.E. the Mesopotamians were basing their new society on metalworking: "It is very clear that the Sumerians placed a very high value on metallurgy."[3] And well they should, because it became the foundation for advanced tools, machinery, and weapons. Aitchison concludes—with admiration for the Sumerians' surprising level of sophistication—that process metallurgy ". . . must inevitably be attributed to the technical genius of the Sumerians."[4]

But what do the Sumerians themselves have to say about their rare talents and gifts for processing and crafting various metals? Their tablets are very clear about how they learned these skills: The gods gave them the knowledge and taught them, just as the gods—the genesis race—laid out the site plans for the temples and ziggurats. The first step was to mark out a building's orientation and set its foundation stone. Then, as tablets tell, a ceremony was performed:

"The king . . . 'the Righteous Shepherd,' 'built the temple bright with metal,' bringing copper, gold and silver from distant lands. 'He built the Eninnu with stone, he made it bright with jewels; with copper mixed with tin he held it fast.'"[5]

It seems from this verse that something fashioned from bronze held the structure in place and that copper, gold, and silver beautified the temple. The tablet's scribe makes it clear that a *Sanug Simug*, a "priestly smith," worked on the temple's façade: "with two hand breadths of bright stone he faced over the brickwork; with diorite and one hand breadth of bright stone . . ." Here and in the preceding verse, "bright stone" is actually a reference to metal. The priestly smith was a master tradesman who obviously knew every facet of this complex art.

The Sumerian tablets are rife with references to the Anunnaki, the working gods who presided over everything from making bricks and building temples to metalworking. Once again we must interpret the word *gods*. Is it possible that those we think of as Sumerian mythological heroes were, in fact, their extraterrestrial mentors and supervisors who had acquired their knowledge and advancements on their home planet?

This possibility is emphasized by several factors. First, the professional names used by the Sumerians in relation to the metal trades—*simug* (blacksmith) and *tibira* (coppersmith and metal manufacturer)—are not original Sumerian words.[6] Linguists talk of there being a substrate language from which the Sumerians borrowed these words, but this protolanguage has not been identified. Second, as the world's first metallurgists, from what human culture could the Sumerians have borrowed these terms? Finally, Mesopotamia lacked metal ores. The Sumerians could not have accidentally discovered metallurgy without centuries of contact and experimentation with raw ores. These practices and skills must have been imported from elsewhere—and those who assisted the Sumerians must have been more advanced, more developed, and conscious of the impact of the gifts they bestowed.

The Sphinx and the Great Pyramid at Giza, Egypt. Some recent studies suggest the Sphinx was built as long ago as 7000 B.C.E. Egyptologists have yet to explain how the massive, precision-engineered pyramid was constructed. Photo courtesy of Martin Gray

The Stairway to Heaven on Mount Tai Shan, China, mountain home of the gods. The emperors of ancient China regarded Tai Shan as the actual son of the emperor of Heaven, from whom they received their authority to rule on earth. At the top of the stairway are the Temple of the Jade Emperor and the Temple of the Princess of the Azure Clouds. Photo courtesy of Martin Gray

The Atlantes crowning the Pyramid of the Morning Star in the ruins of the Toltec city of Tula, central Mexico. These Toltec sculptures, each about 15 feet tall, acted as columns likely supporting a roof at the top of the pyramid. Photo by Will Hart

The Temple of the Inscriptions in the ruins of the Mayan city-state of Palenque in Chiapas, southern Mexico. Did the roof "comb" have a function that modern science has not yet deciphered? Photo by Will Hart

Teotihuacan, the City of the Gods, northeast of Mexico City, Mexico. Built by a pre-Aztec people, the base of the Pyramid of the Sun is nearly as large as that of the Great Pyramid in Egypt. Photo by Will Hart

Aramu Muru's Doorway, near Lake Titicaca in the Hayu Marca region of southern Peru. The large "door" in the stone outcropping has a mysterious keyhole-shaped niche just under 6 feet in height. The age and origin of the monolith are unknown. Photo courtesy of Martin Gray

The Gateway of the Sun, part of the ancient city of Tiahuanaco near Lake Titicaca, Bolivia. Constructed by a pre-Incan culture, the bas-relief at the top of the gate depicts a central figure holding a scepter in each band. His head is surrounded by solar rays and he is flanked by forty-eight warriors. Photo courtesy of Martin Gray

Puma Punka, Lake Titicaca, Bolivia. Some researchers claim that the massive blocks weighing from 100 to 400 tons are the remains of a dock or pier that was part of the 15,000-year-old port city of Tiahuanaco, destroyed by a cataclysm. Photo courtesy of Martin Gray

EIGHTEEN

The Dating Game

When did early hominids first appear? At what point in time did humans originate? How old is the Great Pyramid? How old are the ruins at Lake Titicaca? When did the Olmec civilization emerge? And are any of these and other projected dates and chronologies of prehistory accurate?

The dates attributed to various fossils and to the earliest appearance of human beings and civilization are always subject to change as new findings come to light and old techniques of dating that were once thought to be reliable are found to be less than precise. In addition, and much more problematic, is the practice of shifting dates and chronologies for political reasons or due to the pressure to make new data conform to preexisting time lines and concepts.

The process of dating and creating chronologies needs to be regarded with some degree of skepticism, as is illustrated by what took place after a recent finding in Australia threatened to upset the anthropological "African origin" applecart. It was a classic case of re-dating producing results that did not conform to an established theory.

"Mungo Man Older Than Thought"—so read the headline of the article in the Australian newspaper *The Age:*

> Fresh analysis of the skeletal remains found at Lake Mungo in
> NSW [New South Wales] 25 years ago indicate he may be up to

68,000 years old—making him 28,000 years older than earlier
scientific estimates. The revised dating of the remains by scientists at the Australian National University rewrites the history of
Australia's occupation and has profound implications for
worldwide debate over the origins of modern man.[1]

The article went on to explain that three new techniques were
used to carry out the re-dating. Release of this revised date sparked
a storm of controversy between the multiregionalists, who believe
modern humans migrated from different parts of Asia, and those
who support the "out of Africa" model, which places our origins in
that continent. The latter theory declares that Australia was populated by modern *Homo sapiens* 40,000 years ago.

Interestingly, the re-dating of the Mungo remains was followed
by new research findings in Africa that pushed back to more than
70,000 years ago the date of the appearance of modern human
activities there. An article in the December 2, 2001, issue of the *New
York Times* asserted that "[n]ew discoveries at Blombos Cave, 200
miles east of Cape Town, are turning the long-held beliefs upside
down."[2] Those beliefs dated the earliest evidence of modern human
behavior as having appeared in Europe about 40,000 years ago. The
report went on to conclude that the first appearance of modern
humans points to Africa. So Mungo Man was quickly put back in
his place.

The fact is that now almost every date and time line regarding
human origins and key artifacts is disputed. Several years ago one of
the newest techniques, called thermoluminescence, was used to date
sediment at two sites in Turkey, Jinmum and Durin Yurakh, and the
results shocked the archaeological community. The consensus
expected dates in the neighborhood of 30,000 years old, but the
dates that came back placed the samples at 250,000 years old or
older! The wheels of conventional discontent turned rapidly: Those
unexpected (and unwanted) dates were set aside and a call for a second set of tests was issued. It seems that it is not unusual for tech-

nology to come into question when its results are unexpected or upend longstanding hypotheses.

The most scandalous such case—at least of those that have been made public—involves Virginia Steen-McIntyre, a geologist working for the United States Geological Survey in the 1970s, who was dispatched to Mexico to perform dating tests on specimens of advanced stone tools recovered at a site called Hueyatlaco, near Pueblo. The tools revealed a level of sophistication associated with modern humans, which prompted the anthropologist in charge, Cynthia Irwin-Williams, to expect the stone tools to be less than 25,000 years old, a date predicated on the theory that modern humans crossed the Bering Strait and entered North America around 25,000 years ago at most. Conservative scientists pegged the date closer to the end of the Ice Age, or 12,000 years ago.

Steen-McIntyre performed the tests and even crosschecked her results by using four different methods: uranium series, tephra hydration, fission track, and stratigraphy. She handed the results to the anthropologist, who was shocked. The dates obtained using the latest technology available at the time showed the artifacts to be more than 200,000 years old—nearly 10 times older than expected! To Cynthia Irwin-Williams this result was simply wrong for at least two critical reasons: Modern humans were not in Mexico that long ago (according to the Bering Strait theory) and modern humans did not start making such tools until 50,000 years ago (according to the available evidence).

Irwin-Williams was dissatisfied; she wanted the dates to be placed at less than 25,000 years ago, but Steen-McIntyre refused to change her results. Thereafter she both found it difficult to get her report published and suffered the ridicule of her colleagues, who called her a publicity hound. But that was not the end of the fallout. She also lost a teaching position she had held at an American university. In 1981 Steen-McIntyre wrote a letter to Estella Leopold, associate editor of *Quaternary Research*: "The problem I see is much bigger than Hueyatlaco. It concerns the manipulation of scientific thought through the suppression of 'Enigmatic Data,' data that challenges the prevailing mode of thinking."[3]

Perhaps we have good reason to question the accuracy of the dates and time lines established by orthodox scientists. There are many cases similar to this one—some even more disturbing—and more reasons to wonder why the prevailing theories, dates, and time lines are being guarded so jealously.

I spent a year in the late 1970s researching the Olmec civilization in Mexico. There I noted a time line on the wall of the museum at Villahermosa that put the beginning of the Olmec civilization at about 3000 B.C.E. That date has since been changed to 1,500 B.C.E., a vigorous 1,500-year reduction. I wondered why: Did the old date conflict with a new theory? Whatever the reason, the change supports the idea that all dates and time lines are subject to revision at any time, whether because the methods used to first establish them have been proved inaccurate or because the dates originally ascribed conflict with orthodox beliefs.

In 1996 NBC aired a program called *The Mysterious Origins of Man*. It contained many taboo ideas and anomalous facts that the scientific establishment would rather keep in the closet. Some of the material was based on the book *Forbidden Archaeology,* by Michael Cremo. According to the author: "I told the producers to contact officials at the University of California in Berkeley for permission to film the artifacts stored there. Permission was denied."[4] The producers finished the program by using photographs of the material instead—but that was not the end of the story. The show was well received by the general audience and NBC decided to air it again. Scientists, however, were outraged. Stung by the success of the program and angry about its contents, the scientific establishment swung into action to try to stop the second showing.[5] When their effort failed to sway NBC, they took the campaign to the FCC. Dr. Allison Palmer, president of the Institute for Cambrian Studies, wrote a letter to the federal agency: "At the very least NBC should be required to make substantial prime-time apologies to their viewing audience for a sufficient period of time so that the audience clearly gets the message that they were duped."[6]

We are left to believe that at least some of the members of the scientific community do not trust Americans to discern fact from fiction; therefore we should not be exposed to ideas that contradict the accepted theories of the scientific establishment. In actuality, this episode pointed up the paternalistic attitude of some members of the scientific community as well as their disregard for the First Amendment.

We might ask if chronologies and time lines that are subject to revision have any value at all. Why establish a "fixed" date until that date is absolutely certain to be correct? This question arises especially in the context of news items such as the following from the BBC in 2001, which appeared under the headline "Dating Study Means 'Human History Rethink'": "A complete rewrite of the history of modern humans could be needed after a breakthrough in archaeological dating techniques. British and American scientists have found radio carbon dating, used to give a rough guide to the age of an object, can be wrong . . ."[7]

One hundred years ago French physicist Henri Becquerel discovered the natural radioactive decay rate of uranium. Very soon after this discovery an American chemist, Bertram Borden Boltwood, determined that he could use the predictable decay of radioactive elements to keep track of time. He applied his new technique to the age of Earth, which he estimated to be 2.2 billion years. That came as a shock to the scientific community and to the public, who had long believed it was much younger. By the end of the last century the age of Earth had been more than doubled to about 4.5 billion years. I would not chisel that in stone, however; it could be revised again in another 100 years.

Over the past century hardly a week has gone by without an important discovery about the history of life on Earth making bold headlines. By the middle of the twentieth century paleontologists had uncovered only a few fossils of protohumans. The missing links were many and the time line for the origin of the species went back about 2 million years. Just as the new millennium got under way the latest finding for the date of mammal origins was announced: "Researchers described a fossil that pushes the origins of key mammal features back 45 million years."[8]

Actually, experts have long known that carbon dating is inexact, but they had not realized how inaccurate it could be until a recent study was released in which scientists calculated the age of ancient limestone formations in caves using carbon dating methods and a newer, more accurate method known as uranium dating. They were surprised to find that the carbon dates were off by thousands of years and that the results slipped even more out of synch as older samples were tested. Critics of the carbon dating technique had long contended that it was not accurate and that many ruins and artifacts were far older than estimated by scientists. They argued that the carbon method was based on the flawed assumption that there had been a stable level of radioactive carbon throughout Earth's history. The study showed that the assumption had indeed been wrong and "there may have been much more of it [carbon] in the distant past than previously thought."[9]

Prior to the release of the study—around the time this book was written—the carbon method had been the primary dating technique used by archaeologists to date the artifacts found at excavation sites. The ripple effects that will inevitably reverberate through the scientific community have yet to be translated into revised thinking and adjusted time lines. No doubt many established dates and chronologies will be pushed back even further into the past.

But the inaccuracies of carbon dating are just one point of the debate between the orthodox scientific community and alternative scientists. Many of those outside the orthodox community believe the entire methodology used to fix the dates of ancient ruins is based on assumptions and hypotheses that cannot be proved by any data. It is not possible to ascribe a date to a block of basalt, limestone, or granite rock used to build the Great Pyramid or to a pile of the earth used to build mounds. A geologist can estimate the ages of rock and earth, but such estimates will be in the millions of years, which is not of much help. Archaeologists and anthropologists rely on carbon dating materials found at a particular site to determine the overall period in which that site was built and occupied.

This seems like a logical way to handle the problem, but the results will be accurate relative to the age of the site as a whole only if the materials found at the site correlate to the time when it was built. How can this be known with certainty? Using Tiahuanaco as an example, the only remaining parts of the original structure were monolithic blocks of andesite and limestone and some gravel, but these offered little that could be used to accurately date the original structure and determine when it was occupied.

The next step, then, was to try to locate nearby villages and work from materials found at those sites. But the farther you must travel from the original site to obtain the kind of information needed to date that site, the weaker the resulting date is considered to be. Even if material found at a particular site can be dated, there is no incontrovertible proof that the date corresponds to when the site was constructed and first occupied. The builders and original occupants, for instance, might have abandoned the site, leaving it to be used by a later group of people who left behind their materials for us to find. We know that the Olmecs did abandon their sites after intentionally destroying buildings, burying monuments, and defacing artifacts. But there is no way for scientists to prove that the materials found at the Olmec sites can be attributed to those who built them. At best, the available data support a working hypothesis, a rather tenuous foundation for a time line. Dates for the founding of Olmec sites—and therefore for the Olmec culture as a whole—cannot be stated in definitive terms: The Olmec culture is believed to have been founded in 1500 B.C.E. and is thought to have existed until 300 B.C.E.

It is possible to make a case for almost anything and evidence can always be found to support what we wish to prove. Historians and archaeologists operate similarly to lawyers, often relying on effective or clever argument to convince the jury. This, of course, is not how science is supposed to proceed. The methodology of science is supposed to consist of assembling observable facts into a provable theory that can be independently confirmed. But preconceptions and agendas and the desire to protect them can muddy the process. The preconception and agenda of science regarding the origin of humans and civilization is tied up with the theory of cultural evolution, Darwinism as applied to the development of human societies.

As we have seen, however, there are many enigmas and anomalies that do not fit this accepted model. Tiahuanaco, the Great Pyramid, and the many other megalithic ruins associated with the Indus Valley, Peru, Mexico, Egypt, China, and the Fertile Crescent—along with evidence from around the globe that illustrates the advanced knowledge of early civilizations—reveal legitimate holes in the theory of cultural evolution. Yet it is difficult to challenge accepted theory and make yourself heard.

The late archaeologist Scotty MacNeish, considered both a maverick and a top-notch scientist, wrote 50 books and published hundreds of scientific papers and has been credited with making several important discoveries, such as tracking down the origin of domesticated corn in Mexico. He is convinced that the earliest human presence in North America dates back nearly 60,000 years to New Mexico, but because his theory challenges existing orthodox theory, it will likely get little "air time."

Until the politics of science change or technology reaches an extremely reliable level, the best that can be done is to try to establish the correct sequence of events and disregard any exact dates or inflexible chronologies. Both are written in sand.

NINETEEN

Ages of Ice

We are all descendants of the Ice Age. Surviving icy, frigid climate regimes for extended periods is one of the most serious challenges our ancestors had to face. Just a short time ago on the geological clock, polar bears hunted seals in New York and arctic wolves followed the trails of musk ox along the edge of the ice fields in Illinois. Men clothed in heavy animal skins and whipped by strong winds trudged across frozen landscapes in search of food.

Ice ages have been a fact of life on Earth for millions of years, and during the last 2 million years, our predecessors had to adapt to them. Time and again the ice came, spreading a thick, chilling blanket across the land. In the Arctic or Antarctic and in the glaciers that cling to high mountain ranges we can catch a glimpse of what an ice age looks and feels like. The world's glaciers are, in fact, remnants of the Ice Age, which had already been under way for 15,000 years when the most recent glacial maximum occurred 18,000 years ago. Even as recently as 12,000 years ago a large part of Earth was covered by thick blankets of glacial ice, though the Ice Age was coming to a close and the glaciers were starting to retreat, a process that has gone on almost continuously to this day.[1]

The first of a series of glacial epochs experienced by Earth began about 340,000 years ago, while the second ice age began 270,000 years ago and lasted for 40,000 years. This was followed by another that began 160,000 years ago and ended 130,000 years ago. During the last two glacial epochs, land bridges were formed as sea levels dropped,[2] a dramatic occurrence that resulted from more and more of Earth's water being frozen in the ice sheets that advanced. From about 35,000 to 11,500 years ago sea levels were lower than they are today, and at the peak of glacier advance the sea was roughly 400 feet lower than it is now. At the end of the most recent ice age the sea was 170 feet lower than today, but it has been rising continuously since then.

Of course, life on Earth has had to adjust and adapt to these extreme cycles in various ways throughout the millennia. *Homo sapiens neanderthalis,* for instance, was well adapted to the cold, having survived numerous ice ages during his sojourn on Earth, which started 400,000 years ago. In fact, due in part to their survival, science has greatly revised the portrait of Neanderthals in recent years—they were not the completely dim-witted cavemen that they were made out to be upon our discovery of them.

Roughly 150,000 to 125,000 years ago modern humans began displacing Neanderthals in Africa and Oceania. An article published in *Nature* (May 4, 2000) had this to say:

> The "out of Africa" hypothesis contends that modern humans evolved in Africa between 200 and 100 kyr [100,000 years] ago, migrating to Eurasia at some later time. . . . [T]he discovery of Middle Stone Age artifacts in an emerged reef terrace on the Red Sea Coast of Eritrea, which we date to the last interglacial (about 125 kyr ago) . . . is the earliest well-dated evidence for human adaptation to a coastal marine environment heralding an expansion in the range and complexity of human behavior from one end of Africa to the other. This new, widespread adaptive strategy may, in part, signal the onset of modern human behavior, which supports an African origin for modern humans 125 kyr ago.[3]

Recent genetic studies have presented evidence that appears to show that modern humans, who seem to have migrated from eastern Africa, experienced a "population bottleneck" at some point that dramatically decreased the human population:

> Earlier studies of genetic material known as mitochondrial DNA and micro satellites supported the notion that a small group of primitive humans—5,000 to 20,000—migrated from East Africa, spread around the world, and rapidly expanded in population as they replaced other human populations elsewhere in Africa 80,000 years ago and in Asia 50,000 years ago and in Europe 35,000 years ago . . .
>
> The new study, however, analyzed mutations called SNPS (single nucleotide polymorphisms) in DNA from the nucleus of human cells studied for the Human Genome Project, the effort to map the entire human genetic blueprint. This indicates there was a bottleneck in the human population—what looks like a sharp reduction in the number of people—when ancestors of modern humans colonized Europe roughly 40,000 years ago.[4]

In the December 7, 1999, issue of the *New York Times* Nicolas Wade wrote: ". . . drawing data from 50 ethnic groups around the world, [the study] concludes that the ancestral population from which the first emigrants came may have numbered as few as 2,000 people."[5] Another study showed that this small group headed toward Asia. Regardless of the direction they took, they would not have had long to establish themselves in any new locale because the next ice age began about 5,000 years later (about 35,000 years ago).

The important fact gleaned from all of this is that some pivotal, transformational event occurred about 40,000 years ago, for this is when Neanderthals died out and modern humans became the only *Homo sapiens* species on Earth. One group of scientists is convinced that a major genetically based neurological change took place in *Homo sapiens* around that time, leading behaviorally modern humans to begin innovating more-advanced stone implements and artwork. But what was the neurological event and what caused it? Might this have been the point when a major intervention occurred?

The modern human population is very homogeneous. As individuals our genes differ by only one tenth of 1 percent, regardless of race, gender, or ethnic ancestry. We are all virtually the same at the DNA level. According to a *Discover* magazine article: "Some anthropologists believe that this genetic homogeneity is the result of a 'population bottleneck'—that at some time in the past our ancestors went through an event that greatly reduced our numbers and thus our genetic variation."[6] Nearly every culture has a myth detailing one or more such events or cataclysms that reduced the world's population to a remnant. The Bible's "population bottleneck," for instance, is the Flood of which Noah and his wife and family are the only survivors.

Scientists believe that the "bottleneck" for Earth's population occurred about 40,000 years ago. Archaeologist Stan Ambrose, of the University of Illinois, thinks that a colossal volcanic eruption about 4,000 times more potent than the eruption of Mount St. Helens was the event that caused Earth's population to decrease. About 40,000 years ago Mount Toba in Sumatra erupted, burying India under a layer of ash and, scientists now believe, causing a 6-year global winter that precipitated a mini–ice age lasting 1,000 years.

The notion of a 2,000-person population remnant surviving a world cataclysm 40,000 years ago and subsequently following the migration paths as spelled out in both the "out of Africa" model and the Bering Strait land bridge theory does not seem viable, however. It seems impossible that such a small group of humans beginning in Africa 40,000 years ago could spread throughout the world in both such numbers and such cultural variety within 20,000 years.

Further, why would this small group leave Africa? And if they did leave, why would they have ventured any farther than the next piece of hospitable territory in a world that was large and unfamiliar? If they had traveled far, they would have met impassable mountains, endless seas, and forbidding predatory animals sooner or later. Such a vast dispersal would have required successive generations to abandon what all anthropologists have observed is a prominent trait of human tribes—conservatism.

The premise of our ancestors' migration out of Africa raises other questions as well. It seems impossible to explain why or how our ancestors would have migrated out of Africa during the most recent glacial epoch. We must bear in mind that the most recent ice age began 35,000 years ago and did not end until 11,500 years ago. If humans indeed began leaving Africa 40,000 years ago they— unlike the Neanderthals—would not have had experience with a glacial epoch, for except for its highest mountains, Africa was very little affected by previous ice ages. Assuming they spread north into Europe and China, then crossed the Bering Strait to populate the Americas a mere 20,000 years ago (the somewhat disputed date of humans' first appearance in the Americas is 13,000 B.C.E.), they would have encountered a frigid environment without the skills necessary to survive such extreme cold. In addition, it seems unlikely that they would be motivated to move away from a more temperate region into areas that were much colder.

Geologists now know that following the most recent ice age a massive deluge caused giant floods across North America, Europe, and Asia as the glacial sheets covering North America began to melt. To understand the scale of the flooding, we can turn to the vast region known as the Channeled Scablands in Washington state, which span an area that extends for hundreds of miles, from Spokane westward to the Cascade range. The Scablands were carved out from the post-glacial floodwaters that burst through a natural dam. When the waters receded, they left behind a geological record consisting of bars of gravel and sediment piled 900 feet high, deep gorges etched hundreds of feet into the solid bedrock, and house-sized boulders littering the landscape.

Important to any scenario explaining how humans were able to survive the most recent ice age is an understanding of the mechanism that turns glacial epochs both on and off. Science has only recently been able to relate this knowledge with authority and what the research has found is rather surprising: Ice core samples taken at both poles and in Greenland show that the amount of sunlight shining on the polar region determines when ice ages occur.[7] The last four glacial eras have been directly linked to this phenomenon. Interglacial periods (warm eras between ice ages) occur when the polar region receives more sunlight, and the amount of polar sunlight fluctuates in accordance with changes in Earth's axial tilt combined with its orbit around the Sun.

Our experience of Earth's journey through space is illusory. It feels as though the planet is standing still but we are actually hurtling through the galaxy at about 18 miles per second! As we zoom through space, our spherical spaceship wobbles slightly on its axis of rotation—much like a spinning top might—to describe a cone: Earth is tilted slightly in relation to the horizontal, which is the plane of its orbit around the Sun, and this tilt fluctuates between 22.1 degrees where it is closest to vertical and 24.5 degrees where it is most tilted. It moves between these two extremes in a cycle of 41,000 years and is currently tilted at 23.5 degrees to vertical.

The Earth makes a full rotation around the vertical every 26,000 years as it traces its elliptical orbits around the Sun—a mechanism called *precession*. The shift that results from this has made itself apparent in a number of ways. For example, the North Pole points toward Polaris today, but that hasn't always been the case. The direction in which it points slowly changes. The pole pointed toward Vega roughly 13,000 years ago and it will point toward Vega again 13,000 years from now. The shift can also be observed on Earth by noting the very small changes in the Sun's position at the time of the equinoxes, changes so minute that without modern equipment they are apparent only over hundreds of years.

Modern science now knows that Earth's roughly 26,000-year rotation around the vertical combined with the roughly 41,000-year tilt cycle are the main mechanisms that both start and stop ice ages.

The impact of these mechanisms on Earth's climate is easiest to understand by thinking of the change of seasons and how Earth's axial rotation creates them. In the northern hemisphere, summer comes when the North Pole is tilted most toward the Sun and winter comes when it is tilted away. The process that turns ice ages on and off works similarly, although it is more complex and plays out over a very long period of time. It can be thought of as a very extended seasonal cycle. When the Earth's tilt is less pronounced relative to the vertical, the summers get cooler and ice builds up on the poles year after year.

Once the ice sheets start to build up, they create a positive feedback loop. The increasing reflective property of Earth's surface bounces the Sun's rays back into space, which creates more cooling. As the ice sheets continue to expand, the amount of carbon dioxide in the atmosphere is reduced, which also adds to the cooling process. Over the past 10,000 years we have been experiencing the opposite effect, a warm interglacial era characterized by the "greenhouse effect"—a rising level of carbon dioxide, receding glaciers, and rising sea levels.

The interglacial period that we are still in began roughly 18,000 years ago (when the most recent ice age peaked). Earth's orbit is elliptical, which means that Earth is closer to the Sun during some parts of the year and farther away at other times. The closest approach to the Sun, called the perihelion, now occurs in January, making the northern hemisphere winters slightly warmer than they were 18,000 years ago. The perihelion occurred in July some 18,000 years ago, making the summer warmer in the Arctic at that time.

Once again applying the seasonal analogy to alternating ice ages and interglacial eras, we can see that we have been in the spring/summer phase of the long-term equinoctial seasons for about 18,000 years. As we know, however, the seasons change according to Earth's position relative to the Sun with unerring regularity. We should therefore be near the early stages of the next ice age. That it has not already manifested is probably related to the effect on natural mechanisms of the man-made greenhouse effect.

Certainly, in gaining knowledge of a mechanism as complex as the one that has caused the alternating ice ages and interglacial periods of the past 200,000 years, we have shown the depth of modern humans' astronomical understanding. Such knowledge is the product of thousands of years of civilization. Or is it? As we will see in the next chapter, there is evidence that indicates that ancient people knew as much as we do about the heavens. We have long been aware that the ancients paid a great deal of attention to the constellations, and that Hippoarchus, a Greek, accurately described the cycle of precession. But he made his observations and compared his results to records of even earlier observations made by Alexandrian and Babylonian scholars whose knowledge, in turn, came from Sumer. How did these ancient peoples gain their knowledge?

As with the other technical advancements of the Sumerians, this astronomical and mathematical understanding came from the gods—the genesis race who passed their knowledge to the Sumerians and other ancient cultures via teachings of astrology and the constellations and the positioning of Earth's earliest civilizations close to latitude 30° north, a latitude that is relatively safe from the effects of ice ages. This positioning leads us to the purpose such understanding served: It would allow the ancients, or their descendants, to survive in the future when the ice would once again cover vast portions of Earth.

TWENTY

The Ages of Man:
Linear versus Cyclical Time

The measurement of time is based on Earth's rotation on its axis and its revolution around the Sun, both cyclical phenomena. We use the Sumerian base-60 system to subdivide a day into 24 hours, with each hour made up of 60 minutes and each minute made up of 60 seconds.

We in Western society view time on a grand scale as linear, with a certain starting point from which it progresses until it reaches, theoretically, a certain end point. While we observe cycles that repeat within this great span of time—days, seasons, years, and so forth— overall, we perceive that time moves only forward, in a straight line. Those in ancient civilizations, however, viewed time and history much differently. Not only did the cycle of days add up to the cycles of months, seasons, and years, but there were also other, much longer cycles—cycles of ages in which events occurred and reoccurred. This much more far-reaching cyclical view of time is worth examining to get a sense of how ancient peoples related long cycles to collective human experience.

GREEK AND HINDU PARALLELS

Greek philosophers and poets described these larger cycles as the Five Ages of Man, each of which ends with a great cataclysm.

Hesiod lists the five in his *Works and Days:* the Age of Gold, the Age of Silver, the Age of Bronze, the Age of Heroes, and the Age of Iron. If we use his system of reckoning, we are still in the Age of Iron.

The ancient Hindu Vedic texts describe many cycles as taking place within a very long time period known as a Day of Brahma, which is equal to 4,320,000,000 years. Within it there are cycles of much shorter duration known as the *yugas,* which are subdivided into great and small yugas. The four great yugas roughly correspond to the Greek scheme. The Satya Yuga is the Golden Age, the Treta Yuga is equivalent to the Silver Age, the Dvapara Yuga is the Bronze (copper) Age, and the Kali Yuga is the Iron Age.[1]

The basic belief underpinning both schemes is that human beings devolve spiritually through a series of ages from a zenith Golden Age to the nadir, the Iron Age, when self-centered material-ism prevails. It is intriguing that both the Greek and the Hindu sce-narios seem to agree concerning the description and passage of the ages. Hesiod describes the Golden Age as a time when humans were happy and knew neither greed nor suffering. Earth provided for all of their needs. The *Vedas* describe the Satya Yuga as an ideal time characterized by virtue and wisdom and almost devoid of vice and ignorance.

The Greeks say the Silver Age was when humans invented agri-culture and began to work for food. Humans of this age were power-ful yet deceitful and were lacking in fortitude, resolve, and character. Hardship, suffering, and decay were introduced to humankind until, as Greek legend tells it, Zeus got fed up with the constant complain-ing and bickering of Silver Age humans and decided to destroy them. We can align this to the events in the second and third chapters of Genesis, when the first period in the Garden ends and the gods drive Adam out of Eden, commanding him to toil in the fields to earn his bread. The comparable Hindu Silver Age, Treta Yuga, is characterized by a one-third reduction of the good qualities and virtues of the Golden Age. It was the time when humans invented early religious rites, animal sacrifices, and ceremonies.

Hesiod depicts the Bronze Age as a time of civilization, when humans were strong, productive, and very aggressive. During this era in the history of Western civilization great advances proceeded very quickly and beautiful cities, temples, and works of art were produced. However, for thousands of years wars often broke out between developing city-states and empires. The comparable portion of the Old Testament is likewise full of accounts of tribal war, bickering, infighting, and the spread of pestilence and plagues. The analogous Hindu Dvapara was a time when sensual desires increased, disease began to appear, and injustice spread through human civilization.

It is interesting to note that the Greek system would actually have four primary ages were the Age of Bronze not divided in two, with the second part described as the Age of Heroes. The people of the Greek Age of Heroes were hybrids—half human and half god. They performed amazing feats and lived honorable, fruitful lives. We are reminded of the biblical "sons of God" who mated with the "daughters of men" and produced extraordinary offspring—the giants, or Nephilim, of Genesis.

Both the Greeks and the Hindus describe the Iron Age (the Hindu Kali Yuga) as being characterized by materialism and greed. Kali is literally translated as "quarrel and hypocrisy." In this age labor is degraded into toil for selfish ends; crime becomes commonplace; terrible wars break out; and fraud, deceit, and hatred rule. If all of this sounds familiar, it is because, according to Hindus, we are still living in this age, just as we have been for thousands of years.

THE FIVE SUNS

The peoples of Mesoamerica also had a system that divided human existence into five ages, which they called Suns. The Aztec calendar, or sunstone, is actually the best artifact we have of the system used by the Maya and other ancient Mesoamerican civilizations; although the Aztecs used different names, it depicts the Five Suns and the exact temporal proportions used by the Maya—the implied numerical calculations for both the Aztecs and the Maya are identical, as we know from the chronicles of Bishop de Landa. We should remember that after the conquistadors met both the Aztecs and the Maya and questioned them about their traditions, they destroyed the Aztec temples and the Mayan codices.

The calendar, a 13.5-foot basalt relief weighing 25 tons, is currently housed in the National Archaeological Museum in Mexico City and is both a visual representation of the Mesoamerican creation myth and a very large clock of the Ages of Man.[2] It seems that the cycle of time it presents correlates with the Greek and Hindu ages and agrees with their regard of the present period of time: We are in the final age of a grand cycle.

The stone itself is circular and depicts four suns surrounding a fifth sun, a complete cycle embodying a time span of about 26,000 years, which is equivalent to an equinoctial precession. Each of the four suns—Jaguar, Wind, Rain, and Water—corresponds to a different age of man that preceded Tonatiuh, the Fifth Sun, or Motion. The names of all five suns are significant in that they tell how the ages came—or will come—to an end. For example, the Fourth Sun (Water) ended in a deluge and the Fifth Sun (Motion) is predicted to end in a violent series of global earthquakes and impacts from cosmic objects.

Encircling the sun glyphs on the stone is a ring representing the 20 day signs of the 260-day sacred calendar. A second ring consisting of 52 segments—the number of years in a Calendar Round—lies outside the first. The outer rim of the stone is formed by fire serpents whose tails come together at the top of the stone and whose heads—from which two human heads emerge—meet at the bottom. Each of the serpents is made up of 10 segments labeled with the numeral for "ten" and the New Fire glyph, which together represent 100 calendar rounds, or 5,200 years, equivalent to one sun. Five such suns—comprising a full cycle of the ages of man—thus equals 26,000 years, or an equinoctial precession.

THE LINK BETWEEN THE AGES OF MAN AND THE PRECESSION

As we saw in chapter 19, the precession ultimately controls the geologic pattern of alternating ice ages and the interglacial periods that are characterized by a relatively warm global climate. Given the existence of the Aztec sunstone, we might ask whether the ancients knew of the precession and its effect on these geologic climate patterns, and if so, what this might mean.

As noted above, to the Maya, the 26,000 years of the precession encompassed the cyclical series of five suns or the time equal to a precession. The Hindu Yuga cycle coincides with the zodiacal/precession cycle, which lasts about 2,200 years. The Western system of astrology is also based on the equinoctial precession. It becomes easy to see that all of these many cycles or systems of reckoning converge on the grand astronomical cycle of the precession.

The Sun travels across the sky on a path called the plane of the ecliptic, a great circle that is divided into 12 equal parts of 30 degrees each. Each one of these parts is assigned to one of the 12 signs of the zodiac. The Sun's position at the spring equinox is fixed in each of these 12 parts for roughly 2,200 years. Thus each 2,200-year period represents one of the 12 signs of the zodiac. To move through all 12 signs takes roughly 26,000 years (12 signs multiplied by 2,200 years). A complete zodiacal year is therefore equivalent to the precession.

According to astrologers, we have been in the Age of Pisces for more than 2,000 years and are nearing the Age of Aquarius. (Baby boomers jumped the gun.) If, however, we rewind the precessional clock through the zodiacal year to the era in which civilization began in the Middle East, we find ourselves in the Age of Taurus. Interestingly, artifacts show that during that era the bull played an enormous role in the arts and in literature for several thousand years. Moving ahead in time, to around 1800 B.C.E., the equinoctial sun began to rise in Aries, the Ram—and the Israelites were sacrificing lambs and rams. Jumping forward yet again, Jesus was born shortly after the Age of Pisces commenced—and he is known as the Fisher of Men and is represented symbolically by a fish. All of this seems to indicate that the ancients were well aware of the precession, which can be arrived at by first observing that Earth, the planets, and the stars move in relation to one another in small and large cycles.

It is significant that a number of the world's calendars agree upon the starting date of the present age—what we might call the Age of Civilization. The Mayan Fifth Sun, the Age of Man, started in 3113 B.C.E., roughly 5,100 years ago. At that time, the first civilizations were under way not only in Mexico, but also in Sumer and Egypt and along the Peruvian coast. The Jewish calendar is reckoned from 3700 B.C.E., and is about 5,700 years old. The Chinese calendar is about 4,500 years old and the Julian calendar is roughly 5,000 years old. According to the Hindu calendar, the *panchanga,* or traditional almanac, keeps track of the equivalent years in the Kali Yuga and states that from 1990 to 1991: "5,091 Kali years have passed." By late 2001, 5,102 years of the Kali Yuga, or Iron Age, had elapsed in the Yuga system.

If we turn the Mayan cycle back another 5,200 years we are at another threshold era, the end of the most recent ice age and the beginning of the domestication of plants and animals. If we rewind it 5,200 years from that time, we are very close to the peak of the most recent glacial epoch, which occurred 17,000 to 18,000 years ago.

Clearly, either the ancients were keen observers of the planets and stars for a much longer time than history can establish or they were helped by an older race that already been observing such phenomena for eons. Our ancestors tracked the lunar cycles, figured out the eclipses, and eventually devised fairly accurate solar calendars. Thousands upon thousands of tablets and books dealing with astronomical and astrological data have been unearthed in the Middle East and Egypt and most of the information that is contained in the four surviving Mayan codices deals with important astronomical issues. Scientists have wondered why Mayan and Hindu scales of time extend into the millions of years. But how could these ancient peoples have conceived of such vast cycles of time—and insist that human beings lived through them—if not with the help of those who actually experienced them?

The people of the world's ancient civilizations could not have been on their own in gathering their knowledge of the heavens. While a certain amount of celestial observation was no doubt possible for them, it would have been very difficult to discover the precessional through observation alone. This would have required observing it over its entire course and then observing it beginning again in order to discern its cyclical nature. It would have taken many millennia of tireless sky watching and data recording to chart the patterns of the constellations and the Sun's backward path through the zodiac. It is far more feasible that they were taught—thus, once again evidence points to the role of outside intervention.

Independent researchers have marveled at the precise astronomical alignments of stone circles, dolmens, and major archaeological sites around the world, which are oriented to mark the solstices, equinoxes, and astronomical configurations of various stars and planets. This plethora of evidence has, in fact, led to a whole new branch of archaeology called *archaeoastronomy*. The large number of megaliths and other structures from ancient civilizations suggests that our ancestors were extraordinarily preoccupied with keeping track of the astronomical alignment of Earth and other celestial bodies—and we may ask why.

Of course, as agricultural peoples, the ancients would note the cycles of days, the Moon, and seasons so that they could prepare the land, plant, and harvest at the best times. They learned that these cycles can lead to a successful harvest. Similarly, they must have learned from those who knew—from their cosmic mentors—that the key to life on Earth, even to survival, resided in the positions, periodicity, and motions of the planets, the Sun, and stars.

Observation and recording are two of the primary components

of the scientific method. Our ancestors' observations of the planets, stars, comets, and various natural events that occurred in the world, along with their tracking and recording of the motions of Earth and the interrelationships of Earth and other celestial bodies, might be viewed as steps toward gathering scientific date—perhaps toward predicting certain phenomena. The ancients' celestial observations, their attempts to pinpoint astronomical alignments, and, ultimately, their familiarity with the cycle of precession can all be seen as ways to draw the attention of future generations to the heavens and the cyclical nature of celestial phenomena in order to predict when specific events—perhaps catastrophic events—would occur in the future.[3] By recording their knowledge in permanent records—stone monuments oriented to celestial cycles—they made it available to future generations. These structures, then, were built in part with human survival in mind.

TWENTY-ONE

Cycles of Catastrophe

As we have seen, ancient peoples learned to watch the skies very carefully, aware that the solar system is always in a state of dynamic equilibrium—that it is stable and predictable but has an unpredictable side as well. Comets and asteroids roared by and even smashed into Earth now and then. The phases of the Moon caused the tides to rise and fall. Certain planetary configurations were favorable; others were unfavorable. The universe at large was like Earth, usually calm and restrained, yet now and then capable of great fury delivered in the form of volcanoes, hurricanes, earthquakes, and floods.

Worldwide mythologies speak of repeated cataclysms overwhelming most of civilization and humanity. Not much time has to pass, however, for people to completely forget that our planet is periodically subject to global floods and massive earthquakes, freezing ice ages and the impact of comets, "fires from heaven" and volcanic eruptions that start deep within the planet's superheated bowels.

That this is true becomes very clear from the following lead paragraph to an article titled "Comets and Disasters in the Bronze Age," which appeared in the journal *British Archaeology* in 1997:

> At some time around 2300 B.C., give or take a century or two, a large number of the major civilizations of this world

collapsed, simultaneously it seems. The Akkadian Empire in Mesopotamia, the Old Kingdom in Egypt, the Early Bronze Age civilization in Israel, Anatolia and Greece, as well as the Indus Valley civilization in India, the Hilmand civilization in Afghanistan and Hongshan Culture in China—the first urban civilizations in the world—all fell into ruin at more or less the same time. Why?[1]

This fairly recent global catastrophe has been all but forgotten, wiped clean from the memory of humankind as if collective amnesia had descended upon the world's people as soon as the cataclysm was over. The remnant populations simply picked up the pieces and moved on with hardly a backward glance. Ethnic migrations in all directions followed this great disaster.

Archaeologists have been piecing together the jumbled puzzle of our broken past only over the last century. Excavations from Troy to Israel, from Syria to the Nile Valley have revealed layers of debris and ruin, telling of repeated large-scale disasters: earthquakes, tidal waves, and great fires. From the shores of Mesopotamia's life-giving rivers, the Tigris and the Euphrates, and the banks of the island of Cyprus surrounded by the Mediterranean Sea, to the Indus Valley we find the story of the rise and fall of great cities compressed in buried layers of destruction. The cities of Heracliten and Menthius were found at the bottom of the ocean in Egypt's Bay of Akoubir!

French archaeologist Claude Schaeffer first brought these disturbing facts to light in his seminal volume, *Stratigraphie comparée et chronologie de l'Asie occidentale,* published in 1948. Schaeffer studied the layers at nearly 50 archaeological sites in the Near and Middle East, detecting evidence that the sites had experienced total destruction several times in the Early, Middle, and Late Bronze Ages—and that their ruin had occurred simultaneously each time. He concluded that the only way this could have occurred was as a result of a natural catastrophe. He favored the theory that earthquakes were the principal cause of the periodic collapse of civilization, and many scholars followed his lead. Studies have shown that the "earth changes" in the general region he examined were massive: Parts of what are now the Sahara and the region around the Dead Sea were once farmed; areas formerly fertile and hospitable enough to grow crops were turned into desert.

Schaeffer did not make any connections between the results of his studies and ancient accounts of such catastrophes in even earlier historical and prehistorical times. In 1950, however, Immanuel Velikovsky's analysis of ancient literature led him to conclusions that were similar to Schaeffer's—and the work of both men was initially rejected. In the preface to his controversial book Velikovsky wrote:

> *Worlds in Collision* is a book of wars in the celestial sphere that took place in historical times. In these wars the planet earth participated too. The historical-cosmological story of this book is based [on] the evidence of historical texts of many people around the globe, on classical literature, on epics of the northern races, on sacred books of the peoples of the Orient and Occident, on traditions and folklore of primitive peoples, on old astronomical inscriptions and charts, on archaeological finds, and also on geological and paleontological material.[2]

To the scientific community's ongoing embarrassment and shame, this book was strongly condemned and even banned from libraries. But while his thought-provoking theory was roundly criticized in its day (and it does contain several flaws), his ideas have since been gaining credence. In October 2001 the University of Pennsylvania announced that Dr. Anthony Peratt, a physicist, would "[p]resent new findings that link ancient rock art and Stonehenge to worldwide observations of unusual occurrence." The title of the lecture was "Celestial Catastrophes in Human Prehistory?"[3]

The hunt for the natural causes of human disasters has gained ground over the past 15 years. The publication of the article "Comets and Disasters in the Bronze Age" in *British Archaeology* reveals a strong shift in attitude: Natural scientists have entered the picture and are finding conclusive and widespread evidence "for abrupt climate change, sudden sea level changes, catastrophic inundations, widespread seismic activity and evidence for massive volcanic activity at several periods since the last Ice Age, but particularly at around 2300 B.C.E., give or take 200 years."[4]

The consequences of these natural disasters in ancient times were dire for human civilizations. Populations were drastically reduced: According to *The Cambridge Ancient History* the number of settlements was "reduced to a quarter of the number in the previous period,"[5] and G. Ernest Wright declared that "[o]ne of the most striking facts about the Early Bronze civilization [was] its destruction, one so violent that scarcely a vestige survived."[6]

A thousand years after a major disaster crushed the first civilizations around 2300 B.C.E., another widespread collapse hit the Mycenaeans of Greece, the Hittites of Anatolia, the Egyptian New Kingdom, Late Bronze Age Israel, and the Shang dynasty of China. Astronomers began to home in on the cause of these sudden collapses: the impact of comets and other types of cosmic debris. The idea that an impact by a cosmic object led to the extinction of dinosaurs—presented by Nobel physicist Luis Alvarez in 1980—paved the way for a wider acceptance of the theory that much of Earth's history has been shaped by periodic cataclysms, including those that come from beyond our planet.

It is easy to understand in part why the notion of such catastrophic upheavals in our history might have been difficult for the modern world to accept. While Earth has undergone many dramatic upheavals and catastrophes over its long geological history, compared to ages past we seem to have been living in a warm, hospitable, even gentle era for the past 2,000 years—in a world in which few major disasters have occurred, civilization has spread, and the human population has increased exponentially.

As a result, by the nineteenth century people had become complacent, believing that we live on a very stable and safe planet. This belief was reinforced by the theory of evolution, which insisted that change proceeded in a gradual, orderly fashion. Certainly there was no evidence of the contrary to be found—the only reminders of the Ice Age were far out of sight in the world's polar regions or tucked up on the northern slopes of high mountains. There were no great floods. No comets had collided with Earth in anyone's memory. The age of archaeological discovery had only just begun and no one knew that stories of destruction lay hidden underneath the surface of the soil all over the ancient world.

But evidence of such stories is found not only in the ruins of ancient sites. Studies of tree rings and research on astronomical phenomena also confirm the truth of Earth's catastrophic history. It is not a comforting picture. And although no civilizations have been destroyed in the past two millennia, there have been a number of relatively recent cataclysms that could portend a dark and disastrous future.

Some of the biggest earthquakes ever to rock the planet have occurred in the last 60 years. In 1960 the world's strongest recorded quake—9.5 on the Richter scale—devastated Chile, generating a 30-foot tsunami that wiped out entire villages there, and then raced across the Pacific to kill 61 people in Hawaii. A violent earthquake measuring 9.0 on the Richter scale hit Assam in northeast India in 1950, and a 9.2 quake shook Prince William Sound in Alaska in 1964, killing 25 people and generating a tsunami that took another 110 lives. In 1976 China, prone to large, destructive earthquakes, suffered the most devastating earthquake to hit that nation in the twentieth century, killing an estimated 600,000 people in the Tang Shan province. The temblor leveled a 20-square-mile section of the city of Haicheng. A massive quake in Mexico City in 1985 killed 10,000; one in Armenia in 1988 killed 25,000. Iran; Japan; Taiwan; El Salvador; and Oakland, California, and Seattle here in the United States have all been struck by earthquakes in the recent past.

Volcanoes have also been erupting with greater frequency in the past 400 years—recent times, geologically. In 1783 the Laki volcano erupted on Iceland, resulting in the loss of the island's livestock and widespread crop failure due to acid rain. Almost 10,000 people succumbed to famine. In 1792 an old lava dome collapsed during the eruption of the Unzen volcano in Japan, causing an avalanche and tsunami that killed 14,300 people.

In 1815 the biggest volcanic eruption in recorded times occurred on Sumbawa Island in Indonesia, killing almost 100,000. The effects of the eruption manifested in temporary global climate change. The world's climate was also changed and 36,000 were killed in 1883 by the explosion of the volcanic Krakatoa, another Indonesian island.

The debris from the eruption of Mount Tambora on Sumbawa Island in 1815 took one year to spread around the world, and because of its effects on the world's climate, the following year was known as the "year without summer." Personal diaries and journals agree on the record cold weather of 1816; in New England snow fell in June and frost occurred in July and August. Severe food shortages occurred throughout the world and many died from famine or as victims of related cholera and typhus pandemics.

In more recent times El Chicón erupted in Mexico in 1982, sending enough smoke and ash into the stratosphere to cause moderate cooling in the northern hemisphere. The eruption of Nevada del Ruiz in Colombia in 1985 caused a massive mudslide that buried an entire town, killing 25,000. In 1997 an ongoing eruption on the island of Montserrat rendered two thirds of the island uninhabitable. And in 1991 Mount Pinatubo in the Philippines belched a plume of volcanic ash many miles up into the stratosphere in the twentieth century's most violent eruption. The ash covered a 300-square-mile area around the volcano and 25 million tons of sulfur dioxide were injected into the atmosphere, causing an impact on global weather for a year.

But threats to any planet's stability do not only come from within. In 1994, the comet Shoemaker-Levy 9 sent 21 fragments (the largest was 1.6 miles in diameter) crashing into the planet Jupiter in a cosmic show that still has astronomers talking. But while the impacts were spectacular from our vantage point, we can only imagine the devastation that would result if a comet or asteroid collided with Earth.

Such an event did happen nearly 600 million years ago in southern Australia at a place called Lake Acraman, and the evidence of the collision is still visible. According to the scenario established by scientists, a rocky meteorite roughly 2 miles in diameter traveling at almost 50,000 miles per hour slammed into an area of red volcanic rock 250 miles north of what is now Adelaide. Within seconds the meteor vaporized into a ball of fire that carved out a crater about 2.2 miles deep and 20 miles in diameter. But that was only the beginning. The impact spawned an earthquake that was powerful enough to raise 300-foot tsunamis in a shallow sea 200 miles away. Debris—including sparks—showered the region for many miles and the remains are still scattered across a broad landscape.

One of the largest catastrophes to strike the planet occurred 65 million years ago, according to scientists, when an asteroid 6 miles in diameter punched a crater the size of Belgium into the Earth's surface. The impact sent up a cloud of debris that so altered the world and darkened the atmosphere that 70 percent of all forms of life on the planet at that time—including the dinosaurs—was decimated.

Dr. Victor Clube, of Oxford University's Department of Astrophysics, believes that it is only a matter of time until another comet or asteroid impacts the Earth. He is convinced that collisions of this kind have been regularly occurring events in human history. In a 1990 article from the *London Times* he warns, "The matter requires urgent attention. It is crucial that everyone is woken up to the danger."[7]

His greatest fear is that a nuclear winter is going to be unleashed by what he calls multiple Tunguska bombardment—named for the cosmic explosion that occurred over the Tunguska region of Siberia on June 30, 1908—recalling that when a relatively small object exploded over the region as it approached Earth, the result was the devastation of a 25-mile area. Clube predicts that the particles from the impact of a comet would obscure the sun and produce an age of darkness. According to ancient chroniclers from Peru and Egypt to

Greece, there have been other times in history when the sun was blotted out or stood still and the stars fell to Earth. It seems clear that these are accounts of the impact on Earth of various types of cosmic debris.

These accounts ought to guide us toward a realization of what our ancestors were trying to pass down to us: a warning that the Earth will be visited by periodic cataclysms in a predictable time frame. What is that time frame? If there is a periodicity to earthquakes or volcanic eruptions, it has yet to be established. There is little we can do, then, to prepare for these catastrophes. We are in a better position, however, regarding cosmic bombardment and the cycles of future ice ages. The interface between Earth and the cosmic environment exhibits a certain regularity. According to scientists, Tunguska-like impacts occur every 100 years or so, while a multiple Tunguska bombardment as envisioned by astronomer Clube may occur only once every 3,000 to 5,000 years. The Taurid Complex of meteors, meteoroids, and asteroids, and the comet Enke, have been significant and regularly visible celestial hazards probably from the most recent ice age to the present.

Astronomers used to think the Moon was created from matter spewed out by the young, madly whirling Earth when the solar system was formed. Now they are fairly certain that Earth was struck by another planet that swung around the Sun in an orbit similar to that of our world. The currently accepted theory of the formation of the Moon focuses on a glancing collision between the proto-Earth and a Mars-sized body. As a result of this impact, our current Moon was torn from the body of the proto-Earth and became caught in its gravitational field. What remained of this earlier Earth then settled into an empty space where no planet had been and assumed its orbit as the third rock from the Sun.

This new theory strongly resembles a 5,000-year-old Sumerian account contained in Zecharia Sitchin's *The 12th Planet*. According to the Sumerians, the solar system experienced a major cataclysm in the form of the collision of two planets. The result of the collision was that one of the planets—Tiamat—was split in two. A satellite of the other planet then crashed into one of Tiamat's halves, creating Earth, and the newly formed Earth hit the other half of Tiamat, shattering it and thus forming our solar system's asteroid belt.[8]

Although in the Sumerian account Earth delivers a head-on collision rather than a glancing blow to the ill-fated Tiamat, the story is otherwise remarkably similar to the current theory of the formation of Earth and the Moon. Sitchin concludes with this:

> Moreover, we are offered—for the first time—a coherent cosmogonic-scientific explanation of the celestial events that led to the disappearance of the "missing planet" and the resultant creation of the asteroid belt (plus the comets) and of Earth. . . . We also have the answer to the question of why Earth's continents are concentrated on one side of it and a deep cavity (the Pacific Ocean) exists on the opposite side.[9]

The "missing planet" Sitchin refers to, which he calls Niburia, is known to astronomers as Planet X. According to the Sumerian scenario, the planet that destroyed Tiamat—Planet X—assumed a highly elliptical orbit that sent it far beyond Pluto at its aphelion and well within the orbits of Jupiter and Mars when its own orbit veered closest to the Sun. Astronomers have speculated on the mathematical need for a planet between Mars and Jupiter. Planet X has not been located; any planet that is traveling beyond the orbit of Pluto would not reflect enough light to be seen, even with a powerful telescope. Still, they assume it is there because something is pulling on Pluto, making its movements erratic. According to Sitchin, the Sumerians estimated the orbit of Planet X/Niburia to be the equivalent of roughly 3,600 years, meaning that it is soon to rendezvous again with the inner planets of the solar system.

This return of a planet that engendered the cataclysm from which our planet was created only highlights our vulnerability. On January 8, 2002, an asteroid roared past Earth, missing us by a mere

500,000 miles. The catastrophic results of the impact of such an asteroid would have included large-scale destruction, earthquakes, and tidal waves. This was the second unexpected near miss in a dozen years and it caught astronomers flatfooted; they did not observe it until December 26. When asked what we could have done to prepare for a collision on such short notice, Steven Pravado, NASA's Near Earth Asteroid Tracking program (NEAT) project manager, said: "The answer is not much."[10]

In the past 40 years the number and intensity of disasters has been on the increase. A record number of disasters occurred in the year 2000 and the upward trend is expected to continue, according to research conducted by the world's largest re-insurance agents, the companies that provide insurance to entities like the former World Trade Center. According to the Mayan reckoning, the Fifth Sun is to end in the year 2012, preceded by 8 years of increasing numbers of cataclysms—this cataclysmic "window" is to open up in 2004. Many seismologists, meteorologists, and astronomers concur that our luck is not going to hold out much longer: The planet is due for a major earthquake, extreme storm, or impact from a comet or other celestial object.

Though Solon and Plato recounted similar catastrophes in ancient times, as Solon told his contemporaries, subsequent generations soon forgot that humans had endured them. Perhaps some of these cataclysms were forgotten due to the destruction of ancient records by conquerors such as Alexander the Great and Cortés or to calamities such as the burning of the library at Alexandria.

Given our knowledge of the catastrophe that ended the age of the dinosaurs and the fiery display we witnessed when a comet and Jupiter collided in 1993, it may be in our best interest not only to remember, but also to turn to the prophecies of our ancient ancestors such as the Maya regarding the great cycles or ages of man and our planet's cycles of destruction. For in these prophecies, the genesis race has bequeathed to us some knowledge of our future and the ways we might predict it.

TWENTY-TWO

The End Times

There is an unusual and auspicious convergence among the great zodiacal cycle, the precession cycle of 26,000 years, the end of the Fifth Sun according to Mayan legend, and the final days of the End Times according to the Bible's Book of Revelations.

According to Christian beliefs, following the Second Coming Jesus Christ will reign over a New Kingdom for 1,000 years. Life on Earth will not end; the previous 5,000-year history of the Bible will be wiped away when Christ returns and Heaven and Earth will be made anew. While the beginning of a new age and a new Earth sounds exhilarating and full of promise, if we are indeed nearing the End Times, the pathway to them from this point at the close of the Iron Age or Fifth Sun is set to be rife with terrible conflicts, conflagrations, and disasters.

Revelations 6:12–14 states:

> And I looked when He broke the sixth seal, and there was a great earthquake; and the sun became black as sackcloth made of hair, and the whole Moon became like blood; and the stars of the sky fell to the earth, as a fig tree casts its unripe figs when shaken by a great wind. And the sky was split apart like a scroll when it is rolled up; and every mountain and island were moved out of their places.

The earthquake that seems to be described here is a global disaster of tremendous magnitude, moving "every mountain and island." After a period of time the seventh seal is opened, the results of which are described in Revelations 8:7: "And there came a hail and fire, mixed with blood, and they were thrown to earth; and a third of the earth was burned up, and a third of the trees were burned up, and all the green grass was burned up." The end of the Fifth Sun is described in Mayan and Aztec accounts as a time when the earthquakes will be so violent that they will shake the stars loose and fire will rain down from the sky. The two prophecies are chillingly similar.

Many books have been written over the past 30 years with various predictions relating to the End Times. Certainly the deaths and bombings of the all the wars in the last century and the beginning of this millennium coupled with the dawn of the atomic age at Hiroshima and Nagasaki all point to the kind and scale of devastation and anxiety that would accompany the end of the Fifth Sun.

Likewise the degradation of the earth and its habitats from pollution, development, and other destructive acts of humans; the resurgence of infectious diseases long ago vanquished and the appearance of new viruses and disease; and the rising threat of a new nuclear arms race and terrorism—these have made our planet increasingly dangerous and unpredictable. Nor can we count on stability in our climate. Scientists are warning that unless we put the brakes on our emissions into the environment and focus on preserving the world's forests and green spaces, we are going to experience an unprecedented era of global warming that will melt the ice caps and flood our coastal cities.

It is not difficult to make a compelling case that Doomsday is at hand. But are these the worst of times? Humanity has never before experienced such a benign climate and such favorable conditions as have occurred in the past 3,000 years. The world's population has grown to 6.5 billion and has spread to every corner of the globe. More people are enjoying the highest standard of living in our history, modern medicine has cured many formerly fatal diseases, and we have extended our lives by almost 30 percent over the last 100 years.

Yet for many astronomers and seismologists there is no question that Earth will, at some point, experience a recurrence of the kinds of catastrophes it has suffered in the past. Our history, scientific observation and study, and the law of averages all support this conclusion. The Maya and the biblical prophets also foresaw a calamity of civilization-ending proportions. The question for us becomes: When? While Mayan priests gave a specific date that translates to December 24, 2012, our scientists today cannot say for certain. We can only watch, using our knowledge to predict as much as we can, just as the ancients did.

TWENTY-THREE

Cosmic Ancestry

The first "flying saucer" headlines startled the world on June 26, 1947—we have recently passed the fiftieth anniversary of the dawning of our UFO consciousness. Readers of "The Coming of the Saucers" in *Fate* magazine's first issue learned that on June 24, 1947, Kenneth Arnold, a private pilot, was flying over the Cascade Mountains searching for the wreckage of a lost C-46 airplane. He wanted to claim the $5,000 reward that had been offered to anyone who could locate the wreckage.

Though he never found the missing plane, what he did see put his name in the annals of UFO history. As the pilot was coming out of a turn over Mineral, Washington, he saw nine disk-shaped objects flying at a speed he estimated to be 1,700 miles per hour. The next day he gave his eyewitness account to reporters from the local paper. From there the story went to the Associated Press wire service and within days, as similar sightings were reported around the country, a headline writer coined the phrase "flying saucer," referring to the shape of the spacecraft the pilot had encountered—though Ezekiel's descriptions are actually much more evocative, including his "great cloud with fire flashing forth continually and a bright light around it and in its midst something like glowing metal in the midst of the fire."(Ezekiel 1:4) This seems like a fairly explicit description of a rocket entering Earth's atmosphere, which would be superheated and glowing, as we now know from our own experiences with travel beyond our atmosphere.

Three millennia have passed since the events described in the Old Testament have occurred. Over that time, the theological interpretations of Old Testament scripture have stressed the oblique and the allegorical—so much so that they seem to be missing a truth apparent in a number of Bible verses: We are not alone in the universe and we have been visited in the past. Even New Testament scripture hints at this. Perhaps it is significant that the Star of Bethlehem that so commanded attention moved around in the heavens, unlike other stars: " . . . and lo the star, which they had seen in the east, went on before them, and stood over where the Child was . . . "(Matthew 2:1)

Author of *Chariots of the Gods?* Erich von Däniken was the first modern writer and independent researcher to associate the world's mysterious ancient artifacts with the gods, while author Immanuel Velikovsky appears to have been the first researcher to realize that the Old Testament may have been referring to visitors arriving on Earth from another planet. In an article titled "Nefilim" Velikovsky wrote:

> The story told in Genesis VI about the sons of God *(bnei Elim)* coming to the daughters of men is usually explained as referring to an advanced priesthood that mingled with backward tribesmen. . . . But if we are today on the eve of interplanetary travel, we must not declare as absolutely impossible the thought that this earth was visited, ages ago, by some people from another planet. . . . In my understanding this passage from the book of Genesis is a literary relic dealing with a visit of intelligent beings from another planet . . .[1]

Velikovsy's best-selling book, *Worlds in Collision,* was published years before *Chariots of the Gods?* appeared in 1969. Like Velikovsky, von Däniken based his theory of gods from space primarily on original interpretations of ancient mythologies. His word surely prompted his readers to think and ask pertinent questions about the incredible history of planet Earth and the artifacts that have been found throughout the world. Though his theory was not framed in scientific terms, perhaps it achieved more than any serious scientific theory could have at the time by catching the imagination of the masses.

Certainly that a scientist with Francis Crick's credentials has entered the discussion signals the power of the theory that life was brought here from elsewhere in the universe. Crick was not concerned with the Great Pyramid or other monuments or artifacts that might have been the result of the gods' influence. His notion, presented in the book *Life Itself,* that an advanced civilization had sent rockets to Earth bearing the seeds of life was even more controversial than hypotheses about the origin of the world's ancient monuments. He even went so far as to describe the possible construction of the spaceships that delivered their living cargo.

Astronomer Fred Hoyle and his coauthor N. Chandra Wickramasinghe weighed in with *Lifecloud: The Origin of Life in the Universe.* Just as convinced as Crick that evolution could not have created life as we know it on Earth, they presented the idea that it could have arrived from outer space by riding the pressure of the light waves floating among stars or on comets. According to them, the organisms that arrived on Earth with their genetic code would have been something as simple as bacteria. Both scientists and creationists, however, slammed the theory of panspermia as advanced by Crick and Hoyle.

About the same time that these books were written, the United States launched the space program, landed men on the Moon, and moved space exploration into high gear. Interestingly, despite the fact that our astronauts reported spotting "bogeys"—the NASA code for UFOs—the public was still being told that there was no such thing. Yet the notion of unidentified flying objects that visited from the outer reaches of space captured the public's curiosity. Of course, there were hardened skeptics who did not believe any accounts of sightings, even from the most experienced commercial jetliner pilots or astronauts, and there were UFO enthusiasts who seemed to believe every report, no matter how incredible.

By the late '70s and early '80s, films such as *Close Encounters of the Third Kind* and *E.T.* fueled the subject of life "out there" visiting Earth and it has since become the focus of radio talk shows, a television series *(The X Files)*, hundreds of articles, and dozens of books.

Over the past 20 years certain ideas regarding these visitors have taken hold in the media and the popular mind: In their appearance, aliens are said to be slight, gray, and humanlike, with large heads and almond-shaped eyes. It is perhaps significant that in our conception of them aliens are not men; they are another species altogether. It seems the gods of old have been replaced by beings who are not at all like us. In all ancient accounts, the gods who are said to have come from beyond to teach us are described as human beings. Perhaps, then, those visitors described by alien abductees are not the same as those who visited us in our ancient past.

Another popular myth is that the U.S. government has long known about the existence of aliens and their spacecraft—as evidenced, many say, by the Roswell incident and by comments made by General Douglas MacArthur. Not a man to mince words or bite his tongue, in 1955 MacArthur warned: "The nations of the world will have to unite, for the next war will be an interplanetary war. The nations of Earth must some day make a common front against attack by people from other planets."[2]

Regardless of the nature of our current or future contact with extraterrestrials, recent discoveries are more and more frequently suggesting the truth of the theory that life on Earth was the result of a series of interventions by extraterrestrial civilization. The finding of underwater archaeological sites threatens the orthodox theories of human evolution and history, while other findings have served toward establishing the validity of the theory of panspermia. On December 20, 2001, NASA announced that a research team had discovered carbohydrate molecules (sugars) and several related organic compounds on two meteorites. Though carbon-based compounds such as amino acids and carboxylic acids had previously been found on meteorites, this was the first evidence of the presence of carbohydrates. The discovery provided the first physical evidence that a fundamental building block of life on Earth could have originated in outer space. It also pointed to the possibility that life on other planets could have begun from the same seeds that originated life on Earth.

We have seen that human history has not necessarily proceeded as orthodox models would have us believe. It is full of mysteries and unexpected twists and turns, evidence of genius and sophisticated civilization occurring in an age that would seem impossible based on our prehistory, radical departures from millions of years of development to a course that runs counter to every basic tenet of the theory of evolution. We have seen that millions of tons of cut stone were somehow used to construct pyramids and platforms and other monumental structures by the ancient peoples of Egypt, Mexico, Peru, Mesopotamia, and China for reasons that have remained enigmatic to us. But from study we have discovered that these structures seem to have been placed strategically as geodesic markers, and that highly advanced knowledge of astronomy, mathematics, and engineering was incorporated into their construction.

In a sense, the remains of ancient civilizations scattered around the world are open books in which we can read the evidence supporting the theory that human civilization began as intelligent intervention from an already advanced extraterrestrial source. While these archaeological remains suggest an explanation for the mystery of how civilization exploded into being millennia ago, our cosmic ancestry is cited in ancient accounts from Mesopotamia and Egypt to Mesoamerica and Peru and in the myths and creation stories of these cultures.

We need only look at our more recent history to see how much our loyalty to preconceived models has limited our growth. As long as Europeans believed the sun rotated around a flat Earth, no progress was possible in the direction of accurate mapping or astronomy and no exploration of the wider world could occur. It was only when the model was challenged that we moved forward in our knowledge and understanding.

If we likewise challenge the orthodox historical concept of our origins, the same prize of increased knowledge and understanding could be ours. And to do this we need not accept the concept of spindly, large-headed aliens. As we have seen here, the gods who created modern humans and gave them agriculture and the arts of civilization were described by the ancients as human, although very much advanced. The god of the Bible, Viracocha, Quetzalcoatl, and all the gods of the Sumerians were described as humans—like us.

Today, with our rapidly advancing technological base, we are fulfilling the cosmic mission that the genesis race left to us many millennia ago. We are, in the end, the genetic inheritors or a DNA paradigm that includes space exploration, an ever-expanding knowledge of mathematics and physics, and the ability to manipulate genes in bioengineering. In our pursuit and acquisition of all of these we are echoing the advances that our earthly ancestors attributed to the gods—our cosmic ancestors.

In these early years of the twenty-first century it hardly seems far-fetched to imagine that we might soon be conducting our own genesis experiments on distant planets. What will their primitive inhabitants say of our appearance and conduct? No doubt, that we are gods possessing divine—even magical—powers.

Notes

INTRODUCTION: MAKING THE CASE FOR EXTRATERRESTRIAL INTERVENTION

1. Yahoo Daily News, November 21, 2001.

CHAPTER 1: RECONSTRUCTING OUR ANCIENT PAST

1. Andrew Cawthorne, "Explorers View Ruins of 'Lost City' Under Caribbean," Reuters, 2002.
2. Claire Marshall, BBC News Online, October 17, 2000.
3. Hoda Abdel-Hamid, "City Found in the Sea," ABC News, June 7, 2001.
4. Ellen O'Brien, "Mystery of the Mummies," *Philadelphia Inquirer,* April 15, 1996.
5. News release, Field Museum, www.sciencedaily.com.
6. Koricancha Project press release, Peruvian Embassy, March 23, 2001.
7. Gene Savoy, *Vilcabamba: Lost City of the Incas* (London: Robert Hale, 1970).

CHAPTER 2: MYSTERIOUS ORIGINS: DESCENDED FROM APES?

1. Michael Denton, *Evolution: A Theory in Crisis* (Bethesda, Md.: Adler and Adler, 1997).
2. Charles Darwin, *The Origin of Species* (London: J. Murray, 1897).
3. Louis B. Leakey, lecture, University of the Pacific, February 1967.
4. Richard Milton, *Shattering the Myths of Darwinism* (Rochester, Vt.: Park Street Press, 1997).
5. "A Scientific Dissent on Darwinism," The Discovery Institute, September 24, 2001.
6. Henry "Fritz" Schaefer, in the press release on "A Scientific Dissent on Darwinism," The Discovery Institute, September 24, 2001.

7. Stephen Jay Gould, *Wonderful Life: The Burgess Shale and the Nature of History* (New York: W. W. Norton, 1989).

8. The consensus among Gould's scientific peers was that his new theory was already implied by Darwin's theory.

9. The Evolution Project/WGBH Boston, "The Evolution Controversy: Use It or Lose It," June 15, 2001.

10. "Darwinian Theory and Its Critics," *Tampa Tribune,* October 22, 2001.

CHAPTER 3: ORIGINS II: EVOLUTION OR EXTRATERRESTRIAL INTERVENTION?

1. Fred Hoyle, *The Intelligent Universe* (New York: Holt, Rhinehart, and Winston, 1983).

2. Charles Darwin, *The Origin of Species* (Harmondsworth, Middlesex, U.K.: Penguin, 1985).

3. Michael Behe, *Darwin's Black Box* (New York: Simon and Schuster, 1998).

4. *The Planetary Society*, online editorial, February 2001, www.planetary.org.

5. Francis Crick, *Life Itself: Its Origin and Nature* (New York: Simon and Schuster, 1981).

6. Richard Dawkins, *Climbing Mount Improbable* (New York: W. W. Norton, 1996).

7. Michael Behe, *Darwin's Black Box.*

8. Ibid.

9. Ibid.

10. Ibid.

11. Richard Milton, *Shattering the Myths of Darwinism* (Rochester, Vt.: Park Street Press, 1997).

12. Fred Whipple, "Origin of the Solar System," *Nature* 278.

13. G. Gossen, *South and Mesoamerican Native Spirituality* (New York, Crossroad, 1993).

CHAPTER 4: THE GENESIS ACCOUNT

1. All biblical quotes in this text are from the New American Standard Bible.

CHAPTER 5: GENESIS CONTINUED

1. L. W. King, ed., *Enuma Elish,* vol. 1 and 2: *The Seven Tablets of Creation; The Babylonian and Assyrian Legends Concerning the Creation of the World and Mankind* (New York: AMS Press, 1976).

2. Ibid.

3. Ibid.

CHAPTER 6: SUMERIANS:
THE STRANGE BLACK-HEADED TRIBE

1. Jack M. Sasson, ed., *Civilizations of the Ancient Near East* (New York: Scribner, 1995).
2. Zecharia Sitchin, *The 12th Planet* (Rochester, Vt.: Bear and Co., 1991).
3. Ibid.
4. Sir Charles Leonard Wooley, *Ur of the Chaldees: A Record of Seven Years of Excavation* (Harmondsworth, Middlesex, U.K.: Penguin, 1940).
5. Thorkid Jacobsen, trans. and ed., *The Harps That Once—: Sumerian Poetry in Translation* (New Haven: Yale University Press, 1987).
6. Quoted from "The First Farmer's Almanac" in Samuel Noah Kraemer, *Cradle of Civilization* (Alexandria, Va.: Time-Life, 1978).
7. Zecharia Sitchin, *The 12th Planet*.

CHAPTER 7: EGYPT: MYSTERIES IN THE DESERT

1. The Institut d'Égypte and the Description de l'Égypte, Fondation Napoléon, www.napoleon.org/en/reading_room/articles/files/institut_egypte_description.asp.
2. Herold J. Christopher, *Bonaparte in Egypt* (New York: Harper and Row, 1962).
3. Peter Tompkins, *Secrets of the Great Pyramid* (New York: Harper and Row, 1971).
4. J. P. Lepre, *The Egyptian Pyramids: A Comprehensive Illustrated Reference* (Jefferson, N.C.: McFarland, 1990).
5. John Zajac, "Who Built the Great Pyramid?" *After Dark* 1, no. 2 (Art Bell newsletter), February 1995.
6. *Nova*/PBS Online Adventure, "Mysteries of the Nile: Raising the Obelisk," Public Broadcasting Online, 1995.

CHAPTER 8: THE INDUS VALLEY: THE WATER PEOPLE

1. J. Marshall, *Mohenjo Daro and the Indus Valley Civilization* (London: n.p., 1931).
2. S. Arandara, "The Legacy Left Behind by Mohenjo Daro and the Harappan Civilization," *Sunday Observer* (Sri Lanka), July 25, 2000.
3. Quoted in Tim Appenzeller, "A Mystifying Script: Why Did the Indus Love Baths and Unicorns?" *U.S. News and World Report*, July 24, 2000.

CHAPTER 9: MYSTERIOUS CIVILIZATION X: THE CHINESE PYRAMIDS

1. Hartwig Hausdorf, *The Chinese Roswell: UFO Encounters in the Far East from Ancient Times to the Present* (Boca Raton, Fla.: New Paradigm, 1998).
2. Laura Lee, "China's Secret Pyramids," *Atlantis Rising Online*, Spring 1997, www.atlantisrising.com.
3. Hartwig Hausdorf, *The Chinese Roswell: UFO Encounters in the Far East from Ancient Times to the Present*.
4. Sima Qian, *Records of the Grand Historian*, trans. by Burton Watson (New York: Columbia University Press, 1993).
5. Michael Loewe and Edward L. Shaughnessy, eds., *The Cambridge History of Ancient China* (Cambridge, U.K.: Cambridge University Press, 1999).
6 Zecharia Sitchin, *The 12th Planet* (Rochester, Vt.: Bear and Co., 2002).
7. Jo Lusby and Abby Wan, "The Truth Is Out There," *City Weekend* (Beijing), June 2002, www.cityweekend.com.cn/issues/2002/14/Cover_UFO.

CHAPTER 10: LINKS BETWEEN ANCIENT MEXICO AND PERU: THE MYSTERY OF THE JAGUAR PEOPLE

1. E. Benson, ed., *The Olmecs and Their Neighbors: Essays in Memory of Matthew Stirling* (Washington, D.C.: Dumbarton Oaks, 1981).
2. Michael Coe and Richard A. Diehl, *In the Land of the Olmec* (Austin: University of Texas Press, 1980).
3. Michael Lemonick, "Mystery of the Olmec," *Time* magazine, July 1, 1996.
4. Ibid.
5. Carlos G. Elera, "Puepmape Archaeological Project," unpublished paper, National Museum of Peru.
6. Ibid.
7. M. E. Mosley, *The Exploration and Explanation of Early Monumental Architecture in the Andes* (Washington, D.C.: Dumbarton Oaks, 1985).

CHAPTER 11: CLASH OF CIVILIZATIONS

1. Diego de Landa, *Yucatán Before and After the Conquest,* translated by William Gates (New York: Dover, 1978).
2. Lewis Spence, *The Popul Vuh: The Mythic and Heroic Sagas of the Kiches of Central America* (London: David Nutt, 1908).
3. Ibid.
4. Hernán Cortés, *Letters from Mexico,* translated and edited by Anthony Pagden (New Haven: Yale University Press, 1986).

5. Michael E. Smith, *The Aztecs* (Malden, Mass.: Blackwell, 1996).

6. Lewis Spence, *The Popul Vuh*.

7. John Hemming, *The Conquest of the Incas* (Harmondsworth, Middlesex, U.K.: Penguin, 1983).

8. José Antonio del Busto Duthurburu, *Perú Incaico* (Lima: Liberia Studium S.A., 1981), quoted in Tarmo Kulmar, "On the Role of Creation and Origin Myths in the Development of Inca State and Religion," http://haldjas.folklore.ee/folklore/vol12/inca.htm.

9. Ibid.

10. Ibid.

11. Ibid.

12. Ibid.

13. Graham Hancock, *Fingerprints of the Gods* (New York: Crown, 1995).

14. Hiram Bingham, *Lost City of the Incas* (New York: Duell, Sloan, and Pearce, 1948).

CHAPTER 12: LAKE TITICACA: VIRACOCHA'S HOME BASE

1. Arthur Posnansky, *Tihaunacu: The Cradle of American Man* (New York: J. J. Augustin, 1945).

2. Graham Hancock, *Fingerprints of the Gods* (New York: Crown, 1995).

3. Mark Schwartz, "Evidence from Lake Titicaca Sheds Light on Sudden Global Climate Changes," *Stanford Report,* January 25, 2001, www.stanford.edu/dept/news/report/news/january 31/titicaca_131.html.

4. Ibid.

5. Ibid.

6. John Bierhorst, *Latin American Folktales: Stories from Hispanic and Indian Traditions* (New York: Pantheon, 2002).

7. Monica Vargas, "Peru Finds Pre-Inca Ruins Beneath Lake Titicaca," Reuters, October 30, 2002.

8. *CIA Interactive World Fact Book 1996,* www.geographic.org/geography/cia_world_factbook_1996.html.

9. Alan Kolata, *Tiwanaku: Portrait of an Andean Civilization* (Cambridge, Mass.: Blackwell, 1993).

10. Clark Erickson, "Raised Field Agriculture in the Lake Titicaca Basin" (Philadelphia: University Museum, University of Pennsylvania, 1988).

11. Graham Hancock, *Fingerprints of the Gods.*

CHAPTER 13: MASTERS OF TIME AND PLACE

1. Joseph-Marie Moiret, *Memoirs of Napoleon's Egyptian Expedition* (London: Greenhill Books, 2001).
2. Anthony F. Aveni, ed., *World Archaeoastronomy: Selected Papers from the 2nd Oxford International Conference on Archaeoastronomy Held at Merida, Yucatán, Mexico, 13–17 January 1986* (Cambridge, U.K.: Cambridge University Press, 1989).
3. Anthony F. Aveni, *Skywatchers of Ancient Mexico* (Austin: University of Texas Press, 1980).
4. Justine Shaw, "Maya Sacbeob: Form and Function," *Ancient Mesoamerica,* Fall 2001.
5. Eleanor Robson, *Mesopotamia Mathematics, 2100–1600* B.C. (Oxford: Oxford University Press, 1999).

CHAPTER 14: THE FIRST DIVINE RULERS: MYTH OR HISTORY?

1. American Heritage Dictionary.
2. Garcilasso de la Vega, *First Part of the Royal Commentaries of the Yncas,* translated by Clements R. Markham (New York: B. Franklin, 1963).
3. Ibid.
4. Zecharia Sitchin, *The 12th Planet* (Rochester, Vt.: Bear and Co., 2002).
5. Ibid.
6. L. W. King, ed., *Enuma Elish,* vol. 1 and 2: *The Seven Tablets of Creation; The Babylonian and Assyrian Legends Concerning the Creation of the World and Mankind* (New York: AMS Press, 1976).
7. Ibid.
8. Ibid.
9. Ibid.
10. William H. Prescott, *History of the Conquest of Mexico and History of the Conquest of Peru* (New York: Cooper Square Press, 2000).
11. Peter A. Clayton, *Chronicle of the Pharaohs: The Reign-by-Reign Record of the Rulers and Dynasties of Ancient Egypt* (London: Thames and Hudson, 1994).

CHAPTER 15: THE EVOLUTIONARY STATUS QUO?

1. Robert Fellner, "The Problems and Prospects of Cultural Evolution (part 2)," *Institute of Archaeology* 1 (1990).
2. Ibid.
3. José Antonio del Busto Duthurburu, *Perú Incaico* (Lima: Liberia Studium S.A., 1981), quoted in Tarmo Kulmar, "On the Role of Creation and Origin

Myths in the Development of Inca State and Religion," http://haldjas.folk-lore.ee/folklore/vol12/inca.htm.

4. James C. Cook, *The Journals of Captain James C. Cook* (Harmondsworth, Middlesex, U.K.: Penguin, 2000).
5. Ibid.
6. Ibid.
7. Ibid.
8. BBC News Online, March 27, 2001.
9. Ibid.

CHAPTER 16: ANCIENT ENIGMAS: THE DOMESTICATION OF PLANTS AND DOGS

1. Jack Challem, "Paleolithic Nutrition: Your Future Is in Your Dietary Past," *The Nutrition Reporter* 1997, www.thenutritionreporter.com/stone_age_diet.html.
2. Encyclopaedia Britannica, 15th edition.
3. Loren Cordain, "Evolutionary Discordance of Grains/Legumes in the Human Diet," www.beyondveg.com/cordain-l/grains-legumes-1a.shtml.
4. Daniel Zohary and Maria Hopf, *Domestication of Plants in the Old World: The Origin and Spread of Cultivated Plants in West Asia, Europe and the Nile Valley* (Oxford: Oxford University Press, 2001).
5. "The Origins of Our Daily Bread," *Food Today*, no. 19, European Food Information Council (EUFIC), www.eufic.org/gb/food/pag/food19/food192.htm.
6. M. Smale and T. McBride, 1996, "Understanding Global Trends in the Use of Wheat Diversity and International Flows of Wheat Genetic Resources," Part 1 of *CIMMYT 1995/96 World Wheat Facts and Trends,* Mexico, D.F.: CIMMYT.
7. Zecharia Sitchin, *The 12th Planet* (Rochester, Vt.: Bear and Co., 2002).
8. Ibid.
9. Ian L. Mason, *Evolution of Domesticated Animals* (London: Longman, 1984).
10. Vila Caries, et al., "Multiple and Ancient Origins of the Domestic Dog," *Science,* vol. 276, June 13, 1997.
11. Ibid.

CHAPTER 17: METALLURGY: FROM THE FIRE

1. Robert Fellner, "The Problems and Prospects of Cultural Evolution," *Institute of Archaeology* 1 (1990).
2. R. J. Forbes, *The Birthplace of Old World Metallurgy* (n.p., 1991).
3. L. Aitchison, *A History of Metals* (New York: Interscience, 1960).

4. Ibid.

5. Zecharia Sitchin, *When Time Began* (Rochester, Vt.: Bear and Co., 2002).

6. Jack M. Sasson, ed., *Civilizations of the Ancient Near East* (New York: Scribner, 1995).

CHAPTER 18: THE DATING GAME

1. Janine MacDonald Canberra, "Mungo Man Older Than Thought," *The Age,* May 21, 1999.

2. John Noble Wilford, "Artifacts in Africa Suggest an Earlier Modern Human," *New York Times,* December 2, 2001.

3. Michael A. Cremo and Richard L. Thompson, *Hidden History of the Human Race* (Alachua, Fla.: Govardhan Hill, 1999).

4. Michael A. Cremo and Richard L. Thompson, *Forbidden Archaeology* (San Diego: Bhaktivedanta Institute, 1993).

5. Ibid.

6. Michael A. Cremo, "Colonialism, Identity and Social Responsibility: The History of Archaeology in the Service of Isms," paper presented to the Fifth World Archaeological Congress, Washington, D.C., 2003.

7. "Dating Study Means 'Human History Rethink,' " BBC News Online, June 29, 2001.

8. Kate Wong, "The Dating Game," *Scientific American,* June 11, 2001.

9. "Dating Study Means 'Human History Rethink,' " BBC News Online, June 29, 2001.

CHAPTER 19: AGES OF ICE

1. John Imbrie and Katherine Palmer Imbrie, *Ice Ages: Solving the Mystery* (Cambridge, Mass.: Harvard University Press, 1986).

2. A. Marshak, "Exploring the Mind of Ice Age Man," *National Geographic,* January 1975.

3. M. Walter, "News and Views," *Nature,* May 4, 2000.

4. University of Utah news release, December 23, 2002.

5. Nicolas Wade, "Genes Tell New Story on the Spread of Man," *New York Times,* December 7, 1999.

6. "A Global Winter's Tale," *Discover,* December 1998.

7. Richard Muller and Gordon McDonald, *Ice Ages and Astronomical Causes: Data, Spectral Analysis, and Mechanisms* (New York: Springer, 2002).

CHAPTER 20: AGES OF MAN: LINEAR VERSUS CYCLICAL TIME

1. K. Sherman, "Cycles of Time: Evolution of Consciousness," *New Times,* April 1988.
2. Kay Almere Read, *Time and Sacrifice in the Aztec Cosmos* (Bloomington: Indiana University Press, 1998).
3. Stephen Crockett, *The Prophet Code: Precessional Encryption and the Apocalyptic Tradition* (Mount Gilead, N.C.: Aethyrea Books, 2001).

CHAPTER 21: CYCLES OF CATASTROPHE

1. Benny J. Peiser, "Comets and Disasters in the Bronze Age," *British Archaeology,* no. 30, December 1997.
2. Immanuel Velikovsky, *Worlds in Collision* (Garden City, N.Y.: Doubleday, 1950).
3. Anthony Peratt, "Celestial Catastrophes in Human Prehistory?" lecture, University of Pennsylvania, October 2001.
4. Benny J. Peiser, "Comets and Disasters in the Bronze Age," *British Archaeology,* no. 30, December 1997.
5. Averil Camson, Bryan Ward-Perkins, Michael Whitby, eds., *The Cambridge Ancient History* (Cambridge, U.K.: Cambridge University Press, 2001).
6. G. Ernest Wright, "The Archaeology of Palestine," in *The Bible and the Ancient Near East: Essays in Honor of William Foxwell Albright* (Garden City, N.Y.: Doubleday, 1961).
7. Nick Nuttall, "A Cosmic Trail with Destruction in Its Wake," *London Times,* May 14, 1990.
8. Zecharia Sitchin, *The 12th Planet* (Rochester, Vt.: Bear and Co., 2002).
9. Ibid.
10. Associated Press, "Asteroid Big Enough to Raze France Zips by Earth," *Seattle Times,* January 9, 2002.

CHAPTER 23: COSMIC ANCESTRY

1. Immanuel Velikovsky, "Nefilim," www.varchive.org/itb/nefilim.htm.
2. Gregory M. Kanon, *The Great UFO Hoax: The Final Solution to the UFO Mystery* (Lakeville, Minn.: Galde Press, 1997).

Bibliography

Aitchison, L. *A History of Metals*. New York: Interscience, 1960.

Argüelles, José. *The Mayan Factor: Path Beyond Technology*. Santa Fe: Bear and Co., 1987.

Aveni, Anthony F. *Skywatchers of Ancient Mexico*. Austin: University of Texas Press, 1980.

Behe, Michael. *Darwin's Black Box*. New York: Simon and Schuster, 1998.

Bellamy, H. S. *Built Before the Flood: The Problem of the Tiahaunaco Ruins*. London: Faber and Faber, 1943.

Bierhorst, John. *The Mythology of South America*. New York: William Morrow, 1988.

Campbell, Joseph. *The Hero with a Thousand Faces*. New York: MJF Books, 1996.

Cochrane, E. *The Many Faces of Venus: The Planet Venus in Ancient Myth and Religion*. Ames, Iowa: Aeon Publishers, 1997.

Coe, Michael D. *The Maya*. London: Thames and Hudson, 1991.

Coe, Michael and Richard A. Diehl. *In the Land of the Olmec*. Austin: University of Texas Press, 1980.

Crick, Sir Francis. *Life Itself: Its Origin and Nature*. New York: Simon and Schuster, 1981.

Darwin, Charles. *The Origin of Species*. Harmondsworth, Middlesex, U.K.: Penguin, 1985.

de Landa, Diego. *Yucatán Before and After the Conquest*. Translated by William Gates. New York: Dover, 1978.

Denton, Michael. *Evolution: A Theory in Crisis*. Bethesda, Md.: Adler and Adler, 1986.

Editors of Time-Life Books. *Mystic Places*. Alexandria, Va.: Time-Life Books, 1987.

Epic of Gilgamesh. Harmondsworth, Middlesex, U.K.: Penguin Classics, 1988.

Fiedel, S. J. *The Prehistory of the Americas*. Cambridge, U.K.: Cambridge University Press, 1992.

Gould, Stephen Jay. *Wonderful Life; The Burgess Shale and the Nature of History*. New York: W. W. Norton, 1989.

Gray, Louis Herbert and George Foot Moore, editors. *Mythology of All Races*. New York: Cooper Square Publishers, 1964.

Hancock, Graham. *Fingerprints of the Gods*. New York: Crown, 1995.

Hausdorf, Hartwig. *The Chinese Roswell: UFO Encounters in the Far East from Ancient Times to the Present*. Boca Raton, Fla.: New Paradigm, 1998.

Hemming, John. *The Conquest of the Inca*. New York: Macmillan, 1993.

Hoyle, Fred. *The Intelligent Universe*. New York: Holt, Rhinehart, and Winston, 1983.

Imbrie, John and Katherine Palmer Imbrie. *Ice Ages: Solving the Mystery*. Cambridge, Mass.: Harvard University Press, 1986.

Josephus, Flavius. *Complete Works*. Translated by William Whiston. Grand Rapids, Mich.: Kregel Publications, 1960.

Kolata, Alan. *Tiwanaku: Portrait of an Andean Civilization*. Cambridge, Mass.: Blackwell, 1993.

Kulmar, Tarmo. "On the Role of Creation and Origin Myths in the Development of Inca State and Religion." http://haldjas.folklore.ee/folklore/vol12/inca.htm.

Lemesurier, Peter. *The Great Pyramid Decoded*. Rockport, Mass.: Element Books, 1996.

Leonard, Jonathan Norton. *Ancient America*. New York: Time-Life Books, 1967.

Layard, Austen H. *Nineveh and Its Remains*. New York: G. P. Putnam, 1852.

Loewe, Michael and Edward L. Shaughnessy, editors. *The Cambridge History of Ancient China* (Cambridge, U.K.: Cambridge University Press, 1999).

Marshall, J. *Mohenjo Daro and the Indus Valley Civilization*. London, n.p., 1931.

Miller, Mary and Karl Taub. *An Illustrated Dictionary of the Gods and Symbols of Ancient Mexico and the Maya*. London: Thames and Hudson, 1997.

Milton, Richard. *Shattering the Myths of Darwinism*. Rochester, Vt.: Park Street Press, 1997.

Mosley, M. E. *The Exploration and Explanation of Early Monumental Architecture in the Andes*. Washington, D.C.: Dumbarton Oaks, 1985.

Muller, Richard and Gordon McDonald. *Ice Ages and Astronomical Causes: Data, Spectral Analysis, and Mechanisms*. New York: Springer, 2002.

New American Standard Bible. Grand Rapids, Mich.: World, 1995.

Plato, *Timaeus and Critias*. Harmondworth, Middlesex, U.K.: Penguin Classics, 1977.

Posnansky, Arthur. *Tihaunacu: The Cradle of American Man*. New York: J. J. Augustin, 1945.

Recinos, Adrián. *Popul Vuh: The Sacred Book of the Ancient Quiche Maya*. Norman: University of Oklahoma Press, 1991.

Sasson, Jack M., editor. *Civilizations of the Ancient Near East* New York: Scribner, 1995.

Savoy, Gene. *Antisuyo: The Search for the Lost Cities of the Amazon*. New York: Simon and Schuster, 1970.

Sitchin, Zecharia. *The 12th Planet*. Rochester, Vt.: Bear and Co., 2002.

Sitchin, Zecharia. *When Time Began*. Rochester, Vt.: Bear and Co., 2002.

Smith, Michael E. *The Aztecs* (Malden, Mass.: Blackwell, 1996).

Sparks, H. F. D., editor. *Apocryphal Old Testament*. Clarendon: Oxford University Press, 1984.

Spence, Lewis. *The Magic and Mysteries of Mexico*. Philadelphia: David McKay, 1930.

———. *The Popul Vuh: The Mythic and Heroic Sagas of the Kiches of Central America* (London: David Nutt, 1908).

Tompkins, Peter. *Secrets of the Great Pyramid*. New York: Harper and Row, 1971.

Thompson, John Eric. *Maya Hieroglyphic Writing: An Introduction*. Norman: University of Oklahoma Press, 1960.

———. *Mysteries of the Mexican Pyramids*. London: Thames and Hudson, 1987.

———. *The Rise and Fall of Maya Civilization*. Norman: University of Oklahoma Press, 1954.

Velikovsky, Immanuel. *Earth in Upheaval*. New York: Pocket Books, 1977.

———. *Worlds in Collision*. Garden City, N.Y.: Doubleday, 1950.

von Däniken, Erich. *Chariots of the Gods?* New York: Putnam, 1970.

Waters, Frank. *Mexico Mystique: The Coming Sixth World of Consciousness*. Chicago: Sage Books, 1975.

Internet Resources

The Internet is an excellent place to stay current with breaking news items and developments in the topics explored in *The Genesis Race*. Following is a sampling of informative sites, most of which include links to encourage further exploration.

www.genesisrace.com
I created this site to include articles, current news items, photos, and links related to the subject of *The Genesis Race*.

www.coasttocoastam.com
Art Bell's replacement, George Noory, is maintaining his predecessor's programming and Web site. It includes a schedule of guests on the late-night radio program "Coast to Coast."

www.jeffrense.com
Jeff Rense hosts a popular radio talk show. This site includes stories that you won't find elsewhere about the news-making mainstream media headlines.

www.world-mysteries.com
This extensive site covers history's mysteries from many angles. It includes a large collection of articles and photos.

www.lauralee.com
Laura Lee hosts a radio talk show similar to that of Art Bell and George Noory.

www.grahamhancock.com
This is the official Web site of the author of *Fingerprints of the Gods*.

www.dreamland.com

This site was created by well-known UFO contactee and author of *Communion* Whitley Strieber.

www.atlantisrising.com

The alternative science and history magazine *Atlantis Rising* operates this site. You can download the magazine as a free PDF file.

www.sacredsites.com

This is the spectacular site of photographer Martin Gray, who graciously allowed the use of some of his images in this book. A must-visit Web site if you are interested in archaeology, ancient history, or sacred sites around the world.

www.alternativescience.com

Richard Milton, author of *Shattering the Myths of Darwinism,* includes articles and news items exploring alternative perspectives on many current topics related to science.

Index

BOOKS OF RELATED INTEREST

Ancient Alien Ancestors
Advanced Technologies that Terraformed Our World
by Will Hart

Black Genesis
The Prehistoric Origins of Ancient Egypt
by Robert Bauval and Thomas Brophy, Ph.D.

Gobekli Tepe: Genesis of the Gods
The Temple of the Watchers and the Discovery of Eden
by Andrew Collins
Introduction by Graham Hancock

The Sirius Mystery
New Scientific Evidence of Alien Contact 5,000 Years Ago
by Robert Temple

The Giza Power Plant
Technologies of Ancient Egypt
by Christopher Dunn

Lost Technologies of Ancient Egypt
Advanced Engineering in the Temples of the Pharaohs
by Christopher Dunn

DNA of the Gods
The Anunnaki Creation of Eve and the Alien Battle for Humanity
by Chris H. Hardy, Ph.D.

There Were Giants Upon the Earth
Gods, Demigods, and Human Ancestry: The Evidence of Alien DNA
by Zecharia Sitchin

Inner Traditions • Bear & Company
P.O. Box 388
Rochester, VT 05767
1-800-246-8648
www.InnerTraditions.com

Or contact your local bookseller